Pressing *my* *Luck*

Memoir of a Fleet Street Veteran

Colin Mackenzie

REBEL
MAGIC
BOOKS

REBEL
MAGIC
BOOKS

To Linda

Also by Colin Mackenzie

Ronald Biggs – the most wanted man

Blitz over Balaclava Street (with Hazel Adair)

Contents

1.

Room 909

The rollers from the South Atlantic beat their gentle rhythm onto the bleached white sands of Copacabana, whose dunes were dotted with sunbathers of all colours and sizes. The noise of the traffic careering up and down Avenida Atlantica was a constant drumbeat. Inside my head was turmoil and rising torment.

I was experiencing the worst fifteen minutes of my life, wracked with tension, perspiration, and the knowledge that I might be perceived as the Judas Iscariot of the twentieth century. I would, however inadvertently, be the cause of bringing Ronald Biggs's 3,471 days on the run as a free man to a premature and dramatic conclusion. My heart was beating faster than an eight-year-old awaiting the headmaster's beating at my prep school.

Biggs, a minor cog in the Great Train Robbery, had achieved worldwide notoriety by escaping from Wandsworth jail in the high summer of 1965 to eviscerate the thirty year sentence for his role in the £2.75 million Great Train Robbery heist, worth over £100 million in 2020.

He had successfully eluded all attempts to recapture him, including a dramatic escape from Melbourne in the autumn of 1969 when his whereabouts, and those of his wife Charmian and their three children, had finally been unmasked. Now here he was, four and a half years later, in room 909 of the *Trocadero*, a Copacabana beachfront hotel in humid Rio de Janeiro, singing his story to a *Daily Express* journalist he trusted. Little did he know that his lotus-eating existence was about to be rudely curtailed.

The Metropolitan police had invested hundreds of thousands of pounds chasing Biggs's shadow across the globe since his daring and imaginative leap over the wall of south London's notoriously unpopular prison. They were by turn frustrated and furious that this minor villain, a builder and carpenter from Redhill, Surrey, had escaped their grasp.

So there was more than a degree of satisfaction written across the face of Chief Superintendent Jack Slipper, late of the Flying Squad and the man who first arrested Biggs a month after the 1963 Great Train Robbery, as he spotted the six foot one figure of Biggs on the arm of a twenty-two year old Brazilian media student entering the foyer of the *Trocadero* on the morning of January 31, 1974.

By a signal arranged the night before in Slipper's nearby hotel room, photographer Bill Lovelace was to open the window of room 909, ostensibly to take pictures of Biggs with the background of the most famous beach in the world. This was the signal to Slipper, his assistant Detective Inspector Peter Jones, the British Consul Henry Neil, and a Brazilian plain clothed detective, that their quarry was in situ.

The fact that it took fifteen minutes before they knocked on the door was down to the nerves of the two Scotland Yard men and the inability of the *Trocadero's* elevators to successfully deliver them to the ninth floor of the hotel, a few hundred yards from the celebrated Copacabana Palace where I had originally intended to stay. (It was full to capacity.)

While I waited, I interviewed Biggs as best I could about his life on the run, while my colleague Bill took pictures of blonde Lucia, the latest in a harem of Brazilian girls captivated by Biggs's blue eyes and gringo good looks which defied his forty-six years.

Room 909 was occupied by my friend Constantine Benckendorf, who at nineteen was about to experience his Warhol fifteen minutes of fame. He'd been the catalyst who had brought me into this story some two months earlier. We were neighbours in Battersea, South London, and he came to a pre-Christmas party held in honour of my father, Gordon, who had lived in Brazil for more than forty years, apart from war service in the British army.

Conti had spent much of 1973 backpacking around South America and had succumbed to the delights of Rio. One day he had started talking to a tall Brit with an evident South London accent. The man called himself Michael Haynes and he'd been thrilled to hear a similar accent and to exchange stories about London and the swinging sixties and seventies.

Michael revealed to Conti his real identity, and although the latter was only nine years old at the time of the robbery, he both remembered the event and knew of Biggs's notoriety and life on the run. 'Michael' also said that, since the parole system had been introduced into the British legal system (meaning that a prisoner could apply for release after only a third of his sentence), he was considering giving up life on the run to complete his prison term, which could now be as little as ten years.

Could Conti, he asked, find a journalist willing to do his story in exchange for money for his wife Charmian in Australia and the scoop of his return to Britain? After all, not only had the parole system become part of the fabric of the judicial system, the plain fact was that he was running out of ideas and money to continue his haphazard existence in Rio.

Sure he could, said Conti. But the young student knew no journalists and had forgotten his task until he arrived at my house. I had known his mother Esther, who was divorced from Conti's father, a Russian Count, but had not met Conti until the party when he suddenly learned that I was a journalist on the *Daily Express*.

"I met someone you'd love to meet," he began, upon making my acquaintance. And before he could finish his sentence, I blurted out "You met Ronnie Biggs in Rio, didn't you?"

Conti blushed and countered "How on earth did you know that? It could have been anyone."

I reassured him by saying there were only two good stories currently. One was to find Biggs, and the other was to interview Howard Hughes, the famously reclusive American billionaire who the rumour mill was claiming was dead.

I left Conti alone for a couple of days and then invited him to join me in a local pub. He revealed that Biggs was keen to do a story and to give himself up. I felt a surge of adrenalin and expectation. This could be a life-changing and career-defining story, especially as my employers – Beaverbrook Newspapers – had embarked on a cost-cutting strategy, offering voluntary redundancy to anyone who wished to leave.

I had already arranged for an interview with David English, editor of the rival *Daily Mail*, because of my dissatisfaction with my current role. I had returned from an exciting stint in New York to be placed on the night news desk, a sedentary and largely administrative role I neither desired nor was particularly cut out for.

On my second night on the desk, the *Daily Express* claimed to have a world scoop that it had found Martin Bormann, the notorious Nazi and Hitler's principal lieutenant. We had photographed him on the streets of Buenos Aires where he was allegedly living, having escaped to Argentina with many other Nazis in the immediate post-war months.

Reporter Andrew Fyall and photographer David Cairns had been in Buenos Aires for nearly six months working on the story. It was potentially a huge scoop. My first misgivings arose when I entered the editor's office to tell him that as a fluent Spanish speaker and perhaps the only reporter on the staff familiar with Argentina I should immediately be sent as back-up.

The editor, Iain McColl, who'd arrived twenty months earlier from the *Scottish Daily Express,* which majored in football and murder, looked nervous. "Och, Colin," he began. "This is a very slippery individual and we are not certain yet where he lives; he could be anywhere."

As we claimed to have found and photographed him, I found this observation less than comforting and my concerns were soon to be realised in legal letters. The man pictured on the front page crossing a Buenos Aires street was an innocent Argentine school teacher, and the various important companies we had alleged he was a director of, had no knowledge of Bormann or his whereabouts. For sixty-two year old McColl, manifestly out of his depth, it was a chastening experience and one which cost the paper dearly in libel costs. Little did I know how much this journalistic cock-up would eventually impact me as well.

Conti and I decided to telephone Biggs from my home phone to see if he was still willing to surrender himself to Scotland Yard and return to Wandsworth to complete his prison sentence. Having already served eighteen months, he believed he might have to endure no more than another nine years or so, assuming his escape was penalty free if he gave himself up.

Typically though, Biggs had not paid the telephone bill at his Rua Prado Junior apartment, so we contacted a former American girlfriend called Phylis Huber with whom he had started a building and decorating company called *Planet Venus*. She agreed to invite Biggs to her house the next day.

Meanwhile I had mugged up on the Great Train Robbery, using the library files at the *Daily Express*. I also took in as much biography of Biggs as I could assimilate discreetly. A gentle cross examination would establish whether I was dealing with a chancer or the real Mr Biggs, father of two, married to Charmian Powell and a resident of Redhill, Surrey.

The following day we got Biggs on the phone and I questioned him about his life and about the intricacies of the Great Train Robbery. His high-pitched voice was something of a surprise, but his answers passed muster and it was clear after no more than ten minutes of cross-examination that he was who he said he was.

Now came the moment I had been secretly dreading – what to do with information that could transform the life of not only Biggs but also of me and my family. Should I take the voluntary redundancy package, cashing in on my nine years at the *Daily Express*, and then offer the story to the highest bidder in Fleet Street? Or should I remain loyal to the paper which had taken me on as a raw twenty-two year old recruit?

I turned to my old pal Brian Vine who had taken me under his wing when I joined the paper's William Hickey column in September 1964. We shared a common interest in matters of the turf, had holidayed together, and he had advanced my career when as foreign editor he had sent me to all parts of the world on big stories. Prior to that Vine had been senior foreign correspondent in the New York office and was a man of considerable experience in the machinations of Fleet Street. He might have resembled a country squire (often wearing a monocle for effect) but this masked a keen brain and an electric nose for a story.

"You've got to stay on the paper and be loyal to those who have taught you man and boy to be a reporter," was Vine's initial reaction. "There's no question of this story going elsewhere. We can control the whole thing and you will be properly funded. After all, it would be very expensive to get the story as a freelance, with few guarantees of success."

He was speaking with his *Daily Express* trilby on. By now he was the editor in charge of News and Foreign Affairs – effectively No 3 on the paper. This was a chance, he said, of landing the scoop of the decade and putting to right the humiliation of the Bormann story. So with some trepidation he persuaded me to tell Iain McColl, the editor, what I had discovered.

He also informed Brian Hitchen, the news editor, who until now had been kept in the dark. Hitchen, an experienced reporter newly arrived from the *Daily Mirror*, was clearly unhappy at being left out of the loop thus far. He had been appointed while I was in New York and we barely knew one another. But he swallowed his professional pride and the three of us marched into McColl's office, buoyed by the thought of a great story and hopeful of ending 1973 on a high.

It was immediately apparent that our enthusiasm was unmatched by McColl's dour response. "South America," he whined. "Not again. How do you know it's Biggs? It could be another charlatan."

Despite my protestations that I had done the ground work and satisfied myself that this was no Walter Mitty, McColl insisted I re-interview Biggs from the *Daily Express* office with Hitchen listening on an extension phone. Hitchen – short, balding and claret of face – would prepare the questions and I would ask Biggs to send his finger prints, claiming that the paper had copies of them and those of the other Great Train Robbers.

The following day I arranged for Biggs to again be at the Huber home so that I could talk to him and reassure him that the paper merely wanted to confirm his identity. Most of Hitchen's questions were identical to those I had already asked but Biggs patiently and willingly answered them all again and, crucially, promised to forward his finger prints to my home address in Battersea.

Around a week later I received a small package with a Rio de Janeiro postal stamp and inside was a piece of paper adorned with a toy train and a note which read, "Perhaps not the best set that have been taken, but certainly as good as those found on the Monopoly box and the sauce bottle. Convinced?"

At this point I should have suspected McColl's motives. But naively I passed the letter on to him as further proof – as if it were needed – that this was a genuine Great Train Robber. Big mistake.

Christmas and New Year came and morphed into 1974 without anything happening. I was getting itchy feet and listening to my reporter's instinct that you should never sit on a story, however good it was. There was always the danger that loose tongues could alert the opposition. And then there was the small matter of my interview with David English, by now revitalising the *Mail* and recruiting many of the *Express's* star reporters whom he had known when foreign editor of the paper.

I decided to approach McColl to alert him to the many dangers inherent in inaction and to confirm that Biggs would be paid £35,000 as his part of the deal (albeit the money would go to his wife Charmian in Australia). "Och, Colin. I wish you'd never told me this story," was his astonishing riposte.

I confirmed my job application to the *Mail* and decided to cross Fleet Street to see what English was prepared to offer. Quite a lot, as it turned out. By now my old friend and colleague from the Hickey column, Nigel Dempster, had been handed his own gossip column plus a contract which permitted him four months a year freelancing as an author and television personality. Would I like to run his column during those four months and become a feature writer for the remainder of the year? I assured English I would give it serious consideration.

Having relayed the offer to Vine, who was horrified that I had been to see English, wheels finally started turning at the *Express*. By now it was mid January. I reassured Vine that I had not mentioned the Biggs story to the *Mail*, but clearly this would have been a huge carrot to dangle before English had McColl continued to act like a rabbit frozen in the headlights.

McColl took the news of my visit to the *Mail* badly. He was perhaps unaware that I was answering a pre-Biggs job offer. In the event he set in motion a string of events that was to have huge ramifications for me and for the story. By now he had been in the editor's chair for two years and was receiving regular invitations to No 10 Downing Street and to other big social events. Among them was a boxing tournament where he sat next to the Metropolitan Police Assistant Commissioner, Colin Woods.

Fuelled by some excellent champagne and daunted by the memory of Bormann in far-off South America, McColl decided to enlist some insurance for the Biggs story. "Would you like to know the whereabouts of Ronnie Biggs?" he ventured to his neighbour. "One of my young reporters claims to have located him in Brazil."

The wheels of Scotland Yard worked faster than McColl's, and Hitchen was summoned to the editor's office the following morning, January 18, to be told that the police would like to debrief him and me as to Biggs's precise location. Hitchen's ruddy complexion was all fire and brimstone as he digested the fact that McColl had invited the Yard to the party. Hitchen had thought McColl a plonker, but decided to co-operate as far as he could, provided that the *Express* got the story first.

Meanwhile, Yours Truly was still in blissful ignorance of this turn of events until Hitchen called me at home and summoned me early to the office. "Come on matey," he said. "We're off to see Andrew Edwards (the *Daily Express* in-house lawyer) at his Olympia flat to discuss the legal implications of your story."

In the taxi, I told Hitchen that Brazil had no extradition arrangements with Britain which was one of the main reasons Biggs had felicitously ended up there. We wouldn't be breaching any laws to research the fact that a Great Train Robber had parked his prison uniform alongside Copacabana beach. "We'll have to see," said Hitchen, without mustering his usual serendipity.

By now Vine had despatched himself to New York, ostensibly to cover the first Ali/Frazier fight. He had planned to join me in Rio after it was over, to act as backup and to oversee the story. His absence from the Fleet Street office removed a bulwark of support and influence and left me feeling a little vulnerable. With good reason.

At Edwards's flat, there were three other people there – almost certainly PC Plod and friends rather than legal advisors. Edwards said, "Colin, meet Detective Chief Superintendent Jack Slipper and Detective Inspector Peter Jones of Scotland Yard. This is Commander Ernie Bond of the Met's Flying Squad (the man briefed by Woods)." "We've got a few things to tell you about how we proceed."

Have we hell, I thought inwardly, envisaging my nascent scoop disappearing down Edwards's lavatory bowl. "This wasn't the plan," I began lamely. "I promised Biggs he would be able to give himself up to the British Consulate in Rio de Janeiro."

"No chance of that matey," Hitchen said. "We are going to co-operate with these gentlemen to land our prey. Andrew will tell you how you stand legally and why your hundred per cent assistance is required."

I had few, if any, bullets to fire. But Biggs's precise address was unknown and although I now suspected my phone, and of course the Daily Express phones, had been tapped over the previous twenty-four hours they didn't have Biggs's actual number because he had neglected to pay the bill. All they had was Phylis Huber's number and presumably her address in Jardim Botanico, at least four kilometres from the Prado Junior apartment where the Great Train Robber laid his head.

"Now Colin," Slipper, a moustachioed six foot three caricature of the 1960s Flying Squad, began. "All we need is his address and you can leave the arrest to us. Of course we'll co-operate and let you have the pictures and story.

"Sorry," I said. "That's not an option. Obviously you know he's in Rio. But you don't know his address and I'm not divulging it. I gave him my word that he could hand himself in so that he could get that benefit from the court on his return."

"We don't do deals with criminals," Slipper said. "I suggest you talk to your lawyer here and realise more fully your situation. We are going to run this show, not the Daily Express."

After a few pleasantries, the men from the Yard left. Edwards turned to Hitchen and me and said, "There was really no choice once Iain had spoken to Colin Woods. We are going to be lucky to get the scoop, but having the Yard on our tails is inevitable. Legally we cannot do anything else."

In the cab back to Fleet Street I vented my anger to Hitchen. "How could McColl be so stupid?" I said. "This is the worst situation ever. No one will ever trust the Express again. How am

I going to get the story if they've got there first? It's bullshit and you know it."

To his credit, Hitchen agreed and said. "I'm going to negotiate that you have a week's start before they can lay their handcuffs on Biggs. That's the best I can do, matey." .

My thoughts were in turmoil. Should I tell my wife Tina? I was certain she would recommend contacting Biggs and warn him what was to happen. "Be true to yourself," she said afterwards. I knew what that meant.

What I did was confide in Vine (over in New York) who exploded with rage, and with my best friend on the *Express* James Whitaker, later to become a celebrated royal correspondent. Neither could credit what McColl had done. But both put their heads together to see what was possible and where to go.

By now it had been agreed with Scotland Yard that photographer Bill Lovelace and I would have four days to debrief Biggs before Slipper and Co would make a move. I remonstrated that this was not enough time to take all the necessary pictures and to get the full story of his life on the run, and I knew Biggs was imagining a couple of weeks in Rio's finest restaurants as a precursor to his return to Wandsworth prison. Biggs was on South American time – 'tomorrow' was his watchword. Everything was half speed.

My father Gordon Mackenzie lived in the sleepy town of Aracatuba, a thousand kilometres inland from Rio on the border of Sao Paulo state and Mato Grosso. It was a coffee and cattle area where many of the big farms were owned by the Vestey family for whom my father worked. He had been there since arriving as a 19-year-old in 1930. I contemplated consulting him about the possibility of hiding Biggs and allowing him to go on the run again, if that was what the train robber wanted.

I had four days with him on arrival so I would be able to confront this dilemma with Biggs and ask him in person. It was still Biggs's intention to give himself up. I agonised over whether I should play along to retain the scoop, or confess all and allow Biggs to make up his own mind. It played on my mind and my conscience.

Meanwhile, in order to preserve confidentiality, I was asked to draw £5,000 in cash from the *Express* accounts department, buy three first class return tickets to Rio, flying with *Varig* via Madrid. Normally these would have been provided by the *Express* foreign desk but Hitchen decided that the fewer people who knew of my whereabouts the better. The tickets were for Lovelace, Conti, and me.

It was also decided that two experienced reporters – Arliss Rhind and Struan Cooper – would act as copy takers on the day the story broke, rather than risk a leak from the company's other employees.

A complex coded set of words was created. For example, Rio was to be called Edinburgh, while Biggs was Betchworth (a small Surrey village where I had been brought up). This was some minor insurance against the copy ending up in the wrong hands.

Lovelace, personally selected by me as we had enjoyed some wonderful scoops together over the years, was appraised of the Scotland Yard situation. He could scarcely believe what he was being told and immediately recognised the dangers inherent in having Scotland Yard chasing our tails.

It was agreed that Conti should be kept out of the loop – better that he was an innocent bystander. But it was necessary for him to be there to introduce us to Biggs and to lend credibility to the project. Like me, Lovelace, a veteran of countless big stories and a huge asset to any reporter with his experience and broad shoulders, was incandescent at McColl's naivety and decision to put at risk the success of the project.

It was Lovelace who delivered the bombshell that the arrest was to be brought forward by a further two days. We spent the first day in Rio going to various locations where Biggs had worked and visiting iconic landmarks of the beautiful city, like the Corcovado/Christ Redeemer statue that dominates the City's skyline. We had been unable to call the London office because there was a four-hour time delay on calls – communications in Brazil were definitely third world. So there was mild panic in London as to our whereabouts and safety.

After a long day's filming we bade farewell to Biggs and Lucia, and Bill shot off to Galeao airport with rolls of film to be transported back to London so we didn't alert the local news agency about what we were up to. He found a passenger willing to take the invaluable film to be picked up at Gatwick on arrival on January 31.

Bill's call to the office finally materialised later that evening. Having told them of his Gatwick plan he was told that the arrest was being brought forward forty-eight hours, allegedly because of a chance phone call from *The Sun* to Scotland Yard's press office about rumours that Biggs had been found. He was to go with me to the *Excelsior* hotel where Slipper was waiting with Jones. By this time also, Brian Vine had flown in, having been dragged away from *Costello's*, New York journalists' favourite drinking hole.

Meanwhile Biggs had gone off into the night with Lucia so there was no prospect of warning him about developments. We had arranged for him to come to the *Trocadero* at 10am the following morning to continue the interview and to have more pictures taken.

At the *Excelsior* there was a tangible air of tension with Slipper pacing up and down like an expectant father. He couldn't bear to think that the man he had spent nine years searching the globe for was no more than a few hundred yards from his hotel. "We'll have him tomorrow morning," he addressed the room.

"No, you won't," I retorted. "I haven't begun to get the story off him yet. We've been doing some establishing photos for the last thirty-six hours and every time I've started to ask him where he has been, he says, "Tranquilo, Colin, we're on South American time here. We've got days to sort that out."

At this point Vine intervened. "You've got to do what they say after the Sun's intervention. It's going to be Saturday morning's paper in London and the circulation will never be higher. They've already booked television advertising for tomorrow night and they plan to do a deal with ITN to announce the scoop."

My jaw dropped. Not only had I not had time to properly debrief Biggs, neither Bill nor I had had the chance to put it to the train robber that he could exercise the choice of giving himself up or disappearing into Brazil's vast interior. I glanced at Bill and he was scarcely able to return my look of devastation. We had known Biggs for less than forty-eight hours, but he had engaged both our enthusiasm and our good will in that short time. This would be total betrayal and deceit.

Iain McColl had again taken the side of the Yard, it seemed. The proposition that *The Sun* knew anything was very unlikely – merely a tool to bring forward the arrest to suit circulation and deadlines, and without so much as a word in the ear of the reporter and photographer expected to deliver this massive story.

At this point, Vine took charge. "Colin, this is non-negotiable now. Decisions have been made and you'll do what you're told. You and Bill will just have to co-operate and fix up some signal that Biggs is ready to be arrested. Too much is at stake to leave it another forty-eight hours, and the preparations have been made in London. Friday for Saturday it is, and the paper's circulation will soar above four million again."

"Oh, so that's the fucking reason," I retorted. "Circulation. I can't believe it. What about the story and what about Biggs? I'm telling you in simple terms – I haven't got the story out of him yet. All I really know is what happened up to his leaving Australia, and that's all in the public domain already."

"Don't care, old boy," Vine said. "You'll just have to do your best. The arrest itself will be the main story and his life on the run will be subsidiary. Now what's the plan?"

I looked at Bill, whose broad shoulders had slumped. And that's when the arrangements were made to signal Biggs's presence in room 909. As we trudged wearily back to the Trocadero I turned to Bill and said, "You rest up. I'm going to be up all night writing the background story from what little I've managed to glean. What a fucking cock-up this is." Bill couldn't even bring himself to speak.

2.

The Arrest

The knock on the door sounded just like room service. Bill and I knew better and let Conti open the door to reveal the daunting figure of Slipper, tieless and in a lightweight tropical suit especially purchased for this trip. He walked straight into room 909 without further ado and addressed Biggs who was in Lucia's embrace on the bed.

"Nice to see you again, Ronnie," Slipper began. "I think you'll remember me. It's been a long time."

With Slipper was Inspector Peter Jones, and the British Consul in Rio, Henry Neil, plus a gun-toting, plain-clothed Brazilian detective. Slipper wasted little time in grabbing Biggs by the shoulder and forcing him into the bathroom with the intention of placing handcuffs on him. He wasn't about to start taking chances now. But Biggs would have none of it. He remonstrated with Slipper and struck a deal that if he desisted from handcuffing him, he would "come quietly".

Meanwhile, Jones was interviewing Bill and me, ostensibly to show Conti that we were innocent of any part in the arrest. I was held for around ten minutes before I was free to join Biggs and the police at street level for the iconic picture that Bill took of the Great Train Robber being put into the rear seat of the British Consul's Austin Marina car. He was taken to Catete Palace prison, where the maritime police checked visas and identities of foreigners.

By now I was on auto-pilot. Vine joined me as we put in a call to the office. It was 10.30am Brazilian time and three hours later in London. Vine was able to get through to our New York office somewhat quicker and alerted them to tell London that the story was green to go. But it would be 5.30pm London time before we could start to relay copy. I suggested to Vine that he dictate my overnight story – the full background to Biggs's life post-Australia – from my handwritten notes, while I told the story of the arrest on a separate phone.

That night Bill and I dined alone in a small restaurant on the Rua Nossa Senhora de Copacabana. While the champagne corks burst noisily to life on the editorial floor of the *Daily Express* for the story the UK Press Gazette would eventually christen one of the best ten scoops in Fleet Street history, we could barely raise a conversation. Bill, with tears running down his face, eventually excused himself and said he had to go to bed. I couldn't disagree with him.

Despite promises that my wife Tina would be alerted the moment the story was about to appear, the first she knew of any progress was when ITN's *News at Ten* reported the arrest. She was as shocked as I had been at this dramatic turn of events and was unable to get hold of me although I planned to call her when I could. The four-hour delay was a huge impediment.

Her concerns received further momentum when, three days later, a man turned up on our Battersea doorstep and announced that he was Ronnie Leslie, one of the men who had effected Biggs's escape from Wandsworth prison. He wanted to know how his friend was in a Brazilian jail and how on earth I had discovered his whereabouts, as they weren't even known to Biggs's closest allies. Tina declined all his questions and retreated, shocked, inside the house.

Meanwhile I had even more pressing demands: how to hold off the opposition after the whole of Fleet Street arrived on a damage limitation exercise. *The Daily Mail* had sent its three top reporters from New York plus cameraman Micky Brennan.

David English, its ambitious editor, was doubly incensed that the byline on the story was that of a man he had offered a job to only three weeks earlier.

Vine returned to London within twenty-four hours, having denuded Biggs's apartment of what little memorabilia he could find before the arrival of the train robber's long-time partner and girlfriend, Raimunda de Castro, who had shared the Prado Junior flat with him for the past year.

This signalled the exit of the lovely Lucia, all tears and long legs. She spoke no English but the tableau that played out before her in Room 909 was a universal one that she understood perfectly. Astonishingly, one of the many legacies of her presence on his arm at the time of his arrest was the accusation (in Brazilian newspapers and magazines) that I had hired her as a model for Biggs. They were firmly on the side of the abandoned girlfriend Raimunda, who let slip to me that she was pregnant with Biggs's child.

One lone reporter up against the might of Fleet Street is an uneven battle as I was soon to discover. Ivor Key, the *Daily Express* bureau chief, was eventually flown down to assist me. The *Mail's* Monday edition splashed the exclusive that Biggs, with his wife Charmian, had been plotting a *Day of the Jackal* type return to Australia using the identity of a long-dead Australian baby as the basis for a new passport.

This was discovered after reporter Anthea Disney found a tape in Biggs's apartment, with Charmian suggesting the idea proposed in the Freddie Forsyth best seller. It was a great follow-up.

When Slipper and Jones failed to convince the Brazilian authorities that Biggs should accompany them back to London, they flew home a couple of days after the arrest. Unknown to them, Brennan was in first class with his camera trained on the two men. As soon as Jones arose to go to the toilet, Brennan seized the moment and captured the iconic shot of Slipper asleep alongside an empty seat. The *Mail* were catching up; they'd eventually overtake the *Express*'s circulation a decade or so later.

Back in Rio, I was trying to keep the mercurial Raimunda happy with my rusty Portuguese that was improving by the hour. I had picked up the language during my summer vacations with my father in the 1950s. Raimunda's understandable worry was a financial one. Biggs had supported her after she quit her job as a nightclub hostess. How was she to survive, especially as she couldn't go back to work pregnant? That was her constant and irritating refrain from the moment I first met her.

I tried to reassure her that the *Daily Express* would look after her without the slightest evidence that the promised £35,000 would be forthcoming. Indeed, I learned that in London the paper was denying that any money had changed hands. And they were right. Once control of the story had been levered from my grasp the question of reward had been ignored.

Furthermore, Scotland Yard had issued a press release claiming that they had worked in conjunction with the *Daily Express* to locate Biggs in Brazil. It was quickly corrected and amended to deny this version, but the damage had been done. Rival papers immediately took the view that the *Express* had tainted the reputation of Fleet Street by such an act of betrayal. And who was in the immediate firing line? Moi.

On February 5, my thirty-second birthday as it happened, my father flew down from Aracatuba to Rio to see what all the fuss was about. He had known nothing of the story prior to its publication and was more than intrigued to find his only son at the centre of a media maelstrom in Rio. I was door-stepping the prison when he arrived for one of the more unusual birthday parties of my life. After finally being allowed to see Biggs for ten minutes I was able to reassure him that he was being sent up to Brasilia, Brazil's capital, where his case would be reviewed over three months. I assured him that I would get him a good lawyer and that with Raimunda's pregnancy confirmed his chances of remaining in his newly adopted land were improving.

On the morning of Biggs's arrest, John Monks, the *Daily Express* man in Australia was waiting outside Charmian's house in Dandenong, in Melbourne. When he knocked on the front door and announced that her husband had been arrested in Rio, Charmian knew that the long sojourn on the run was over. She almost felt a sense of relief, except for the fact that she would never have advised him to give himself up she later told me. At this stage however she had no knowledge of how her husband had been found.

She had done a deal with the Packer press in early 1970 to serialise her story when her whereabouts in Melbourne had been discovered, and she turned to them again to get an airline ticket to Rio to see Ronnie. Little did she realise that the reunion would be played out at a press conference in front of the world's media. This was in Rio on the fifth day of Biggs's detention. However her presence in Catete prison was detracting from the sub-plot of Raimunda's pregnancy which was playing to a receptive Brazilian audience and readership.

After the press conference, I was able to get alongside Charmian to explain the sequence of events and to try and persuade her that the only way of rectifying matters financially was to let me do a book and that we would split the royalties. She agreed to this and invited me to Dandenong so that I could meet her children and debrief her on the whole saga. She had a far more retentive memory than her husband about the entire saga.

The following day I flew to Brasilia where Biggs had been taken for a three month stay so that his identity and history could be properly verified by the Brazilian authorities. I secured the services of a local lawyer, Dr Jose Pertence, who for a fee of $4,000 would set to work to see if he could secure Biggs's right to remain in the country and be a hands-on father to the child Raimunda was expecting in August.

Almost three months later, Biggs was released and given temporary residential status so that he could support his unborn child. He was required to live with Raimunda and be her partner. This was the signal for another Fleet Street bun fight as other papers tried to get an interview with the world's most wanted felon. This time I had some backup, with the broad shoulders of colleague Mike O'Flaherty deployed to protect our asset in a flat I had rented for Biggs.

Meanwhile, Charmian, with whom I had spent most of April in Australia researching the intricacies of the Biggs story, had decided to fly herself and her two sons Chris and Farley to Rio to effect a romantic and, so she hoped, permanent reconciliation with the Great Train Robber. At my own expense I installed her and the boys in a hotel alongside the fashionable beach area of Leblon.

Unfortunately, Charmian's very presence in Brazil was putting at risk the prospect of her husband's long-term future which depended on Raimunda giving birth to a Carioca (Rio-born) child. Biggs was between a rock and a hard place, desperate to retain the love of the woman who had been at his side for fourteen years and keen to re-establish himself in the eyes of his two boys. On the other hand, Raimunda was the darling of the local press and was a needy and whining presence in his life. He couldn't win, as he had to protect the woman he called the "chosen vessel" so that he could retain his liberty.

After ten days, Charmian realised she was in a lose-lose situation and said she'd like to come back to London with me and see her parents, two head teachers based in Reigate, Surrey, with whom she had severed contact following her 1960 marriage to Biggs. She and the boys accompanied me on a British Caledonian flight to Heathrow to spend a week in Britain unspotted by either the media or the police.

Among her various odd jobs was to visit the offices of an East End legal practice Biggs had used during his trial. The managing clerk was one of four people to whom Charmian had entrusted a quarter of their Train Robbery loot. I drove her down to Wapping where the offices were situated and waited outside while Charmian tried to extract the best part of £30,000 from this man who was shocked to his core to see her.

Needless to say, he came up with all manner of excuses as to what had happened to the money, including the old canard of a failed garage investment. But Charmian was not prepared to budge until he at least raided the "petty cash" where he was able to find £10,000. She agreed to settle for this amount on that day but threatened to return for the rest later in the week. In fact she was more than happy with the £10,000 and felt it might be dangerous to transport more than that sum by plane back home to Melbourne.

Charmian re-established contact with her parents who were thrilled to meet their two strapping grandsons. Then it was home, where she completed her degree course prior to becoming a university lecturer.

Back in Brazil, Biggs was trying to get his life together, acting as a tourist magnate which provided him with some sort of income. Raimunda gave birth to Mikezinho in August, a boy whom Biggs raised until he was an adult and who remained devoted to his father until the latter's death in London in 2013.

Although Mikezinho achieved some fame and income from a brief stint as a teenage pop star in a group called *O Balao*

Amarello (the yellow balloon), Biggs struggled to earn enough to live, even though tourists paid him to cook churrascos (barbecues) while he related the stories of his life on the run.

In 2001, having suffered three strokes (the latest of which removed his powers of speech), he decided to give himself up so that he could have medical treatment in Britain. He did a deal with *The Sun* which paid Mikezinho £125,000 for the scoop. He was flown back to Northolt airport in Rupert Murdoch's private jet and was formally arrested and taken to Belmarsh prison to serve at least ten years of his thirty year sentence.

Eventually, largely because he posed little or no threat to the public, he was released early on the grounds that he had cancer and little time to live. He and the alleged Libyan bomber of the *Pan Am* jet, Abdelbaset Ai-Megrahi (who had prostate cancer), were released on the same day in 2009. The latter lived for another three years while Biggs achieved his stated aim of outliving the Libyan by surviving in a North London care home until November 2013.

3.

Arrivals

I was born on February 5, 1942, a contribution to the Mackenzie diaspora, named after the founder and head of the Scottish clan. My second name was Gordon after my father, a Lieutenant in the Royal Scots Greys, who had volunteered for army service from his home in Brazil eighteen months earlier. My arrival hardly rivalled that of the United States into World War Two following Pearl Harbour a couple of months earlier, but it was important to my mother Hazel.

Within a week, my worrying pneumonia was arrested in full stride due to the miraculous healing powers of penicillin which had only recently become widely available, to the great relief of Hazel who had given birth to me in Middlesex.

The crunch of Hitler's bombs was ever present even though the Blitz was officially over. The Battle of Britain may have been won in the warm haze of September 1940 but the Luftwaffe was still active, even randomly attacking the small suburb of Hatch End where I lived with my mother and maternal grandmother, Alma Hamblin.

Gordon Mackenzie had volunteered, along with his fellow "cowboy" and best friend from Brazil, Murray Pearman. They wandered up Whitehall in July 1940, having arrived by White Star liner from Rio de Janeiro, in the hope of joining a cavalry regiment. They soon learned that volunteering wasn't as easy as might have been imagined. Offering their services as good horsemen had been met with some hilarity. They were eventually directed towards the Royal Scots Greys, a cavalry regiment, and sent up to Edinburgh for training. Within two weeks the regiment had foresworn horses in favour of tanks.

Gordon, whose parents lived in a grand house in Hatch End (his mother Elsie was a cotton mill heiress from the Garnett family of Clitheroe, Lancashire) had met the pretty, vivacious Hazel Hamblin, who was driving an ambulance even though she had never passed a driving test. Gordon, nine years her senior and possessing a dashing Errol Flynn moustache and a scarlet MG sports car, was mesmerized. Within weeks they were engaged to be married.

Hazel, an only child, was born in Darjeeling, Northern India, within distant sight of the magnificent Mount Everest. Her father was Edward Willetts, an engineer who built the celebrated railway from Calcutta to Darjeeling, a not inconsiderable feat traversing the foothills of the Himalayas. Within nine months of Hazel's birth Mr Willetts had abandoned his wife and child, leaving the latter pair to return by slow boat to the UK with few prospects of advancement in a world which frowned upon divorce.

Hazel's mother Alma attracted the attention of a neighbour, Cliff Hamblin, who soon promised marriage. Hazel took the surname of Hamblin and the divorce trauma was left unacknowledged. An only child, she was educated privately at the local day school, Woodridings, where coincidentally she met and befriended Gordon's youngest sister Lorna.

Hazel was a bright child, readily passing all her exams with ease. English was a favoured subject and it was little surprise to her mother when, in the immediate post war months and years, she rose to become one of radio and television's best known and ground-breaking scriptwriters under her nom de plume Hazel Adair. Having contributed to radio programmes, she turned her attention to the nascent world of television writing for children's programmes such as *Saturday Special* and *Whirligig*. By the early 1950s she was a fixture at Broadcasting House, the *BBC* headquarters off Oxford Circus.

Gordon had been educated at Malvern College and was keen to explore the world after leaving school. No academic, he was an action man, keen to serve King and Empire in some capacity. In 1929 he was offered a position to assist a rubber planter in Malaya. But the imminent economic depression put paid to a life in Kuala Lumpur. Instead he took a lowly position in a stockbroker's office in the City of London, a role he hated.

A year later he met a fellow Old Malvernian, Ronald Vestey, who was running Union International, a company expanding into South America, buying big cattle and coffee ranches in Argentina and Brazil. "Would young Gordon fancy the life of a cowboy in Brazil?" "You betcha" was the approximate reply. And so in early 1930, Gordon made his way by sea to Rio de Janeiro, then capital of the world's fifth largest country, and a place that he was to make his home until his death in 2001. On his arrival in Rio he transferred to a train which made laborious progress over the next three days to Mato Grosso in central Brazil. His first job was as an assistant to a farm manager, most of whose peons – cowboys – were native Brazilian Indians. For a man with little Portuguese, this was an even bigger test as the locals spoke only Guarani Indian.

For Hazel, life living with her mother in a cramped first floor flat in the suburbs was proving to be both boring and testing. Mr Hamblin had also done a runner by the outbreak of World War Two and Hazel soon realised that she would be the wage earner as her mother had been brought up to be little more than "her indoors." Meeting the glamorous and tanned polo-playing Gordon Mackenzie seemed like a positive solution to gaining her freedom. If this sounds a little cynical it was eventually to prove to be the reality of the marriage.

Following their October 1940 nuptials in Edinburgh, where Gordon was training with his regiment, the ambitious Hazel made it crystal clear that she was not prepared to be wed to a mere trooper. Gordon was exhorted to become an officer and within weeks he was at Sandhurst Military Academy in Surrey alongside notable elements from the movie industry such as David Niven and the Boulting Brothers. He was later commissioned and sent to Ulster for further training.

Hazel, now pregnant, was back in Hatch End living with her mother. It wasn't quite the scenario she had envisaged. She wasn't even able to return to her old job as an ambulance driver due to her condition. Life was claustrophobic and testing, to say the least.

By late 1942, Hazel, her mother, and the baby were invited to join mutual friends in Barton-on-Sea, a quiet little village in Dorset. The friend, whose husband was serving in the army overseas, had a baby the same age as me. It was an ideal arrangement, especially as the Luftwaffe's bombs still seemed attracted to Hatch End, despite the pretty London suburb having no strategic relevance at all.

My first memory as a child was the arrival of Canadian troops billeted in Barton-on-Sea in early 1945. D-Day was long gone but reinforcements were constantly being transported by ship to Southampton and Portsmouth. They had bountiful supplies of *Hershey* bars that they were willing to share with a gobby three year old.

My sole skill – apart from *Hershey* hustler – was recognising the myriad different aircraft flying over our house. Without even seeing them, I could identify Spitfires, Hurricanes, Halifaxes, Wellingtons, and so on, just from the timbre of their engine noise. It's not a skill I have been able to parlay into good use in later life, but I am adept at recognising voices.

By 1946, my father was de-mobbed and ready to return to Brazil. He had enjoyed a relatively undramatic war in terms of action but had been part of Monty's army fighting through North Africa and then on into Italy. An acting Major, he was still in Milan when the war ended.

Was Hazel returning to Brazil with him, went the conversation. No, she wasn't, was the instant reply, which rather startled the war hero. Hazel had ambitions to both act and write for the *BBC* and she had no intention of becoming a fazendeiro's wife in the dark interior of Brazil. Of course, I didn't witness this conversation, nor was I aware of its significance until years later. Although I knew who my father was, I had not knowingly met him until he came home on leave in 1949.

He took me to see all his relations scattered across the UK in Sussex, Yorkshire, and the Lake District, and then we had an enjoyable week's holiday in Kent.

During Gordon's stay, he agreed to do the decent thing and divorce Hazel. In those days, the only grounds was adultery, and to this end an actress friend of Hazel's consented to accompany Gordon to a room in the British Rail hotel at Victoria station, witnessed by a private detective who could give evidence to this effect. My parents were divorced, although I, aged seven, was unaware of it.

My mother and I returned to Hatch End. Hazel was appearing in and writing intimate revues in the West End. In 1948 she was invited to submit some scripts for *Children's Hour* radio. Until then virtually all the writing for the *BBC* was undertaken by men. Soon Hazel was commuting regularly to Oxford Circus.

I was enrolled in Wellington school, a hundred yards from the cramped first floor flat we were still living in. Further down Wellington Road was Greylands, the large mansion owned by Gordon's parents; after my grandfather George Mackenzie died in 1944 the house was sold and became an old people's care home.

As an only child, I made much of my own entertainment. Rationing was the norm until the Government ended it in 1954. Sweets rationing was a hardship that ensured obesity was a factor of the future and not of immediate post war Britain. And yet for the most part, children were happy and fulfilled. I enjoyed regular visits to my mother's office in Broadcasting House. At six and seven years of age, it was safe to send your children alone on the tube. Toys were a luxury and some of mine had been fashioned in wood by German prisoners of war; I felt lucky to play with them.

Christmas celebrations in 1949 were tempered by the news that I was to be sent away to boarding school. The Vestey company which employed my father in Brazil was willing to pay private school fees to compensate ex-pats for their time abroad. I was to be sent to Lambrook preparatory school, where my father had spent 1920-25, whether I liked it or not. I would then go on to his old public school, Malvern College, when I was thirteen, provided I wasn't too stupid to pass the entrance exams.

4.

Lambrook, unhappy school days

Lambrook was a feeder prep school for Eton, Harrow, and Winchester. Occasionally more minor public schools such as Sherborne and Malvern would feature as well. It had high academic standards and was better at sport than most of its nearby rivals which included Ludgrove (where Princes William and Harry were educated), Sunningdale (Prince Michael of Kent and racehorse trainer Henry Cecil), Papplewick, Heatherdown, and St George's Windsor. The Ascot Enclave, some called them.

Today, Lambrook has 550 boys and girls, some boarders and some day pupils, and is evidently well thought of. When I arrived in January 1950, it had 110 boys, all boarders, most of whose parents were well-heeled and often aristocratic. My mother's 1935 coffee-coloured Austin Ten seemed more than a little out of place parked alongside the Rolls-Royces and Bentleys in the car park when I arrived nervous and deeply unhappy that my comfortable life and routine in Hatch End was being eroded.

Any hopes that "the happiest days of your life" might materialise in the Winkfield Row prep school were dashed within three weeks of my arrival. I was not yet eight years old when I suffered, with almost half of the school, from what Headmaster Archie Forbes described as book inspections. This meant that if your handwriting was below par you were subject to a beating at the Headmaster's hand.

This was not the slipper I might have expected but a riding crop on bare buttocks. The first time I received this attention I screamed, so shocked and upset was I. That was the one and only time I made a noise as I never again (there were around ten such episodes) wanted to give the Headmaster that pleasure. As we had to swim naked in the school swimming pool on a daily basis, it was more than apparent from the weals on the buttocks of many boys exactly whose handwriting was deemed inadequate.

Two weeks later, I was sat in the main hall writing my weekly letter home to my mother when a second traumatic event took place. Religiously copying the sports results, must have sent my blessed mother to sleep, even if she could read my "poor" handwriting. But I persevered and then addressed the envelope to Mrs Mackenzie, 10 Wellington Rd, Hatch End, Middx.

As I handed it to the Headmaster, he shouted, in front of the entire school "Why have you addressed this to Mrs Mackenzie, Mackenzie? You know perfectly well she got divorced and remarried two weeks ago and is now Mrs Marriott."

The fact is that I didn't know my mother had remarried. In her mind I had suffered enough trauma being sent away to boarding school, even though she knew nothing of the sadistic headmaster's beatings. She had planned to inform me of her nuptials at the end of my first term when I went home. In 1950, divorce was social suicide and relatively rare. It stigmatised families and was another shock to my system. No wonder I started biting my nails.

Ronnie Marriott who had fought with distinction in the RAF during the war was known to me as a friend of my mother's. I wasn't unhappy that she had chosen him to replace my father who in truth I hardly knew. But it was a lot to confront, adding to my misery at Lambrook. Other boys looked at me with pity and amusement – a divorced mother no less!

Early in 1950, the new Mr and Mrs Marriott moved to Redcliffe Gardens on the borders of Chelsea and Fulham. It was not far from Stamford Bridge, the home of Chelsea Football Club, of which I have been a fan for the last seventy years. We had a maisonette at the top of a Victorian building – definitely a step-up from the flat in Hatch End.

Later that same first term at Lambrook, I was beaten again. This time Forbes's wife Elsie was the culprit, reporting me to her husband for failing to eat all my spam fritters. The rule was that you had to eat everything on your plate because of rationing. I wasn't alone but it was a severe test as you had to wait until evening in your ice cold dormitory for the punishment to be delivered after you got the summons to the headmaster's study.

For some ludicrous stiff upper lip logic, I never revealed to my mother how unhappy I had been during my first term at Lambrook. Why I didn't put up more resistance to returning there for the summer term, I can't remember. Eventually I suppose I got used to it, the saving grace being that I was sporty and soon represented the school at cricket and soccer, becoming captain of both teams in my final year. I also boxed (it was compulsory) and was unbeaten. Eventually my sporting prowess won the respect of my peers and of the Head Master, but it was hard gained.

In 1952, to my horror, Archie Forbes invited Hazel and Ronnie to the school to read some chapters from their new children's book "Stranger from Space" based on a children's television serial they had written. Instead of pride, I was hugely anxious, especially after one of the younger schoolmasters asked for my attractive mother's telephone number as he had fallen "under her spell".

In August of that year I acquired a half-brother in the noisy form of Charles Marriott. To assuage my doubts about having to share my mother with another, my father Gordon arrived somewhat felicitously on leave from Brazil to take me on a tour of the relatives and cousins around Britain. My full appreciation of Charles was delayed for a few weeks.

Later that year, the whole of Central London turned dark at midday. It was the result of extreme pollution caused by the many coal and wood fires that were the norm in people's homes. Few enjoyed central heating in the post-war austerity. This phenomenon, led to legislation which would eventually ban domestic fires while factories had to pay attention to their own pollution.

The Queen's Coronation followed in the summer of 1953 and we were all allowed to go home from school for a week's holiday. We already had a television set because of my mother's work but for many millions this was an excuse to buy their first "haunted fish tank," as the box became known.

Another half-brother arrived in the Spring of 1955: Craig. By now we were living in the pretty Surrey village of Betchworth in a thatched ranch house called Nutwood purchased by Ronnie and Hazel for a princely £4,000. Our immediate neighbour was Donald Campbell, who spent his life breaking speed records on land and water. Hazel was completing a script of *Mrs Dale's Diary*, the daily radio soap, even as Craig was being born.

Gradually, my sporting prowess at Lambrook won the approval of Forbes and his formidable wife and I was left relatively untouched by the riding crop. I almost enjoyed my final two years there, although I was somewhat puzzled by one event. The whole school had to sit around the radio as it relayed the results of the 1951 General Election which saw Winston Churchill returned as Prime Minister. Every time a Tory was successful, we were encouraged to roar our approval. When Labour or the Liberals won a seat, we were exhorted to boo loudly. Extraordinary in hindsight.

I have since learned from contemporaries in other boarding prep schools in the 1950s that my experiences at Lambrook were not that unusual although perhaps exercised with a degree of cruelty at the upper end of the spectrum. It doesn't excuse the behaviour of Forbes and his ilk. I still believe the practice reeked of abuse.

5.

Marvellous Malvern

I was fairly confident that Malvern could not be as cruel an institution as Lambrook although I had no proof that my hopes would be realised. Founded in 1865, Malvern was a typical Victorian public school whose location was determined by the Great Western Railway which provided access to pupils and parents. Its principal buildings were neo-Gothic, much admired by the poet John Betjeman, who I would later meet when he was guest speaker at Parents' Day 1960.

I had been assigned to House No 8; boarding arrangements divided the 650 boys into ten different houses. This was the house that my father and two uncles had attended in the 1920s. The house master was George White, known to his sixth form classics pupils as Wagger White. It was not long before I discovered the cane had not become redundant although it was used sparingly and more gently. The head of house, the senior prefect, was also allowed to administer corporal punishment, albeit via the slipper. Fagging, when new boys perform tasks such as cleaning prefects' shoes, was still rampant.

Academic standards were high at Lambrook, where masters deemed I was not suitable scholarship material for Malvern. We used to practice for Common Entrance, the exam for entry into public schools, by taking the bespoke Winchester exam papers which were more testing than CE papers. Whether or not this influenced my teachers I don't know, but I sailed into Malvern and was soon promoted to the scholarship class which meant that I took O levels at fifteen, and A levels at seventeen.

I soon found the atmosphere at Malvern conducive to hard work and the sporting facilities were wonderful. I was a reasonably good soccer and cricket player, having captained Lambrook at both, but not good enough to make the 1st XI at either sport at Malvern. I played both sports for my house but my attention was drawn to the fives courts, the rackets courts, the squash courts, and the tennis courts.

Boxing was also compulsory and I carried my unbeaten record through, eventually suffering defeat at the hands of Geoff Irvine, who later won a blue at Oxford, and Pat Orr, later an international rugby player for England. I was competing in the annual quadrangular competition with nearby public schools Downside, Clifton and Cheltenham. I always felt it was a little unfair that the monks of Downside would sit ringside holding their rosaries and blessing their boys in the ring. Boxing is hard enough without competing against God!

Malvern had wonderful views over the Vale of Evesham as it was sited at the base of the famous hills. The town was also home to a dozen girls' public schools. Crocodiles of girls enjoying exercise on the hills could be viewed from the boys college. Some of the more adventurous souls would dive bomb the crocodiles from higher up in the hope of making an impact. The level of success was on the lower side of minimal but it made for interesting viewing.

These girls' schools were well aware of the threat posed by the college and resisted most attempts for social interaction. It wasn't until 1960 when I was head boy, that a dance was arranged with Malvern Girls College in our gymnasium. The level of scrutiny and supervision by the girls' chaperones was such that any prospect of romance was stamped on from the first to the last waltz.

Of the 700 pupils at Malvern in 2020, 300 are girls. The major effect has been to elevate the academic level of the college. Surprise, surprise. What it has done for relationships between the sexes I have no idea. But as a relic of the 1950s I can attest that the average teenage public schoolboy of my era had little or no knowledge of girls as objects of desire. More's the pity.

I found it easier to make real friends at Malvern than at my prep school. Mike Manson arrived the same day as I, studied the same specialities (French and Spanish), went on to Oxford with me and, poor chap, even became best man at my wedding. We enjoyed an immediate affinity although I had no idea he was Jewish until one day he went missing from Chapel and revealed to me that he had been excused that daily chore because of his religion.

Malvern's headmaster was Donald Lindsay, a very good public speaker and quite inspirational. He missed his vocation which would have been to be a Shakespearean actor. Later he was able to live this dream vicariously when his son Ian became a thespian.

Mens Sana In Corpus Sanum – healthy mind, healthy body – was the unspoken ethos espoused by Malvern even if the official school motto was *Sapiens Qui Prospicit* – wise is he who looks forward. There were six lessons a day followed by at least two hours of sport: soccer in the Autumn term, rugby in the Spring term, and cricket in the summer term, all compulsory.

The school has now turned exclusively to rugby in the winter terms which is a great shame as historically Malvern had one of the best public school soccer teams in the country, hardly losing a match in my five years at the school.

Malvern was not as academically rigorous as, for example, Winchester, Eton, or Marlborough, however there were some very good teachers there, notably Tony Leng who taught French and Spanish at 0 and A level. He successfully navigated both Mike Manson and me into Oxford University for which we owed him a tremendous debt. He later became House Master of School

House whose pupils included the BBC's arch interrogator Jeremy Paxman. The latter claimed not to have enjoyed Malvern much, but he admired Tony Leng and was at his funeral in 2005 where Mike and I both met him.

During the late 1950s my mother Hazel was breaking glass ceilings at the *BBC* and at *ITV* where she and Ronnie separately were responsible for the first two programmes ever broadcast by the independent channel *Associated Rediffusion* in September 1955. Ronnie directed an advertising magazine while Hazel co-wrote the first ever daily soap called *Sixpenny Corner*. Sadly, and largely due to costs, it folded after only three months. But it was the precursor and trail blazer for later shows such as *Coronation Street* and *East Enders*.

Because of the demands on her time, not to mention bringing up my two half-brothers, I rarely saw my mother outside of school holidays. While some parents would attend frequently to watch their sons' sporting triumphs or take them out for Sunday tea, my mother and stepfather rationed their Malvern visits to no more than once a year. It was a little disappointing but had the effect of driving my ambition to get noticed by them and by my peers at school. In hindsight I never felt unloved but possibly a little unappreciated and that made me try even harder.

I sailed through 0 levels, although chemistry proved to be a subject too far. It was a late decision by the school to make linguists take that subject as well as physics and maths. We had no more than a few months to master it and I was less than keen as I was determined to do languages at A level. There were no grades at 0 level in 1957 but eight out of nine passes were enough to qualify for the sixth form where I would concentrate on French, Spanish, and Latin.

By now I had espoused fives, squash and tennis. Soon I was captain of all three sports which was thrilling but time consuming. I even tried my hand at rackets, surely the fastest indoor sport of all. The cost (I used to break three rackets a week) was worrying and I eventually gave it up. If only I had known Lord Vestey was picking up my school fees (as my father's boss) I wouldn't have worried but I was ignorant of this fact until many years later.

At home, Nutwood had ceased to be a thatched ranch-style house and was now topped with red bricks above the lengthy six-bedroomed building which overlooked two Surrey beauty spots in Leith Hill and Box Hill. In the summer holidays, when not commuting to Brazil to see my father, I picked apples from the extensive orchard and sold them to passers-by for 4d a pound, less than 2p in today's money.

I had joined Reigate tennis club but getting there was difficult with two working parents and local bus services something of a mirage, but I discovered that the beautiful Sonia Macintosh, the girls' junior champion, lived only half a mile away and I was able to get a lift with her on most occasions. We even began a rather tepid romance, largely because I was so shy around girls. The tennis was going well, however, boosted by a very good coach called Peter Cawthorne who saw some promise in both of us. We were both good enough to compete in the Surrey championships and later Junior Wimbledon.

My first visit to Brazil occurred when I was twelve. Four weeks in a far-off land was both exciting and a little daunting. I was put in the charge of *KLM* staff on the lengthy DC 6 flight from London, flying via Amsterdam, Frankfurt, Lisbon, Dakar, Recife, Rio de Janeiro, and finally Sao Paulo. By the time the Cruzeiro DC 3 landed at Aracatuba's tiny country airport I had been careering around in an aircraft for over fifty hours. Talk about jet lag.

Aracatuba, a thousand kilometres inland from both Rio and Sao Paulo, was the gateway to Brazil's Wild West. It was the centre of the coffee and cattle region with many of the latter raised in the Mato Grosso further inland before being trained to Aracatuba where Lord Vestey's rich farms fattened them up. They were then transported by rail to the slaughterhouses or frigorificos in Barretos and Mendes nearer to Rio.

In those days the Vesteys owned more than fifty farms in Argentina and Brazil. Some of them were in excess of a hundred thousand hectares in size and it was my father's job to fill them up with cattle to be fattened up for another Vestey company, Dewhursts, the butchers. To do this he flew from farm to farm, usually by small Cessna, buying up cattle from local Brazilians. The reason he became so popular with the local fazendeiros was that he always paid up on time and the cheques never bounced.

On my second visit to Brazil when I was fourteen, I accompanied my dad on several of these trips and was even allowed to fly the Cessna, although I wasn't permitted to land or take off.

I fell in love with Brazil, with its subtle rhythms, wonderful soccer, and crazy multi-ethnic people. About a third of Aracatuba's two hundred thousand population were Japanese. They were attracted there after the war and encouraged to farm, mostly vegetables and sugar cane. They prospered, as they worked harder than most of the locals, and Aracatuba soon had a Japanese cinema and many Japanese restaurants.

With my Spanish and French, I could understand a lot of what the Portuguese-speaking Brazilians were saying and I gradually picked up the local patois. Wandering into town and sitting at a bar it was easy to strike up conversation especially when I mentioned the name Mackenzie. It seemed the whole town liked and trusted my dad. I never knew if I was speaking to a millionaire or a humble peon. It was exciting.

My father had a black housekeeper called Dona Maria Silva who had two children, a boy called Benedito one year younger than me and a daughter Sueli who was nine years my junior. Benedito and I played football a lot. He was quite a scallywag and later became the chairman of an important logistics company in northern Brazil.

Dona Maria was illiterate and would have been astonished to learn that her granddaughter is now one of Rio's top plastic surgeons, exemplifying the possibilities that exist in Brazil for anyone with ambition. Sadly, too few get the chance.

Sueli, now 68, studied hard, speaks fluent English and recently graduated from London University's School of Oriental and African Studies with a Master's degree in Comparative Religion and Politics. She was on a scholarship, funded by Britain's Foreign Aid programme, and fulfilled her own dreams of becoming a graduate. She is a wonderfully kind person who has helped many Brazilians and Americans through her work for religious organisations.

In 1960, I saw Pele, the world's greatest footballer, represent Santos against our local team Presidente Prudente. Pele had just turned twenty and had been the hero of the Brazilian team two years earlier when the World Cup was played in Stockholm.

In 1959 I took my A levels. I was already Head of House but never expected to be made Senior Chapel Prefect. Donald Lindsay could not have timed his invitation to become Head Boy more infelicitously. He summoned me to his study ten minutes before I was due to sit my Latin examination. While flattered to be asked I was terrified at the prospect of such advancement with the attendant duties of public speaking and welcoming of distinguished guest speakers to the school.

I spent the first fifty minutes of my ninety minute exam in a state of shock, committing nothing to paper. It was no surprise to me a few weeks later when I was deemed to have failed my Latin exam, although an unwelcome shock to my Latin master. Luckily, my French and Spanish A levels were unaffected as I had already taken all the papers before Donald Lindsay's intervention.

My house master, George White, who at sixty-five was in his final year at Malvern before retiring, was thrilled to have his Head of House be appointed the Senior Chapel Prefect. He had taken a shine to my ability as a squash player, able to lose to him at appropriate moments.

I felt I would never again have such command over my contemporaries as I had as Head Boy of Malvern. The masters left much of the school's disciplinary matters to the prefects. And I had the last word in who would be appointed prefects, who would be captains of most sports and so on. It was heady stuff although I hope I never let it enlarge my ego.

Donald Lindsay even gave me the keys to his Wolseley, ostensibly to meet and transport guest speakers from the train station to the debating hall, such as Father Trevor Huddlestone, who fought so gallantly against apartheid, the aforementioned John Betjeman, and Jodrell Bank supremo Bernard Lovell.

Father (later Bishop) Huddlestone was an inspirational figure who opened our eyes to the horrors of apartheid. He also played some wonderful music and introduced us to the melodic "click" songs of the incomparable Miriam Makeba. He brought along some LP records of her music which sold out within minutes.

In December 1959 I sat the entrance exam for Gonville and Caius College, Cambridge. The weather was freezing and the room I was allocated seemed even colder. The rejection slip came through after Christmas and I knew I had underperformed.

I was seventeen and had the benefit of a second chance at Oxbridge the following year. For once, my academic ambitions were realised, unencumbered by shocks or other interruptions.

In 1960, refreshed by a summer holiday with my father in Brazil, I sat the entrance exam for Oriel College, Oxford. Within a couple of weeks, I had the offer of a place at this ancient academy founded in 1326 where the likes of Sir Walter Raleigh had lain his cloak. With undisguised joy I returned home to tell my mother the good news.

"How are you going to pay for that?" was the surprise reaction and one I had least expected. No congratulations, no celebrations, and no prospects.

I had just left Malvern and was planning to spend January through to October on a mini gap year, perfecting my Spanish with a job in Barcelona. A member of Reigate tennis club had contacts with a Catalan import/export firm called Carlos Rafael Mares who would be delighted to provide me with employment for six months starting in March. Gracias. The pay was a modest 700 pesetas a week – about six pounds – but rent was cheap and you could live quite well on that money in those days.

Hazel and Ronnie decided to adopt three girls to add to the three boys in their household. The original intention was to adopt one – Janet Coyne – who had a marvellous singing voice. They had been taking her out for weekends from the Surrey County Council orphanage where she lived. Her mother was alive but Janet and her two siblings, Carol and Maria, had been put into care.

For some reason my mother had imagined that I would become a wage earner and, in all probability, quit the family nest once I had left school. This failure of communication was shocking and despite my letters home detailing my Oxbridge ambitions the message had gone missing like a bottle in the ocean. What to do?

The cost of a year at Oriel in 1961 was around £500 of which £370 was room and board while the remainder was to enable you to buy the necessary books. Hazel and Ronnie had two boys at a fee-paying prep school, while two of the three newly adopted girls were bound for Elmhurst Ballet school which was also fee-paying. My prospects looked bleak.

I applied to the Surrey County Council for a grant. To my astonishment, the Surrey Education Committee were responsive to my letter and agreed to grant me a state scholarship of £500 a year. I wouldn't be costing my mother a single pound. Relief all round and a great thank you to a system which, sadly, has largely gone missing for the modern student.

6.

Oriel College

Gap years and foreign travel are the norm for many university-bound teenagers these days. But in 1961 it was relatively rare and I felt very privileged to enjoy work experience in Barcelona. Carlos Rafael Mares turned out to be a much respected and well-liked company, most of whose employees were more comfortable speaking Catalan, the local dialect/language of Cataluna, than Castilian. They took pity on me however, and usually spoke colloquial Spanish when I was with them.

My principal job was to translate documents from Spanish to English to be sent to customers abroad. It was more difficult to learn the formal language of business than to translate. Working hours in the winter months were 8am to midday, followed by four hours siesta, and then three more hours from 4pm to 7pm. From April onwards it was "horas de verano" – summer hours – of 8am to 2pm. The rest of the day was yours.

I was living in the Barrio Gotico, a working class area down by the port. Due to my impecunious state I was sharing a room and rarely was the same person there from night to night. Nevertheless, in those gentler times, I never suffered any losses from theft or had cause to doubt the honesty of my many different roommates. I was paying twenty-five pesetas a night to share, roughly three shillings or 15p in today's money. This left me with 500 pesetas a week, £3, to spend on food and fun.

I used the time to visit local beaches and to acquire a tan and meet people. I came across one of the *KLM* air hostesses who had been on my last flight from Sao Paulo the previous September, a lovely Dutch girl called Gerda. Because of the length of the flights in that era you sometimes got to know crew members and I had fallen under her spell and asked her out to dinner on our arrival in Amsterdam. She had politely declined, but I could tell we had a little connection.

One day on the beach in Sitges I heard my name called in a delightful Dutch accent, and there she was, taking three months off from work to add Spanish to her portfolio of language skills. She was five years older than me and definitely out of my league. But I decided to take the plunge and we enjoyed a wonderful summer romance until she had to rebase to Amsterdam in June. I was no longer a virgin soldier.

A taste of business led me to wondering if I should continue with my plans to read French and Spanish at Oxford or whether to transfer to Philosophy, Politics, and Economics (PPE). I figured that I could keep my language skills alive by visiting France and Spain as often as I could while broadening my work possibilities with a different degree. Oriel agreed immediately to let me do this. I was unaware at the time that many prime ministers and government ministers used PPE as the gatehouse for a career in Westminster.

Oriel is the fourth oldest college at Oxford, blessed with three charming quadrangles and home to around 300 undergraduates. It is one of the smaller colleges, famed for the rowing prowess of its students. Being head of the river, as Oriel frequently was, led to rumbustious suppers with attendant drunkenness and lewd behaviour. Rowing was not a sport I was familiar with and having seen its participants throwing up after training sessions it held little appeal for me.

Oriel was also the alma mater of Cecil Rhodes who had colonised a large swathe of southern Africa and had become immensely wealthy towards the end of the 19th century. He had endowed the Oriel cellars with enough wine for a hundred years or more and the dons were still benefitting on the high table. Far more importantly, he had provided the funds for Rhodes scholarships which enabled students from poorer backgrounds to enjoy an Oxbridge education. Former US President Bill Clinton was one such beneficiary, and while I was at Oriel we had at least six African Rhodes scholars from countries as diverse as Ethiopia and Ghana.

Five other Malvernians joined Oriel in 1961. One was Jonathan Foden who had been in my house but with whom I had not been particularly friendly; we became roommates and best buddies and had a bedroom each and a shared sitting room.

He was reading geography and became a government agricultural advisor in Malawi. Tragically he lost his arm in a traffic accident in the late 1970s and had a blood transfusion in the local hospital in Blantyre. The blood was polluted and poor Jonathan contracted Aids. He died in Britain six years later. He would have been proud of his son Giles who became a respected journalist and novelist and whose *Last King of Scotland* was a best seller, later made into a movie.

The first objective at Oriel was to pass prelims – exams taken in March to demonstrate that you had been attending tutorials and lectures. If successful, you faced no further examinations until your finals two and a quarter years later. Another bonus of passing prelims was to be allowed a car, not that I was the proud owner of such a luxury item. But Jonathan Foden did have a car – a glorious 1929 Lee Francis open grand tourer complete with dickie, a passenger carrying boot which opened to the elements.

To his shock, but my indecent delight, Jonathan failed his prelims which had to be retaken in June. I passed and was therefore eligible to own and drive a car. Generously, Jonathan leased me the Lee Francis for our first summer term, and it was my passport to success with women.

My endeavours began somewhat disastrously when I invited a lovely Danish PPP undergraduate from Somerville College, Anne-Marie Olesen, to dinner at the fashionable Elizabeth restaurant. The bill was £4-15 shillings (£4.75), a fortune. I had only £4 on me and had the humiliation of having to borrow 15 shillings from my date or face washing up for the rest of term at this smart restaurant. The days of the credit card and bank overdrafts lay in the future.

Anne-Marie thought the whole episode was a hoot, but as a very inexperienced suitor I took it badly and felt ashamed. I also felt that she was probably First Division to my Third Division North, which was true on several counts. We agreed to remain just friends.

One of the freshmen at Oriel was Maurice Manasseh, a very talented cricketer. He was to change my life when he took me to a betting shop. I had little or no knowledge of horseracing, having attended a race meeting only twice in my life. We were on our way to play football and we popped into this hole in the wall situated down a little side street. Maurice, a veteran punter, had sniffed it out.

Years later, as racehorse owners, Maurice and his brother-in-law Bobby Lorenz would win the prestigious Lincoln handicap.

"Come on Colin, have a little yankee and I'll win you a few quid," Maurice said. He promptly wrote out a betting slip with four horses listed on it and added, "This is a yankee bet. You have six doubles, four trebles, and an accumulator, and if all four win you'll get a tidy sum. If you do it for five bob (25p) it will cost you £2 fifteen shillings (£2.75)."

Off we trotted to Ifield Rd where the soccer match was to take place, returning three hours later before the final selection was due to run. To my amazement, the first three had won at odds ranging from 6-4 to 7-2. We waited for the last one, a 5-2 shot.

In those days there was no commentary, let alone television pictures from the tracks. You waited for the telex machine to spill out the result which the board man would transfer in chalk to the results board.

My life might have turned out very differently had the final selection been unplaced. But it duly won and one dirt poor undergraduate was richer by more than £150.00. These were riches far beyond my modest dreams. The adrenalin rush of a bet would stay with me for the next sixty years and fuel an ambition to one day become a racing correspondent. Had I lost money on my first real investment on the turf I truly believe I would have gone into business or been something in the City.

I promised to share my bounty with a few new friends in Oriel by holding a cocktail party. We had already discovered Cyprus sherry; an entire bottle was no more than six shillings or 30p. Beer was cheap in the Junior common room bar, but Jonathan and I decided to have the party in our rooms despite the presence on our staircase of the Regius Professor of History, Hugh Trevor Roper, later Lord Dacre of *The Hitler Diaries* fame.

His rooms were on the same floor and his front door faced ours. Luckily, we were aware that he seldom visited Oriel, preferring the more rarefied ambience of nearby Christ Church college where he taught. This was just as well because certain of our friends, it can now be revealed, burst into his rooms and drank all his Spanish sherry and port. This raid was only brought to his notice a full twelve months later by which time Jonathan and I were lodging in a different quadrangle.

Another of our friends, also reading PPE, was Nigel Lindsay-Fynn who was sharing rooms with a Yale graduate called Len Bickwit. Nigel took one look at his sparsely furnished drawing room and immediately fitted a plush new carpet with Lintafoam underlay. It turned out that his father Basil owned Lintafoam and

Nigel was not planning three years of austerity as an undergraduate. A grand piano was miraculously installed in their first floor drawing room as well to enable the talented Nigel to tickle the ivories.

Bickwit, who couldn't believe his luck at having his quarters upgraded at no cost to himself, went on to become my tennis partner, and we played for Oriel as the number one pair. He became a great friend, went on to Harvard Law school and eventually landed a job in Washington with a top legal firm. When Senator John Glenn, the first US astronaut to orbit the Earth, was standing for the Democratic nomination against Ronald Reagan in 1984, Bickwit was his legal counsel. Glenn eventually lost out to Walter Mondale who came a poor second to Reagan in the subsequent election.

Another lifelong passion was ignited when I was invited to watch several Orielenses playing bridge, a game I was unfamiliar with as a teenager. Watching the play and the gambits was thrilling and a group of novice players was formed to while away the cold evenings in college. I was hooked and still am.

Our 1961 intake of PPE students failed to impress philosophy don Mr Robinson who promptly opted for a sabbatical, subleasing his undergraduates to a lady in St Anne's College. Dr Eric Hargreaves, who had been a government advisor during the Depression years of 1929 and was a disciple of John Maynard Keynes, took on Economics while our Politics tutor was Hugh Seton-Watson.

I doubt I made a mark on any of them, but unlike my good friend Manasseh, I did at least turn up at lectures and tutorials. When asked for my friend's whereabouts I came up with a range of excuses, from ill parents to cricket coaching. How he got away with it I'll never know but Maurice surprised even himself by graduating with a Fourth Class degree, exclusive to a small minority and better than a pass degree.

There can be few more glorious places in the UK than Oxford in summer. Free of the burden of exams, proud lessor of a vintage car, with unlimited tennis and village cricket, provided Salad Days for this Oriel student. There was even a Commem Ball to plan for, the only question being who to ask as my partner?

My first visit to the Wimbledon championships, which I have rarely missed since, was in June 1962 when Oxford's tennis captain, Tim Phillips, asked if I would like a job answering the public telephones in the press room. I jumped at the chance and realised after two days that the public phones rarely, if ever, went off. My press pass allowed me free entry to the Wimbledon grounds where I witnessed a host of wonderful matches on the outside courts.

The following year, that job went to someone else and I applied to Messrs Walls for a job as an ice cream salesman. I must have been rather useless because I was sacked after three days. But again, I retained my Wimbledon pass and was able to repeat the feat of twelve months earlier.

Following Wimbledon, there were the immense possibilities offered by a four-month summer vacation. Nutwood was now somewhat overcrowded with five children so I determined to spend the time abroad. And with this in mind my old school chum Thom Keyes came to the rescue. His father was an American doctor living in Las Vegas and he had two small children who needed babysitting through July and August.

Thom, who was at Christ Church, was planning to tour America that summer and agreed to provide me with an introduction. He would join up with me on September 1 to drive back across to New York where Len Bickwit's parents had offered to put us up. Perfect.

We booked a charter flight to New York and Thom drove us to Nevada and the hot sands of Las Vegas. I was welcomed into the Keyes household and somehow got a job as a medical orderly in the Southern Nevada Memorial hospital. My principal job was to wheel burns victims to a vast bath where they could be washed and treated. It was humbling to witness their courage as they sought to get over their life changing injuries.

I'd had some success at the hospital with a couple of nurses. I was even invited to have dinner at the home of one whose parents accused me of being a communist when I revealed I was at Oxford. It was a lesson that we and the Americans may share a common language but we enjoy very different perspectives of the world. In 1962, barely five per cent of Americans even had a passport, let alone accurate knowledge of the politics of other nations.

Once in New York we were on safer ground, politically and philosophically. I fell in love with Audrey Hepburn who was starring in *Breakfast at Tiffany's* which I insisted on seeing four times in the local cinema. The Bickwits couldn't have been kinder.

At Oriel, second year students were still able to rent rooms in college and were only decanted into the town for their third year. Other colleges had different arrangements. While this was a pleasing and satisfactory deal, I began to have second thoughts as December arrived with blizzards and a cold spell which refused to relax its icy grip until early March. Horseracing was cancelled for two and a half months because of freezing conditions while football and most other outdoors sports were aborted. Oriel, founded in 1326, had not done a lot to improve its plumbing arrangements down the years. Jonathan and I had a shared bathroom in the second quad apartment that we now occupied. But it was incapable of adapting to the cold bite from the east. Pipes froze and very soon arrangements had to be made to utilise a modern building several hundred yards away to wash and shower. We accepted this at first, but two solid months tested our resolve.

For my twenty-first birthday, there were a few drinks in the Junior Common Room bar. We were able to run up an account which had to be settled before the end of term. Dad had remembered the occasion and sent me a cheque for £100 which I parlayed into a scarlet 1935 MG TA similar to the one he had driven during the war.

At last I had wheels of my own, albeit ones which would cause me heartache as I was no mechanic. Glamorous as she looked, my MG was a madam; God bless Jonathan Foden, who enjoyed fiddling around underneath vintage cars, even fashioning a new exhaust as mine had rusted to pieces.

Most sport was cancelled but I was able to indulge in some fives and squash, winning a Squirrel (second team blue) playing against Cambridge. My bridge improved too, as the freeze nullified much of the socialising outside college. One bonus emerged as there was little else to do but study. A brief moment of relief occurred each Saturday evening when many us sat down to watch the new satirical programme *That Was The Week That Was* hosted by David Frost. It was new, fresh, and uproariously funny, and caused me to wonder about a career in television.

With this in mind I submitted a few articles for *Cherwell*, the student newspaper. I was less successful with *Isis*, the rather more intellectual university magazine. I figured having a few articles published might help with job interviews eighteen months down the line.

The summer of 1963 was spent in a haze of tennis, girlfriends, and wonderfully scandalous news stories. The Profumo Affair had reared its head, with the Minister of War, Jack Profumo, found to have shared a lover – the young and beautiful Christine Keeler – with a Russian military attaché/spy, Yevgeny Ivanov.

By August a group of villains had electrified the criminal underworld and the rest of society by pulling off the Great Train Robbery, removing nearly £2.7 million in used bank notes from Her Majesty's Mail train. The audacity of the crime astonished the public who were seduced into believing the caper had a Robin Hood element to it. Once the identity of the villains was discovered, that notion gradually evaporated, but the caper continued to resonate glamour. In many pubs and nightclubs in London there would be a surreptitious "nudge nudge wink wink", "I may have been involved in the Great Train Robbery". and "I knew Mr Big".

Through summer, I worked at the *BBC* television headquarters at White City. I was a runner on the weekly soap *Compact* written by my mother and Peter Ling. It featured life on a women's magazine, and it was massively popular. Many of the cast became household names including Ronnie Allen, later to star in *Crossroads*, and Carmen Silvera, the much-loved put-upon wife in *'Allo 'Allo*.

In 1963 the majority of television output was live and sometimes performed in front of audiences. *BBC1* was in its pomp and although *ITV* and *BBC2* were by now rival channels, it remained the most popular. It had begun life before the war in 1937 and in those pre-war days the signal was disseminated from Alexandra Palace in North London and reached barely 20,000 homes with a television. By 1963 there were audiences of fifteen million plus watching *Compact*.

By October, I was acutely aware that my scholastic indolence was a threat to the quality of my degree. It was entirely self-inflicted and there was no one to blame but myself. Rather naively I had imagined that a tennis and a boxing Blue might make up for my academic deficiencies in the minds of would-be employers. So I joined the OUBC, the Boxing Club. A large Etonian called Dan Meinerzthagen, later to gain fame as a friend and confidant of Lord Lucan, was the captain and heavyweight. I scaled eleven stone and was a natural middleweight.

My first bout was held in the Oxford Town Hall in a match against the Channel Isles. Nervous but fit, I examined my opponent carefully across the ring. If he was a Channel Islander then I was Dick Turpin. The heavily muscled and smiling opponent, not dissimilar in looks from a young Frank Bruno, was actually from St Lucia. Happily for me, he had done little boxing and barely touched me during the three three-minute rounds. I was happy to get out of the Town Hall with a points win and a few cheers ringing in my ears.

Like most of my generation I will never forget where I was when the assassination of President Kennedy occurred in November 1963. I was walking across Oriel Square to have a pint in the Bear pub when someone shouted the dread news. It was very sobering and those in the pub drank to the man whose reputation was unsullied in the minds of students who admired his rhetoric and the democratic views he espoused.

My boxing career lasted through to March, a few days before the Varsity match when the aforementioned Meinerzthagen and I were sparring in the gym. He was at least two stone heavier than me which was not of massive importance as long as I could keep him at arm's length. However, he landed a pile driver on my proboscis which promptly splintered, necessitating a visit to the Radcliffe Infirmary. No Varsity match for you, said the doctor unfeelingly, and no Blue to compensate for the pain.

Now it was down to tennis and David Faulkner, my new landlord. The latter responded very generously to my pleas for help with economics and philosophy; the politics section intrigued me and I was up to speed on that subject. An American publication called *Philosophy Made Simple* was easy to digest and assisted to some extent; economics was a subject David Faulkner loved and enjoyed teaching me.

As the dread days of Finals approached, I was gradually getting there even if the effort felt like a marathon runner who had started three miles behind the field. Thank you, David Faulkner, for getting me over the line.

I was elected to Vincents, the Blues club, where among many fine sportsmen I met Jeffrey Archer who ran the 100 metres for the University's athletics team. I encountered Jeffrey again in the 1980s when we regularly played squash at Dolphin Square. By then a successful author he was kind enough to recommend a novel written by my wife Tina called *Memory and Desire*.

I had met Tina Fonseca and her elder sister Jose in 1964 at a party in Oxford. They were eighteen and twenty respectively and were at secretarial college in London. To call them Oxford groupies would be unkind, but both these good-looking girls could recognise a party opportunity. Not for nothing were they later christened by me the Fun Seeker girls.

My MG proved to be something of an aphrodisiac to girls of this age, being far too shy to imagine that pretty girls would be attracted to me, reflecting my constricted upbringing as a public school boarder still unused to social interaction with the opposite sex.

Jose, as the elder, was more forthcoming and we started dating, albeit at fifty miles distance. She was my partner at the 1964 Oriel Ball following the completion of Finals. As her surname indicated, she was of Portuguese extraction, her father Amador's family owning the Port company of that name in the earlier part of the century. He himself was born in Ireland and now practised law with offices in Ebbw Vale, Newport, and Abergavenny.

Jose was gorgeous, dark, with false eyelashes adorning her huge almond eyes. I was smitten with this girl who would go on to become joint owner of *Models One,* the agency which was the hub of "Swinging London" in the late '60s and '70s.

A trip to the 1964 Cheltenham Gold Cup in my MG almost brought a premature ending to the nascent relationship with Jose, as I hadn't legislated for the extreme cold, the snow, and the fact that my MG did not possess a heater.

After a tortuous journey to Cheltenham, Jose was frozen, unimproved by the fact that my budget ran to two tickets in the humblest of enclosures in the middle of the track. After race two, Miss Fonseca was stamping her elegant feet and demanding a lift back to Oxford in any vehicle other than a 1935 moving refrigerator. My first ever visit to the home of jump racing was spent finding her a lift with a friend and losing my only bet on *Mill House* who was odds on. He was beaten by the legendary *Arkle.* This episode should have cured me of my love for the sport of kings. It certainly cured Jose's but I remained a faithful lap dog to the ups and downs of the thoroughbred jigsaw.

As I bade farewell to the university that had been my home for three years, my final act was to find someone to take over my room in Holywell Street. A student activist called Tariq Ali was keen to have the room and his supplications were soon accepted by the Faulkner family. Little did I or they know that they were housing someone whose name would become a byword for protest over the remainder of the 1960s.

7.

Fleet Street & William Hickey beckon

From July 1964 onwards I was applying for jobs. I still wasn't certain what I wanted to do but filled in a form for a *BBC* traineeship, one of 1,500 applications from Oxbridge graduates alone, for seven positions. I knew my fate before too long as my resumé failed to reflect any theatrical or artistic experience.

Having a BA Honours degree but no training in any trade or profession is no great incentive to a would-be employer, especially as I had no first class degree to dangle before them. Some companies had head-hunted bright students even before they graduated, but I had not caught the selector's eye.

I wrote to about fifteen provincial newspapers with a view to training as a reporter. Those that replied indicated that they were not interested in graduates, preferring their trainees to be straight out of sixth form. Somewhat panicked by this response, I wrote to the editors of the *Daily Express* (circulation 4 million) and the *Daily Mail* (about 1.4 million).

I was bowled over when I received replies in the affirmative from both newspapers and was asked to present myself for an interview. At the *Express,* editor Bob Edwards was on vacation so I was cross-examined by his deputy Peter Baker. His first question was "Are you a nosey bugger?" Luckily for me I made the correct reply, "very nosey". He offered me a position on the William Hickey gossip column then and there.

My chat with the *Mail* was more circumspect. I knew that an Oxford acquaintance of mine – Nick Lloyd (later Sir Nick Lloyd, editor of the *Express*) – had been offered a job there. I was interviewed by the managing editor who promised to think about it.

There was no argument though – the *Express* was by far the bigger paper and the major mid-market publication and broadsheet of the 1960s. Lord Beaverbrook, its pioneering owner, had died three months earlier but his son Sir Max Aitken was carrying on the tradition of this great paper by employing more reporters than any other paper, with more photographers and more staff generally. I might get lost in the vast marble edifice christened the Black Lubianka by *Private Eye* but I would have my foot in its magnificent vestibule which commanded the eastern end of Fleet Street.

I was not a regular reader of the *Daily Express* while at Oriel, nor was I familiar with its infamous gossip column 'William Hickey' where I was to start my career. The William Hickey column had been created in 1933 by the Labour MP Tom Driberg. Beaverbrook loved employing people of the opposite political persuasion to him; his principal cartoonist, Giles, was a card-carrying communist until his death.

William Hickey was a pseudonym, named after an 18th century diarist, as was the custom among many newspapers of the time. *The Mail*, for example, used the name Paul Tanfield or Charles Greville. It was only after the *Daily Mail* and the *Daily Sketch* merged in 1971 that firstly Paul Callan and then Nigel Dempster garlanded the gossip column with their own by-lines.

On a sunny day in September I ventured into the *Express* office from my Betchworth home, awed by the noisy ambience of a working newspaper and the super-confident staff. The William Hickey office had twelve reporters, plus the editor, Dennis Blewett. It was hard to find a chair or desk space but within a couple of days one of the twelve, a young reporter called Nigel

Dempster, decided to up sticks because he had found work in New York.

I nabbed his desk space and office chair, grateful to establish some kind of residence in this teeming office, full of talented but under-employed reporters. Blewett was horseracing mad. When he learned that I was going down to Wales to see my girlfriend and her parents in Abergavenny via the stables of trainer David Gandolfo who had a runner in the Capital and Counties hurdle at Newbury that Saturday, I was invited to find out if his runner *Hopeful Lad* was fancied.

Gandolfo, in the infancy of his long career, was then training about twenty jumpers at Burford in Oxfordshire. His main patron was Phyllis Amey. Her son Grahame was a friend from my Oxford days and keen on Tina, the younger Fonseca sister. Gandy, a general pessimist, offered little prospect of victory for his horse who was to be ridden by Eddie Harty.

I duly imparted this intelligence to Blewett who was grateful that he could rule out at least one horse from the fifteen contesting that valuable televised race. In Abergavenny I felt I had better watch the race and was somewhat relieved when Peter O'Sullevan's mellifluous tones reported that *Hopeful Lad* appeared to have got the better of his rider and was twenty-five lengths clear of his field after half a mile.

I was a little more concerned when The Voice of Racing announced that as they turned into the finishing straight *Hopeful Lad* was still twenty lengths clear and was showing little sign of stopping. By the finishing post, *Hopeful Lad* was still fifteen lengths clear, had broken Newbury's long-standing track record for a two mile hurdle, and was returned at 33-1. I thought twice about turning up for work the following Monday.

Years later David Gandolfo told me that Eddie Harty had been contemplating returning to his native Ireland because of lack of success in England. He had gone to Mass that Saturday morning to pray to God to help his career along. Little did he realise that his success almost led to my immediate departure from my first real job! It's now history that Eddie became stable jockey to Toby Balding and won the Grand National in 1969 on *Highland Wedding*.

Blewett behaved very well when I returned to the office, forgiving my naivety. And he behaved even better a few days later when I was up before the editor Bob Edwards because someone I had written about objected to the story. Edwards had no idea who I was as it was his deputy who had offered me the job.

The doughty Marchioness of Dufferin and Ava had complained that I had described her as Lady Dufferin and Ava. That was the argument – there was nothing wrong with the actual story – it was just her title. Luckily Edwards saw it as the minor infringement that it was and I was forgiven. The only bonus was that he now knew who his latest recruit was.

As a Hickey reporter you were supposed to source stories as well as to stand them up. As to the latter requirement there was a standing dish of a phrase used by the likes of Brian Vine and Dempster: "Never ever be conned old boy". In other words, if you were told to do a particular story about a marriage break-up, you persevered until you had established its veracity.

There were some reporters better at this than others. Geoff Levy, later a distinguished feature writer on both the *Express* and latterly the *Mail*, was a past master at persuading a dowager that news of her failed marriage deserved a wider audience. He would dissect her words with the skill of surgeon and present the story as if it were her own idea.

Soon I was in the rhythm of the column. *The Sporting Life* was my constant companion as, quite apart from the form guide, there were often stories to be expanded upon. Cries of "There are no stories in the Wye card" were jokingly directed at me by my colleagues. The irony was that Wye, in Kent, had succumbed to the developers a few years earlier and no longer existed as a racecourse.

My love for a punt led to the nickname "The Betchworth Kid" after the movie the Cincinnati Kid premiered that autumn. Until I found my first flat in December 1964, I was commuting from my parental home in Betchworth. Years later on my sixty-fifth birthday, syndicate manager Henry Ponsonby promised to name a horse after my nickname if I took a ten per cent share. It was one of my wiser decisions as the *Tobougg* gelding won eight races and nearly £200,000 in prize money, giving our partnership loads of fun.

One of my first stories was to find Old Etonians to recall memories of their first day of school as new boys. It was mid September and start of the Michaelmas term. Among many I tried, I telephoned Harold Macmillan who had been prime minister only twelve months earlier before resigning following the Profumo Affair and because of prostate problems.

He had returned to his first love as chairman of his family's publishing company so I duly put in a call to Macmillan headquarters. The switchboard put me through to the Chairman's office and instead of the expected secretary I was through to the great man himself. "Thank you for your question, Mr Mackenzie," he droned, in that laid-back patrician accent. "But as a publisher you will be aware that my reminiscences are copyright."

It was a short conversation but gold dust as a quote. And to think that I had just spoken to a prime minister of this great nation. This was heady stuff and something that would never happen nowadays as men of his stature surround themselves with PR enablers and annoying buffers.

A week later I discovered that Field Marshal Lord Montgomery – 'Monty' to men like my father who had served under him during World War II – was learning how to do the football pools. He had telephoned John Moores, Chairman of Liverpool-based Littlewoods, to ask if he could send his best lieutenant down to his Hampshire home to show him how to fill in the Treble Chance. The Treble Chance was a low stakes method of predicting football draws. Success would produce winners of around £70,000 to £100,000, worth fifty times that amount in today's money.

I related the story to Blewett who advised me to get all the details into one question because Monty was famous for putting the phone down when tackled by journalists. Getting my thoughts and breath together, I got through to the great man at his mill house and posed the longest question of my emerging career. "Quite right," said Monty with his Jonathan Ross speech impediment. It was all I needed and another lead story was acquired for the column.

My next encounter with *Daily Express* authority occurred after my first four weeks on the paper. I was summoned to the managing editor's office to explain my expenses which I had submitted for the first time. I was terrified that I had stolen a couple of shillings unwittingly in my weekly tally of around £2-19-6d.

"You'll get us all into trouble if you go on like this," said the managing editor in a broad Lancashire accent. "You've got to put in at least £15 or we'll all be found out!"

A lesson learned. I was at this stage not on the staff but freelancing on a daily basis for £5 a shift or £25 a week. With my new found expenses profit I was on in excess of £30 a week which compared favourably in 1964 with the pay of most graduates of my acquaintance. My temperamental MG was soon traded in for a more reliable and modern Mini in which I commuted from Betchworth until finding a flat in Bayswater.

In October 1964 I was sent on a mission to discover what 0 levels Prince Charles had achieved at Gordonstoun earlier that summer. Hickey had learned that one of his contemporaries at the Scottish public school, and a cousin, Prince Alexander of Yugoslavia, was attending the world premiere of *Goldfinger*, the third and latest James Bond movie, at the Empire cinema in Leicester Square.

The *Daily Express* had acquired a ticket to this prestigious event and I was tasked with tracking down Prince Alexander and acquiring the necessary intelligence from him. Not easy. It wasn't until the film was over that I was able to get alongside the Prince on his way to the toilet. I joined him to have a pee and said how much I had enjoyed the film and what a wonderful escape it was from school.

"How did you get on with 0 levels?" I enquired all innocence. "Terrible," he replied. "I fluffed four of them and only got three. Luckily my cousin did rather better."

"Oh, who is that?" I asked. "It's Prince Charles, who got five 0 levels which put me to shame," he replied. "I just hope my father doesn't find out."

"What were they?" was my final question as we exited the toilet. And to my astonishment he reeled them off.

Outside in Leicester Square, Brian Vine was waiting to hear what news I had, as the editor was holding the front page in readiness. I relayed all the information I had gleaned from Prince Alexander for my first real scoop in the *Daily Express*. Sadly no one thought to put my byline on the story even though I had been the vital conduit to the facts.

William Hickey usually produced two columns a day, one for the early editions which went to the outposts of the nation, and a later edition for the Metropolis. This meant that the "dirty dozen" reporters were sent out at 6pm to trawl the nightclubs, embassies, casinos, and restaurants for stories. A terrible hardship but someone had to do it.

We learned of diplomatic parties at foreign embassies through a magazine called *The Diplomatist,* whose editor Remy Hefter was not averse to tipping us off with good stories. I often went along to Millionaire's Row opposite Kensington Palace where the Russian embassy was situated to go to one Independence Day party or another. Helen Styles was an Australian journalist who joined the Hickey gang shortly after I and we regularly went as a duo.

Helen could charm the diplomatic pants off most attachés who tended to be more indiscreet to the female of the species. She was our honeytrap. I also befriended a few diplomats, including Russia's cultural attaché Igor Kazinsky. On my second visit to the embassy he invited me to lunch at a famous Chinese restaurant in Gerard Street. I was more than happy to accept.

On the second occasion that I was his lunch guest, at *The Gay Hussar*, he inquired if I would assist with political information. He could not comprehend that a Fleet Street journalist was not in the pay of the government and privy to government secrets. However exciting the prospect of being a double agent might have seemed, I decided to end this particular game of diplomacy early. In the immediate future I left it to Helen to be our Russian correspondent.

Early in 1965, Dennis Blewett was replaced as Hickey editor by Richard Berens, an Old Etonian who had been No 2 on the *Daily*

Telegraph's gossip column Peterborough. He was another racing man and owned a horse called *Man of Kent* who was moderate enough to cost me several weeks wages over the next two years as he refused to win when the money was down.

Berens was a member of *Boodles*, the St James's gentlemen's club. In the early days of his editorship he would bring back wonderfully gossipy stories from clubland which certainly enlivened the Hickey output. Unfortunately, as he soon learned, Boodles members grew increasingly unhappy that one of their members was being indiscreet in print about them and his sources began to ostracise him.

Nigel Dempster also reappeared in the Spring of 1965 to rejoin the column. He had failed to crack New York and was forced to earn a modest wage as the doorman of the *El Morocco* club.

Watching the man who would later become the prototype for a gossip columnist in the 1970s until his untimely death in 2007 was educational. He had been a deb's delight in his late teens and knew many of the girls about whom we were writing. There was some mystery over whether he had been at Eton but later he admitted that he had been at the perfectly respectable Sherborne where he had played rugby to a decent level.

He once told me that he was dancing with a pretty debutante in the Savoy to the Joe Loss orchestra when he swung her past the celebrated band leader. "Good evening Loss," shouted Nigel to the arm waving conductor who immediately wheeled round and said "Evening, My Lord!"

At this stage of his career Nigel was still reluctant to admit to his friends that he was a gossip columnist. Often, when interviewing for a story in the office, he would telephone and say "This is James Hamilton of Queen magazine" before launching into his enquiry. Needless to say, this was not the norm at the *Express* and Nigel eventually received a warning when the powers that be learned of his subterfuge.

An example of how luck plays a part in the gathering of news or gossip occurred when I met a twenty-two year old American tourist at a party. Shannon was on a whistle stop, eight week tour of Europe with a week in London. She was pretty, and qualified for the Mackenzie chat-up lines which were serving me increasingly well as I recorded my twenty-fourth birthday.

After our first meeting Shannon said she would have to get the tube home to her digs which were near Tower Bridge. I duly put her on the Circle Line to this destination. Following our second date I vowed to take her back to her lodgings with the nefarious ambition of taking the relationship a little further. Which is when she told me she was staying as a paying guest in the Tower itself.

Although my hopes for the night's denouement were frustrated, it transpired she had answered an advertisement in a New York magazine which offered rooms for £25 a week in the actual Tower of London. Please apply to the offices of the Governor, Sir Thomas Butler, which she had duly done.

Logging this information, I made further enquiries the following day back in the Hickey office, only to discover that Sir Thomas's office not only denied the possibility that this was true, it was specifically disallowed on security and other grounds. A third date with Shannon, while I waited outside the Tower's gates to meet her, established beyond doubt that she was one of several young Americans staying in this ancient monument which housed not only the Crown Jewels but was also the scene of many an execution, notably that of Henry VIII's wife Anne Boleyn.

Something wasn't quite right I surmised, while writing the story that this landmark tourist attraction was the most exclusive B&B in the capital. Little did I anticipate that this item would be picked up by Labour MPs in the House of Commons who enquired if Buckingham Palace was to be the next iconic building to be offered to Britain's tourist trade.

Sir Thomas was forced to come clean about his little "earner" and was severely admonished for his illegal entrepreneurship. If truth were told he was lucky to stay in the job and indeed he resigned the following year.

Another old friend joined the column during late 1965 when diplomat's son Peter Tory, who had been at Malvern, finally drew stumps on his promising acting career to become a hack. At school he was regarded with some awe following his Henry V and other leading parts. He went on to RADA and then joined the Royal Shakespeare company with whom, in 1962, he toured the Soviet Union.

Peter never quite made the acting game pay and was usually cast as a Shakespearian spear shaker, his words not mine. He recalled to me how he spoke the line "Edmund is here, My Lord" with differing emphasis on each word at successive performances to keep himself awake. His sister Wendy was also an actress and would eventually marry Derek Fowlds who went on to great fame as Basil Brush's partner and then Sir Humphrey's sidekick civil servant in *Yes, Minister* and *Yes, Prime Minister.*

Peter admitted, shortly after becoming a Hickey hack, that he had been the glamorous Julie Christie's lover while on tour in Russia. This startling piece of intelligence raised our esteem of our new colleague, not to mention our envy of him.

Julie Christie was the direct reason that I acquired my first by-line in the *Daily Express*. In 1967, attending the premiere of *Far from the Madding Crowd* with co-star Terence Stamp, she was photographed outside the cinema with her mini skirt caught by the wind, Marilyn Monroe style.

This photograph was bounced off the Moon, a technical first, all the way to Mexico City, where it was published simultaneously with my byline on the picture caption. A copy of this photo story remained displayed on the wall of the *Wig & Pen* club opposite the Law Courts in Fleet Street for the next thirty years as a memento of this ground-breaking, technological advance.

There was an element of public school bullying among the dozen talented Hickey hacks with too little to occupy their time. Chief among the victims was David Pitman, younger brother of the paper's political columnist Robert Pitman. Pitman junior, an Oxford graduate, would have been better suited to being the literary editor or some similar position. He wasn't a natural at diplomatic receptions or mixing with debutantes at parties. And he was fair game for the likes of Dempster and Vine.

One day they tied his ankles with rope which they strung up over the hat stand in the office. It has to be said that Pitman must have co-operated in this exercise to some masochistic extent. The minute his telephone rang the guilty pair jumped to their feet and tugged at the rope so that the hapless hack's feet were practically at ceiling level and he was upside down.

To his lasting credit Pitman clung to the telephone and was heard to say "I'm sorry, Your Royal Highness, I didn't quite catch that." It turned out that Prince Richard of Gloucester was returning his call about a new appointment that had been made for him by the Queen.

Peter Tory couldn't believe his eyes or ears when this outrageous behaviour took hold. He shared a flat with Robin Hawdon, an actor turned scriptwriter, and he would routinely ring home to let Hawdon listen to this puerile activity with a view to replicating it in a play or television series. Seemingly it was too ridiculous for the powers at the *BBC* and *ITV* to believe.

Meanwhile I was pursuing what I hoped to be a path out of Hickey and on to more serious matters. But it was taking time. By the summer of 1966, childhood friend David Leon, and I had sold our Bayswater flat to Geoff Levy who installed his future wife Stefanie there. We moved to a swish address in Belgravia, none other than Eaton Mews West. It may have sounded smart with its Belgravia telephone number, but the reality was a bath in the kitchen (making it possible to toast your bread from the bath) and an ever-leaking roof.

My old friend Len Bickwit had completed his law studies at Harvard and was in London for the summer prior to starting his legal career in Washington. None other than ex-Vice President Richard Nixon, who had narrowly failed to win the vote to be governor of California that summer, was seeking to add Bickwit to the roster of lawyers at his new legal practice. It would be a further two years before he stood for the presidency.

Nixon was in London, staying at *Claridges* with his wife and two daughters, and asked Bickwit to come and see him with the prospect of luring him onto his staff. Len said he would come and see him but only if his Oxford pal Colin Mackenzie could interview him at the same time. He must have been keen to recruit Len because he immediately consented.

Meeting Nixon was one of the great disappointments of my burgeoning career. He was boring and repetitive, droning on and on about completing his world trip by visiting the Chinese and also seeing American troops in Vietnam. He was still smarting from losing the presidential election to John Kennedy in 1960. I carefully harvested a dozen paragraphs which the paper duly published but it was not my finest hour.

Later that summer I interviewed another President, Janio Quadros of Brazil, a true reformer who was ousted after only a couple of years for being too progressive for that country's establishment moneyed figures. He was quite riveting in his views but sadly the paper wasn't that interested in a failed South American president and my efforts went unpublished.

Rumours of my prowess in the boxing ring led to my assignment to accompany celebrity lawyer David Jacobs when he served divorce papers on the actor Richard Harris who was known for his mercurial Irish character as a member of Hollywood's Rat Pack. Jacobs – no relation to the disc jockey of that name – was meeting the actor at Heathrow off an inbound aircraft from Los Angeles and he took me to the airport in his chauffeur-driven Rolls Royce.

Nervous as I was, Richard Harris could not have been more charming or co-operative, admitting that it was entirely his fault that his lovely wife Elizabeth had called time on their marriage. Somewhat relieved, I climbed into Jacobs' Rolls Royce so that he could decant me at the Notting Hill home of Mrs Harris to update her and get some further quotes.

Dressed in a smart suit and coat I thought I resembled a typical solicitor. But when I pressed the doorbell of Elizabeth Harris's smart town house, a red haired, freckle-faced five year old came to the door, took one brief look and before I could open my mouth, shouted up the stairs, "Mum, the fucking press are here!" So much for my attempts at sartorial elegance.

I occasionally visited the *Casanova*, a Mayfair gambling emporium run by a lady called Pauline Wallis, whose brother Tommy was a senior figure in the Jockey Club and whose nephew Stephen would go on to run Newmarket racecourse. Pauline was Irish and liked to decorate her club with eligible young men while she fleeced willing Arabs of their fortunes. If I dropped £100, she would be in no hurry to hassle me for the money.

One of her regulars was Jack Meyer, headmaster of Millfield public school where promising sports stars of the future could win scholarships. The Somerset school had a high reputation for excellence. And Meyer, not the best player of chemin de fer in the world, would sometimes bet a parent a whole term's school fees on the chemmy table with unpredictable and expensive results for the school. I'm afraid this was too good a story for a hack to ignore and it got a wider publication.

One of his pupils, Johnny Nelson, son of racehorse trainer Peter Nelson, told me years later that Meyer actually transferred him from The Hollys house at Millfield to Meyer's own house in order to get information from him. One day, thirteen year old Nelson was summoned to the boss's study and asked about his father's three runners at Kempton the following day. Relieved that he wasn't there for other reasons, young Nelson borrowed the headmaster's phone and spoke to his father who said all three horses had chances and represented each way bets and were doing their best.

Peter Nelson himself did not bet, nor did Johnny or his brother Charlie who was also at the school. So Johnny was unaware of the results from Kempton until the Headmaster had him in the following evening thanking him profusely as all three had won!

"He wasn't a bad man at all," Johnny recalled. "He offered plenty of scholarships to good sportsmen whose parents couldn't afford the school fees. He brought the school up from nothing and made it a great place. When my father's horses all won, he offered me a sherry and said a big thank you."

On another occasion, I was sitting at the chemmy table when some villains broke into the club and tried to hold up the clients with what appeared to be fake guns. At the table was Lord Lucan and the Tory MP for Portsmouth Brigadier Terence Clarke, an old war hero who was having none of this interruption. Instead of cowering behind the furniture as punters debated what to do, Clarke shouted at the dealer "Banco!" It made a very good headline in the William Hickey column twenty-four hours later.

In late 1966, by which time I was squiring Jose's younger sister Tina, I was despatched to my old stamping ground Oxford for the premiere of *Dr Faustus* at the New Theatre, starring Richard Burton and his wife Elizabeth Taylor. We watched the performance – Taylor was surprisingly good for someone with limited theatre experience – and then repaired to the after party at the Randolph Hotel.

Knowing few of the people there we sat at a table with a quiet Welsh couple who, it turned out, had been friends with Burton in the far-off days of his childhood immediately after and during the war. As Tina had a Welsh heritage, we managed to find a common interest. Conversation was in full flow when Burton hove onto the scene and plonked himself at our table to greet his oldest friends. We were introduced and Burton assumed we were friends of his friends.

La Taylor wasn't very happy about this arrangement as she wanted to dine with the producer and theatrical angels who had backed the production. But her charms and entreaties were lost on her husband who eventually told her, "Look I'm catching up with old friends to talk about rugby. You can either join us or fuck off."

At this point she demanded a taxi back to their hotel while the rest of us drank on into the night. At some point I brought up the subject of an interview with the great man who simply said "Meet me at the Bear in Woodstock at 10am and I'll give you half an hour."

Sometimes it is better to be lucky than rich, I thought to myself. And at 10am there was the great Richard Burton at his breakfast table clutching a bottle of vodka and offering me any cereal I wanted. He gave good interview.

"Elizabeth has surprised me, you know," Burton told me. "I knew she was a bloody marvellous screen actress, but she has had very limited experience on the stage. She is really good in this play and I expect we'll do others in the future. She had a lot riding on this and it takes guts to perform in front of the critics. I've had years of experience and I still find it nerve wracking."

The next time I met the Burtons was two years later when despatched to the Tower of London to interview the stars of *Where Eagles Dare*, who included Burton and Clint Eastwood. La Taylor had insisted on bringing her pet dogs with her and so, due to Britain's strict quarantine regulations, they were officially banned unless she was willing to put them into quarantine. So the Burtons hired the largest yacht seen in the London basin and moored it beside Traitors Gate, the biggest floating kennel in the world.

By 1967 I was getting itchy feet and Bruce Kemble, the *Express* education correspondent, was anxious to recruit me as his No 2. There were rumblings of student unrest – largely because of the on-going Vietnam war – and the paper was getting increasingly interested in student politics. Despite my pleadings, I was told to sit tight on Hickey for the time being.

By doing so I became involved in two of the best stories I had ever done. For the first time, the Miss World competition was to be televised live, and also for the first time there was betting on the event, initiated by Ron Pollard of Ladbrokes. In the end all the major bookies were taking bets.

I was instructed by Berens, a keen betting man, to go to the preliminary Miss World parties from which I could report. I was also to determine who was going to win – not an easy task when there were no fewer than seventy-eight possibles. Jokingly, I think, he suggested that if I came back with the wrong intelligence my job would be forfeit.

I had about ten days of preambles with which to work. Early on I determined that one of the prettiest girls was Miss Peru, a dark-haired beauty from Lima. The downside was that she spoke not a word of English and some of my colleagues from other papers suggested that this deficiency would count against her.

Nevertheless, my penchant for the South American look won the day and once Berens was alerted to this, he decided that the *Express* would orchestra a Miss World coup. I collected £5 from twenty different reporters on the paper and placed the £100 bet in Joe Coral's betting shop on Fleet Street at odds of 16-1. The manager, Alf, who knew my propensity to back losers on the turf, thought this was just another mug bet. In truth, I thought so myself.

Come the big day, the identities of the Miss World judges were announced – some of them, such as society photographer Patrick Lichfield, well known to the Hickey team. Five Hickey reporters were assigned to interview the judges in advance about their role and to drop a not too subtle hint that Miss Peru was a stunner who deserved to win. She had attracted some press attention – not least in the *Express* – and her odds had tumbled to 10-1 joint favourite.

As the contest was reaching its closing moments, I was relieved to see that Miss Peru was in the final eight contestants. This was the moment when Eric Morley, chairman of the Miss World contest, stepped in to announce the winners "in reverse order". Third was Miss Guyana (later to become the wife of actor Michael Caine), second was Miss Argentina, at which point my heart sank. Surely there couldn't be a South American clean sweep?

But there was. In first place, to my eternal relief, was Madeline Hartog-Bel, the aforementioned Miss Peru. Job safe, and a handy sum to be picked up from Joe Coral the following morning. Cries of "steward's enquiry" from Alf, the manager, were drowned out by the stentorian tones of Vine who bellowed "pay up, pay up". I won £80 for myself and £1,600 for my colleagues. For ten minutes I was the hero of the hour.

Miss Guyana, Shakira, had been sharing a hotel room with Miss Cyprus, a delightful Greek-speaking girl called Lalla whom I had befriended in the line of duty. I even got a picture caption of Lalla, the daughter of a Limassol police chief, or so she said, into the Hickey column. She looked buxom and quite fetching.

On the day of publication, the Hickey office received a telephone call from film star Warren Beatty who was staying at the Dorchester hotel. He was interested in meeting Lalla with a view to casting her in one of his movies. I was deputed to drive Miss Cyprus to the Dorchester to meet this Hollywood icon. Two days later a tearful Lalla asked me to collect her from the hotel saying, "This Warren, he not very nice!"

Towards the end of 1967, the British economy was sliding towards oblivion. The pound had been devalued by a Labour government whose popularity was waning by the day. A £50 foreign travel limit had been placed on tourists and businessmen by the Financial Secretary to the Treasury, Harold Lever.

I fielded a phone call from Gstaad shortly before Christmas 1967 to the effect that Lever, whose third wife Diane was the daughter of a Beirut banker, was playing high stakes backgammon in the foyer of the Palace Hotel. What's more, he appeared to be losing thousands of pounds to his opponents who included the Greek playboy/journalist Taki Theodoracopulos.

Taki, who later gained fame as the author of the *Spectator's* High Life column, was both an excellent tennis player and an accomplished backgammon player. He had been winning thousands of pounds at the expense of a man who was supposed to be on a £50 foreign travel limit. This was dynamite.

I managed to locate Taki who was staying in the Palace hotel and he named the other backgammon players as well as confirming that Lever was the big loser over the past few days. This was an important story and far bigger than just a piece of William Hickey gossip – it merited a front page splash. Enter Derek Marks, the tall, bespectacled editor of the *Express* who had been a political correspondent in his former life.

Marks was intent on killing the story. After consulting with his contacts at No 10 Downing Street he had decided the story wasn't worth the telling as Mrs Lever had funds of her own from the Lebanon which were paying for her husband's losses. Apparently Downing Street had even threatened obliquely that the *Express's* lobby privileges would be in peril if we went ahead with a story like this which could damage the Labour party beyond repair.

I could scarcely believe my ears, nor could my Hickey colleagues who had been privy to this great scoop. But Marks was the editor and what he said was final. I was seething and even more determined to widen my journalistic remit by leaving the gossip column. A few days later I did something for the first and only time in my life: I gave the entire story to *Private Eye* who disseminated it to a wider audience in their Christmas edition a week later.

What to make of the William Hickey column I was to leave after three and a half years? Its content was somewhat dated, concentrating almost exclusively on a diet of aristocratic misdemeanours which was having increasingly little relevance in a more equal society. But it was an entertaining and vibrant work place, albeit one where bullying was not entirely absent.

As an apprenticeship for journalism it was without parallel. Many of its staff – Messrs Vine, Dempster, Levy, and Tory for example – went on to enjoy great careers in Fleet Street. Patrick Robinson, who had joined from the sports department of the paper, became a celebrated and successful author.

The stories we published were not easily sourced or stood up. The skill level required to survive could exceed that necessary in other areas of reporting. I have never regretted the graduate training it gave me in the university of life.

It was also an entrance exam for one of the great clubs of the writing world – Fleet Street. This no longer exists as an entity as all the great national newspapers have left the 'Street of Shame', as *Private Eye* christened it, to ply their trade in boroughs as diverse as Wapping, Lambeth, and Kensington.

Meeting great legends such as crime writer Percy Hoskins, racing correspondent Clive Graham, foreign correspondent Vince Mulchrone, sports writers Hugh McIlvanney and Ian Wooldridge, in *El Vino's*, the *Cheshire Cheese*, or the City Golf Club was a rite of passage denied the young reporter today.

The boozy four hour lunch is a relic of another century. Today's national newspapers are battling for their very survival, certainly the print versions. There are few lunch breaks, no smoking or drinking, smaller expense allowances, and zero atmosphere in mostly modern offices. I fear for the sub-editors glued to their screens 24/7 – repetitive strain syndrome may be around the corner. It's a tougher, less exciting world out there for the modern newspaper reporter in my opinion.

The poet Humbert Wolfe summed up the scallywags on Hickey rather well when writing;

> You cannot hope to bribe or twist
> Thank God! The British journalist

But seeing what the man will do
Unbribed, there's no occasion to.

8.

Marriage & education

Jose Fonseca and I went our separate ways at the end of 1964. The somewhat erratic hours of a reporter played havoc with our social life. Equally Jose was finding her size four feet in the competitive world of modelling. By 1968 she had established *Models One* with her business partner April Ducksbury, with offices in the Fulham Road and a roster of beauties who would soon become household names: Jerry Hall, Sue Murray, Marisa Berenson and Ingrid Boulting, for example.

In 1966 I met up again with the Fonseca sisters at a party in Bayswater. Tina, by now nearly twenty-one, had blossomed into a beauty. Our previous friendship developed into a full-blown romance as the year progressed, especially after she decided to travel to the West Indies that summer and on to Los Angeles where she stayed with my mother Hazel. Her absence made the heart grow fonder.

Hazel was joint chairman, with Denis Norden, of the British Writers' Guild, which was having talks with their Hollywood counterparts. She had already taken on Lew (later Lord) Grade over repeat fees for writers. With *Crossroads* a great commercial success, made by Grade's *Central TV*, she had a weapon, i.e. withdrawal of labour unless writers achieved what was already the norm in the acting profession. Grade backed down quickly.

The Americans were debriefing Hazel on the whys and wherefores of her success. Striking was still a relatively alien modus operandi for the free market American spirit. And many Hollywood writers were still recovering, emotionally and financially, from the appalling treatment by Senator Joe

McCarthy whose campaign against perceived communist leanings caused immense hardship among the profession.

Tina and I grew closer and closer until we decided to get married on St David's day, March 1 1968, at the Carmelite church off Kensington High Street. It was a Friday and the eve of the rugby international between England and Wales, so the Abergavenny contingent of friends and relatives were more than happy to enjoy a wedding in London rather than in the more bucolic environs of Monmouthshire.

Most of my Fleet Street friends and colleagues pleaded work commitments in order to avoid the two-hour nuptial mass which had me on my knees, as neither Tina nor I, a non-Catholic, knew quite when to stand or pray. Unsurprisingly they found themselves available for the 6pm kick-off of our reception at 30 Pavilion Rd near Sloane Square. Tina looked radiant in her Ossie Clark wedding dress. Ossie, a dear friend, had even designed the dresses for the bridesmaids.

My father-in-law, Amador Fonseca, insisted on paying for everything and instructed Searcy's, the catering company which owned Pavilion Road, not to stint on the champagne. He hadn't quite catered for the voracious thirst of rugby fans which was more than matched by that of Fleet Street's finest. It was no surprise when supplies ran short and an emergency visit to Searcy's cellars was needed.

Our wedding passed in something of a haze, although I do recall making a speech. My best man, Mike Manson, read out some telegrams, including one of Brian Vine's better efforts. "Congratulations Colin, you have finally backed a winner, signed William Hill, Joe Coral and Cyril Stein."

Two months later, following a honeymoon in Tunisia, my bride was pregnant and I was the proud owner of one third of *Mount Etna*, a grey gelding racehorse previously owned by the Queen

Mother. He had been sold out of Peter Cazalet's stable to Alan Brush, a gravel pit millionaire who in turn found him too moderate to persevere with. He was a gift horse to Brian Vine, his best friend public relations chief David Wynn-Morgan, and me.

Vine had the inspiration to send him to the West Country maestro Les Kennard to be prepared for a seller at Newton Abbot when the jump season recommenced at the end of July. Kennard trained on the Quantock Hills in Somerset and enjoyed a reputation for being able to "get one ready". Conditional jockey John Williams, claiming a 7lb allowance, was tasked with landing a coup for us city slickers.

My excitement matched that of my wedding day. Nerves were jangling, money was invested, and the car journey to Newton Abbot seemed shorter than the four hours that was the reality. Halfway through the race, *Mount Etna* was twenty-five lengths clear of his field. "Not too far, John," was the shout from one of our neighbours in the grandstand.

Mount Etna, his white tail gleaming in the July sunshine, remained that far clear until the winning post. It was John Williams's first ever winner and he went on to a successful career as a flat jockey. It was also my first winner. In various partnerships and syndicates since that great day I have enjoyed a further seventy-one wins. But somehow you can never repeat the adrenalin surge of the first triumph.

Sadly Mount Etna never won again. It was as if he knew he had done his job because he never tried very hard again. Kennard found him a good home later that year and that concluded my owning career for the next five years while I became the proud father of three girls.

Catherine Maria Fonseca Mackenzie was born on December 6 1968 at St George's hospital adjacent to Hyde Park Corner.

Despite her slight stature, Tina was in labour for no more than three hours. I was able to be present at the birth, unusual in the 1960s, and my joy was unconfined. Within twenty-four hours I was able to take mother and baby out of the hospital to drive them down to Wales to stay with the Fonsecas until after Christmas when our newly acquired Battersea house would be ready for occupation.

The pride was immense and then the responsibility for another human being pierced my heart. A little piece of me was breathing quietly in her mother's arms as we motored, in those pre M4 days, via Gloucester to Abergavenny. I'm sure every father feels the same but the senses were waylaid in a manner that far outpaced my excitement as a racehorse owner.

After Christmas we moved into our new home, an end of terrace Edwardian monstrosity with no fewer than seven bedrooms and three bathrooms. There was scope to let a flat on the first floor which we duly did to mitigate part of the mortgage.

We paid £6,900 for the house which changed hands in 2019 for nearly £10 million, thirty-six years after we had bailed, before serious property inflation took hold. Meanwhile Tina was expecting our second child later that October.

We rented our flat to film producer Ken Harper and his glamorous second wife Pam Hart. They had met on the set of *Summer Holiday*, the Cliff Richard musical, in which ballet-trained Pam was lead actress and a dancer.

Unknown to this reporter, Pam had had a famous previous lover in the priapic form of Tory minister Alan Clark who described her as "the love of my life". This emerged only in 2009 when certain love letters were found. For around a decade I had unknowingly been party to a good gossip story.

We provided the Harpers' London pied-a-terre. They had a charming cottage in Chipping Warden in Oxfordshire where naughty Ken, sadly no longer with us, grew his own cannabis. No wonder he was always giggling, even when chairing the wine committee at the Garrick Club of which he was a proud member.

My new career as an education correspondent began with a front page splash when Essex University students rioted while being addressed by a junior government minister, Labour's Fred Willey. He was at the university with four other MPs, all members of the select committee on education, namely Ronald Bell, Arnold Shaw, Kenneth Marks, and Gilbert Longden.

The students were clearly up for a fight and having heckled the minister throughout his speech, which he had to abandon before its conclusion, they sat down to prevent the MPs from leaving the hall. Bell, a Tory, complained that he was "in severe physical danger" as students tried to rip off his trousers. The Labour MPs among them were slightly more tolerant.

It was pure luck of course. I was the only Fleet Street hack present in the university's main hall when the riot started. It was impossible for the MPs to complete their visit. There had been significant anti-Vietnam war demonstrations in Paris where the Sorbonne was in shut down, but this was a British first, at an institution known for its left wing activism.

My colleague Bruce Kemble's desire to widen his personal education fiefdom on the *Express* was bearing fruit sooner than he could have hoped. And very soon the protest virus had come even closer to Fleet Street when the London School of Economics, based in the Aldwych less than a mile from the *Express* building, went into lockdown. There were protests on the street and banners, preventing the teaching staff from entering the building.

Having led a relatively alcohol-free life and still mustering only twenty-six years on the planet I could get away with being a student. As instructed, I put on student apparel and wandered into the main building as if I belonged there. Soon I bumped into a lone member of the teaching staff who was still in situ, Dr Bernard Donoughue, made a life peer in 1985 by the Labour party. He would later be an advisor to the Wilson government, and following that helped Robert Maxwell's attempts to make the *Mirror* group the pre-eminent newspaper giants of Fleet Street.

Donoughue, I soon discovered, was a turf aficionado. This small connection emboldened me to reveal what I was up to in the LSE building and he felt able to lend the use of the telephone in his office to file reports to the office down the road. I slept in the building for two nights and received a "herogram" from editor Derek Marks when I returned to the office on the third day.

In 1969 the Education Correspondents Group – around thirty hacks from different papers – invited the newly elected shadow education minister to a lunch. Her name was Margaret Thatcher.

The majority of us were left-leaning by political inclination although my views were coloured, to some extent, by those of Bruce Kemble who was a bullish proponent of the comprehensive system of secondary schooling. I could see the merit of this system too, although the reality often failed to match the rhetoric.

Mrs T had been in the job only a few weeks but had clearly done her homework. And no, she was not in favour of the comprehensive ideal, having been a product of the grammar school selective system herself. She had read chemistry at Oxford, thanks to the sterling efforts of the teachers at her selective secondary school in Grantham, Lincolnshire, where she was brought up.

Only one among us – Rod Tyler of the *Daily Mail* – appeared to agree with her strident views on the aspects of the education portfolio that we quizzed her on, and over the next few years Rod would have little cause for regret as he parlayed this support into a friendship, eventually writing an esteemed biography of the Iron Lady.

Jack Straw, later an integral member of the Blair Government, became president of the National Union of Students. He was eloquent and persuasive and I had several conversations with him which convinced me he was a leader of the future. It required extreme tact and diplomacy to run the NUS at this time because the militants demanded so much, and yet at the same time he was fighting the government for improved grants and funding for his members.

In July 1969 there was but one topic of conversation – the extraordinary fulfilment of the late president Jack Kennedy's ambition to put a man on the surface of the moon. Like so many around the world I was transfixed by the prospect and even more amazed that the whole enterprise would be televised live.

That July night I stayed up to watch every millisecond of the events as they unfolded. It was riveting television – a one-off, as if you were a member of Columbus's crew discovering America. The tension and the stress were felt by viewers but not, seemingly, by Neil Armstrong and his crew who were calmness personified, despite things going disastrously wrong immediately prior to landing. Armstrong had to land manually following a computer glitch and the fuel needed almost ran out.

"This is one small step for man – one giant leap for mankind" was to become the headline in the newspapers of some 200 nations the following day. Even the Russians, who had lost the space race to be the first on the moon, offered congratulations through gritted teeth. It was a time for the world to unite and salute a wonderful achievement.

I went to the office without threatening my pillow overnight. But I also knew that the odds of my being in the paper the following morning were 1,000-1 and drifting because of the all-consuming coverage of the moon landing.

And so it proved. But it didn't stop me and many colleagues from visiting *El Vino's* that lunch time to celebrate the most monumental feat of the 20th century and the one event that would remain with my generation for life.

On October 24 1969, Tina and I welcomed our second daughter Tara into the world, born at home in little more than two hours. She was and remains a wonderful addition, dark haired and pretty as a picture while Catherine was a lovely redhead. Some of our friends joked that she was an Irish twin, a sibling born less than twelve months after her predecessor.

Two babies under twelve months old was quite a strain, especially on Tina. We had arranged a maternity nurse from a recommended agency. But when this harridan arrived, she expected staff (me) to provide a cooked breakfast before she would start work. She lasted only forty-eight hours before I had to ring the agency and explain that we had no staff or need for an elderly disciplinarian.

Not to be beaten, the agency sent along a young, eccentric and fun-loving nanny called Alice Hamburger who, despite her valiant efforts to lose weight, rather resembled her surname in stature and shape. She liked nothing better than to invade our bedroom at 7am, and sit on our bed wearing a mini skirt that barely merited the name to discuss fashion and gossip.

The blessed Alice was only supposed to work for us for a couple of weeks until Tina was strong enough to cope. The *Daily*

Express had not recognised the notion of paternity leave in the 1960s and I could assist only when I wasn't working. It was hard on Tina. But Alice told us she was having such a good time that she would stay on, without pay, for another three months. As funds were short (I was earning around £2,000 a year at this time), we agreed.

My education role gradually petered out after the Tories and Edward Heath came to power in a shock general election win in 1970. Students were becoming less militant and education wasn't at the forefront of day to day news. I was co-opted onto the news rota and this move initiated my career on the road and abroad.

There was one other education story that I was to cover three years later in 1973 when the communist Romanian government of Nicolae Ceausescu invited education correspondents, together with junior education minister Norman St John Stevas, to fly to Bucharest to inspect the "wonderful" education system of that country.

The aircraft was an elderly Vickers Viscount turbo prop with passenger seats so crammed together that there was little or no leg room. I was squeezed into a middle seat between the flamboyant junior Minister and a member of his civil service staff. Comfort-wise it seemed a very long flight even if the extrovert Minister himself was quite entertaining.

Extraordinary as it seems in hindsight, Ceausescu was held in some regard internationally at this time. He was even being talked of as the Henry Kissinger of Europe as he tried to intervene in the Israeli/Egyptian war which had flared up that summer. A meeting with this man, who ruled his country with a fearful abuse of power, was not on our schedule but seemed to me the only point of being there.

After three days of traipsing round schools and universities, being told how wonderful the skills of Romanian students were – they were certainly better linguists that most other Europeans – I was frustrated and let my opinions be known rather loudly at a British embassy reception.

Whether the conversations in that building were bugged I don't know but the following morning I received a note through my hotel door to the effect that I and the man from the *Daily Telegraph* could submit some questions which the president would answer. Geronimo!

We got together and submitted thirty questions, ranging from why Romania had so few consumer goods in its shop windows to how the president was going to solve the Middle Eastern crisis. Two hours later we were summoned to the president's palace and told to wait in an ante room. An aide emerged a few minutes later with a piece of paper on which only half our questions were listed – the President had disallowed the rest. There was no point in protesting – it was that or no interview at all, we were told.

He was small, dark, and rather menacing – almost a Hollywood version of a tyrant – and sat behind an enormous desk. There were no handshakes, just a reluctant effort to be done with the interview. Virtually all the questions about Romania had been eliminated but at least he was willing to talk (in Romanian which had to be translated for us) about the Middle East crisis and how happy he was to help.

After half an hour we bowed our way out of the building and compared notes as my shorthand was limited at best. There were no tape recorders allowed and mobile phones were decades away. In the end there was a half decent story which I was able to file to London. Another president was logged in my cv.

It took another sixteen years for democracy and the rule of law to catch up with Ceausescu and on Christmas Day 1989 he was found guilty of treason in a one hour trial. He was shot by firing squad moments later, demonstrating a certain lack of decorum that had characterised his own reign of terror.

9.

News, foreign & a third child

Being one of thirty *Daily Express* news reporters in 1971 was rather like being in a long taxi rank at Waterloo station. You waited your turn while the bosses digested all the stories that needed coverage. It was clear from the outset that I had to prove myself all over again. I may have been a leading light on the William Hickey column and done tolerably well as an education correspondent; I still had to earn my spurs at what the news editor termed "proper reporting".

At that time there were eight-hour shifts – not a problem in themselves unless your shift started at 8pm and lingered long into the night until your release home at 4am. You were there in case the world came to an end at this ungodly hour. Ex Hickey editor Dennis Blewett was on duty in Prague in the autumn of 1968 when Russian tanks invaded the city at 1am to end the Prague Spring of Alexander Dubcek.

Dubcek had come to power the previous April in a popular uprising against communism. He led a government which was going to end repression and gradually introduce western-style democracy. It took about five months before the Russians, who controlled the Eastern bloc countries, could react. And they did so with force and menace.

Blewett seldom rose before midday and was always awake long into the night, hence the story that shocked the world. He managed to get it into the last edition of the *Daily Express* which was seen only in central London. Indeed it was often known as the Ludgate Circus edition because that was the scope of its circulation. But at least the paper could crow about its "scoop". Dennis's reward for this great story was to be transferred to

Moscow where he spent the next twenty years, enjoying a torrid romance with the Olympic gymnast Olga Korbut.

Many was the time in the summer of 1971 when I would get home at 4.30am only to be woken an hour later with the dulcet cries of two hungry babies, aged two and one. It took a good story for me to be released from these shifts which lasted most of that summer. The problem was that I would follow what was nicknamed the "dogwatch" shift with one that started mid afternoon the same day. I was young and I was fit but this taxed the metabolism.

The one bonus of these late shifts was to get to know the landlord of *Poppins*, the pub beneath the *Express* building run by an inveterate punter and character called Bob Mason. Unless there was an important story on the go, the late shift would gather in *Poppins* to pass the time. There you would often meet the clubbable Clive Graham, the paper's leading racing correspondent known as The Scout, who liked to pass on his best intelligence to the publican.

The cricketer Dennis Compton, who worked for the *Sunday Express*, was another regular who also liked a bet on the horses. And when in England, Keith Miller, the wonderful Aussie all-rounder and friend of Compton's, would also seek wisdom from Clive Graham.

Clive's partner on the paper was racing legend Peter O'Sullevan who kept himself to himself. I got to know Peter later in our careers and there was no more charming or interesting person. But he was too shy and reserved to decorate the bar in Poppins, unlike his Old Etonian partner who loved the cockney banter of Mason and his wife Marie.

Contrary to belief at the time, Clive and Peter were close friends. Peter was a loner and liked to drive himself everywhere in his Jaguar. But at the racecourse and whenever they socialised, they were a tight team. When Clive was diagnosed with cancer in 1975, until his death two years later, Peter would frequently be at his bedside reminiscing about former triumphs and disasters, usually of a punting variety.

I felt privileged to be sat near Peter at Clive's memorial service in St Martins-in-the-Field where John Lawrence (later Lord Oaksey) and the BBC's Cliff Morgan gave wonderful tributes to a man who had decorated the *Daily Express* for the past twenty years. His daughter Penny worked in the fashion section of the paper during his latter years and Clive was always proud of her contribution to journalism.

Bob Mason would later carve his name in racing history and lodge his name in the *Guinness Book of Records* when in 1978 he sued William Hill for the unusual offence of slander. Mason had long been a thorn in the side of Hills for being a winning punter. Every weekend he would place a football bet in their Chancery Lane betting shop and then go home to his house on the Thames at Wraysbury. These football bets were unusually successful and Hills decided that there must be some form of collusion with the betting shop manager, despite the bets being registered twenty-four hours before the Saturday results they had predicted. Bob would pick up his winnings on the Monday when he returned to work at the pub.

One Monday morning in the autumn of 1978, just as he was picking up his winnings from the betting shop, he was accosted by two ex-policemen now working for Hill's security team and frogmarched out of the shop without being able to collect his winnings. Not unnaturally Bob protested long and hard and then telephoned John Santer who was the Hills public relations man and a regular in *Poppins*. Santer had been Clive Graham's driver in his previous job and had worked on the *Express*.

Santer tried his hardest to dissuade Hills from their decision to defend their actions in the High Court but its leading lights were convinced they were onto a fraud. Santer knew that Bob Mason was one of the shrewdest punters in London, whether on football or on horses. He also knew that Hills wanted rid of him as a customer.

Mason's only son John was a successful businessman based in Germany and was incensed at the notion that his father, a Freeman of the City of London, was being perceived as a fraudster. He said he would bankroll his father if he wished to take Hills to court for slander. Mason senior claimed, probably correctly, that a number of his customers (including Bruce Matthews who was Deputy Chairman of Rupert Murdoch's newspaper empire) had witnessed this event which could have only one meaning – that he was being dishonest.

When the case came to court a few months later I was asked to be a character witness on Bob's behalf. I remember being cross-examined by Richard Hartley QC, for Hills. He later became a friend and a racehorse owner and shared ownership of the 2011 Welsh Grand National winner *Le Beau Baie*.

In 1998 Hartley would defend the *Sporting Life* in a libel action over the horse *Top Cees* which was alleged by the paper not to have tried in the Swaffham handicap at Newmarket. He won the competitive 1995 Chester Cup next time out a few weeks later, a result greeted by boos in the winner's enclosure on the Roodeye. The litigants were trainer Lynda Ramsden, her husband Jack, and champion jockey Kieren Fallon who had ridden the horse in both races. The *Sporting Life* lost the action in an expensive trial which sadly presaged the demise of the paper.

As in so many civil court proceedings, Bob Mason's case dragged on for more than a couple of weeks and I was at the Cheltenham Festival of 1979 when I learned of Bob's victory.

The jury decided that Bob had been traduced and he was awarded £70,000 plus costs, a sum which was for several years the largest slander award ever made under British law.

By the summer of 1971 my career began an upward curve again with my first big foreign assignment. Timothy Davey was a fourteen year old who had been arrested in Turkey for selling twenty-five kilos of hashish. It was an extraordinary amount even in those flower power days and it turned out that he was trying to financially support his hippie mother Jill and three younger siblings who were roaming the Middle East as a family.

Young Davey was the fall guy for his mother who hot-footed it back across the Syrian border to safety. Meanwhile Timothy was taken initially to jail in Ankara and a couple of weeks later to prison in Istanbul. He would stand trial in March 1972 and was sentenced to six years, before being released early on compassionate grounds in May 1974.

I flew to Ankara where I door-stepped the prison. After being permitted a very brief word with the young man it was decided by the office that I should attempt to get into Syria and track down Jill and her tribe of youngsters.

I flew by internal *Turkish Airlines* to Adana on Turkey's southern Mediterranean coast, fifty miles or so from the Syrian border. Felicitously, my passport still had my profession down as "student" which helped me cross the border. At that time, Syria was politically isolated, its sole true ally being communist China. They were not receptive to journalists and would have found the notion of tracking down a drug smuggler as little more than a cover for spying.

As I booked into the finest hotel in Aleppo I was struck by the absence of tourists and by the fact that the only guests there were Chinese generals. Syria and China were about to sign some military accord, I was told by the hotel receptionist. After I filed copy to the *Express* office, I became aware that my conversations were being monitored.

The friendly receptionist, who had believed my passport description of student, was now being monosyllabic and distant. The atmosphere was cooling and rather than call the office back I telephoned my wife Tina to get in touch with the *Express* to inform them what was going on. They told her that my quarry, Jill Davey, was now thought to be in Beirut, capital of the neighbouring Lebanon.

Digesting this information, I was wondering how to get there when a large Mercedes drew up at the hotel and out stepped the familiar face of Michael Brunson of *ITN*. He was accompanied by two large Italians, his cameraman, and a sound man. After I told him that the Davey family had hightailed it out of Syria to Beirut, Brunson suggested I get my luggage and join him in this huge car. I didn't need a second invitation.

Hard as we tried, we never caught up with Jill Davey and her brood. We looked everywhere for about three days when I finally had to admit defeat. The office told me to take the next flight home. Meanwhile Mrs Davey and co were actually plotting to help Timothy escape from his new Istanbul jail dressed as a girl. This escapade failed miserably and caused his sentence to be harsher than it might have been.

Part of young Timothy's experiences were used to inspire the movie *Midnight Express,* about life for drug smugglers in a Turkish prison. The film starred Brad Davis and John Hurt and was released in 1978. It was directed by Englishman Alan Parker.

Meanwhile I wasn't quite sure what reception I would get back in Fleet Street having failed to locate Jill Davey. In fact the foreign editor was pleased that I had got into Syria; apart from

Brunson no other news organisation had managed it. I was now eligible for other foreign sorties.

I hit the front page of the *Daily Express* on September 13 with an extraordinary story which was subsequently made into the 2008 movie *The Bank Job* and several documentaries. Radio ham Robert Rowlands came to the *Express* on the afternoon of Sunday September 12 bearing a tape recording of what he believed to be a bank robbery going on somewhere in the vicinity of his Wimpole Street flat.

He had first reported what he'd heard, which seemed to be a lookout reporting to his bank robber colleagues, on the previous evening but the local police had taken little notice. Then Rowlands began to record what he was hearing on a tape cassette. On the Sunday morning he had plenty more material and he decided to ring Scotland Yard instead.

This time the Yard took his recordings more seriously and searched 750 banks within an eight mile radius of Wimpole Street. If only they had concentrated on nearer banks – which Rowlands advised them to do – they would have had more luck. In frustration, Rowlands decided to come to the *Daily Express* to see if we could help.

After I listened to the recordings, it was crystal clear that something highly illegal was going on. It was also obvious from the gang's conversations that bank vaults were in the process of being robbed. We decided to publish that there was a bank raid going on which would become apparent only when the managers opened the vaults on Monday morning. It was a great scoop and by 9.30am that Monday, the full extent of the gang's work became visible.

There were rumours that secret photographs of Princess Margaret in the compromising company of show business villain Johnny Bindon were in one box. I believe that to be erroneous, cooked up to sell the movie. However another box was owned, embarrassingly, by none other than the Lord Chancellor, Lord Hailsham, the country's leading law officer and a senior member of Edward Heath's Cabinet.

Two hundred and sixty-eight boxes had been emptied of their contents so there was no knowing how much had been stolen. Estimates varied from £1.5m to £4m and I suspect it was much higher than that. Eventually, Rowlands, who now lives in Spain, was awarded £2,500 by Lloyds Bank, even though the police considered charging him with technical "telegraphy" offences. Thankfully for Rowlands they never proceeded with what would have been "sour grapes" charges.

In April 1972, Tina and I welcomed our third and final daughter into the world at a nursing home in Lambeth. Although Tina could have had baby Georgia at home, she decided she needed some rest while I and another maternity nurse looked after the older two in Battersea. Georgia, the spitting image of Tara, was an unexpected and delightful surprise.

With two babies in two years Tina had decided Roman Catholicism was not receptive enough to birth control and decided to foreswear her religion. But despite our best efforts, Georgia had defied the odds and presented herself as a 9lb arrival, dwarfing the birth weights of her siblings. Three girls – was I a lucky chap – and the *Express* took pity, offering me three days paternity leave to cope.

A few weeks later I was covering Wimbledon, a dream opportunity for a player and fan. Within a couple of days I had a front page splash – largely thanks to Tina who had heard BBC commentator Dan Maskell referring to the advertising on American doubles star Rosie Casal's dress.

In 1972 the Wimbledon dress code – which always insisted on whites throughout – was very strict about the presence of advertising of any sort. *Robinsons'* squash drinks beneath the umpire's chair were about the limit of their scope. But apparently Casal's dress was interwoven with the insignia VS for *Virginia Slims* cigarettes.

I missed the first edition of the *Express* but when Tina relayed the story to me after I got home, I filed the copy which made the front page in the tennis-mad *Express*. I guess it was a slow news day but I was thrilled to have my second splash story and it soon led to others.

'Black September' was a terrorist organisation largely peopled by German activists who had been bombing major installations throughout Europe and they had been considered the prime movers behind the appalling slaughter of Israeli athletes at the 1972 Munich Olympic Games. So when France discovered a cell in their country which included an English girl called Dr Diane Campbell-Lefevre they decided to deport her forthwith and let the UK authorities deal with her.

In March 1973 photographer Bill Lovelace and I were despatched to Paris to locate this girl and gain the first interview with her – no easy task. Luckily for me, Lovelace, experienced and broad shouldered, had been based in Paris for three years during the '60s. More importantly he had contacts with both *British Airways* and *Air France* which led us to the correct flight and timing, the 4.15pm *Air France* flight to Heathrow.

In 1973 there were few short haul flights with pre-selected seats; you walked to the aircraft and simply found the best seat you could. Luck, which always plays a part in scoops, dictated that I spotted this young-looking, thirty-one year old in the reception lounge having her handcuffs unsheathed by two plain clothed Sûreté detectives. I had my quarry; now it was a matter of staying close and parking myself next to her on the aircraft.

I knew that rival colleagues from the *Mail,* the *Mirror,* the *Times* and the *Guardian* had booked business class seats in the belief, not entirely unfounded, that she would be at the front of the aircraft to facilitate her exit on arrival at Heathrow, presumably escorted by Special Branch.

I had little difficulty in plonking myself next to Campbell-Lefevre who had selected a window seat in coach and was hiding behind large dark glasses. Bill Lovelace was in a seat immediately in front of mine so that he could take a photograph of the two of us in conversation. So far so good. It was just a matter of timing and/or whether this lady would open up to a "surprising" co-passenger.

The *Mail*'s Bill Lowther solved the problem for me – unknowingly. Ten minutes into the forty-five minute flight he emerged from business class, saw my face, and realised who I was sat next to. He stopped and began to try and ask questions of the girl who burst into tears. Meanwhile two cabin stewards heaved Lowther away from our row and forced him back into business class.

Now I was able to console my neighbour who was gradually drying her face. Comforting her as best I could she started to open up about her predicament at which point I revealed that I was a *Daily Express* reporter. Cue more tears. But I tried to be as reassuring as I could, pointing out that she could have her say before Special Branch took over once the aircraft had landed. She lit up another *Gauloise,* the cigarette of choice for girls of a certain age in that era, and she started to speak about how and why she had joined Black September. She seemed a nice middle class girl from Surrey, not your average militant. She had just spent five unhappy days in a Parisian prison. I wondered if she had been brainwashed, but at this point she decided not to say much more, especially as the aircraft was already beginning its approach to Heathrow. On landing, two Special Branch detectives entered the aircraft, found her, and escorted her off the plane before the remainder of the passengers could leave. Lowther asked me for a quote and I replied, "Not possible this time, I'm afraid."

The following morning the *Daily Express* splashed the story on the front page. The *Guardian*'s first edition claimed that the girl had been secreted away by the police without giving an interview, so in later editions we published Bill Lovelace's picture of me talking to the girl which proved, beyond doubt, that the interview had taken place.

Curiously it seems as if Special Branch merely escorted her to a domestic flight for Manchester from where she disappeared. Her parents could offer no clues as to what had happened. Years later she emerged as a leading psychology lecturer. It makes one wonder if Special Branch had actually placed her within Black September as a potential mole.

By June 1973 I was looking forward to reprising my role as the *Express* news man at Wimbledon. Most of the good players had gone on strike, ostensibly to improve their prize money. Luckily for us news hounds there was a seventeen year old Swede called Bjorn Borg who was not yet a member of the ATP, the Association of Tennis Professionals, which was orchestrating this industrial action.

Wimbledon was a sell out as usual and there was in influx of young girl fans who thought Bjorn Borg was more attractive than any of the Beatles. Borg mania was born and it was an extraordinary sight. However much male fans might have worshipped at the altar of Maria Sharapova and other East European beauties in subsequent years, their adoration was dwarfed by the pop star frenzy lavished on the ice-cool Borg.

I was just getting into my stride covering this phenomenon when I received a call from the office to get myself off to New York forthwith. My old friend and colleague Nigel Dempster, doing a stint as a foreign correspondent for the *Daily Mail* in the Big Apple, had come up with a scoop that the second marriage of Richard Burton and Elizabeth Taylor was over.

On arrival in New York, where the *Express* had offices on West 42nd street in the *Daily News* building, I learned that La Taylor was holed up in the fashionable village of Quogue on Long Island. I rang the home and was told by the voice on the other end of the phone that Miss Taylor was not there. I was pretty certain that it was Elizabeth's voice pretending to be a Latin American maid.

I recalled that Bill Lovelace had been drafted in as best man at the second marriage four years earlier. Through the *Express* foreign desk, I located Bill on an assignment in Hawaii and he agreed to call Elizabeth and get her to take my call. He was as good as his word, and once I had reminded her of our meeting in Oxford when she was in *Dr Faustus*, she was as good as gold and talked about the sad break-up of her marriage and what her plans for the future were.

She told me, "I still have great ambitions to be in good movies. It's sad that Richard and I won't be together again, but that's life isn't it? I so enjoyed hearing from Bill again. He's a handsome chap and we had a lovely dance in the Dorchester after Richard and I married for the second time."

Bill was a handsome chap who died far too young. He had an enormous influence on me and helped me so much in Brazil. It was like having a great reporter at your elbow as well as one of the world's greatest press photographers. While colleagues at the *Daily Express* had been drowning in champagne the night of the Biggs arrest, Bill and I had had a reflective dinner together, shocked at the turn of events.

For three months I had a full and fulfilling time in New York. *Daily Mail* bureau chief Dermot Purgavie was on furlough in London for eight weeks and I was able to rent his wonderful East 65th street penthouse apartment. We may not have been highly paid hacks in those days but the expense allowances were very good. I never needed to touch my salary the whole time I was abroad.

There was one story dominating the news schedules on a daily basis – the Watergate scandal. This was two years before the impeachment of President Richard Nixon but the evidence of his criminality was mounting, and this was the story that just kept giving.

Two Washington Post journalists – Messrs Woodward and Bernstein – had discovered that the offices of the Democratic committee for the election of the president, in the Watergate building, had been raided by burglars. They were on the case, as the burglary seemed to have been committed on the orders of senior Republican figures within the White House.

I went to Washington once for the hearings but it soon became clear that it was much easier and more efficient to watch PBS live on television to get the updates. "Follow the Money" was the mantra adopted by the interrogators and it paid constant dividends.

Apart from the regular plane crashes, murders, and features on places like Rikers Island prison, there was one stand-out event I was called on to cover: a Pittsburgh concert by the heavy metal group *Led Zeppelin*.

I was invited by the group to go to Newark airport, New Jersey, to join them on their customised "Starship" Boeing 707 – complete with jacuzzis and large double beds – to fly to Pittsburgh where they would perform at the Three Rivers baseball stadium in front of 40,000 fans. I confessed to bureau chief Ivor Key that I was not familiar with the group's music or personnel. "All the better; you can be objective" said Ivor.

Having established that I was to meet their manager Peter Grant at the airport, I quickly boned up on the names of the group – lead singer Robert Plant, guitarist Jimmy Page, bassist keyboard player John Paul Jones, and drummer John Bonham. I knew nothing of their music at all.

Once at Newark I realised what a big deal this was. There were a dozen groupies pleading to get on the plane which was a monument to excess. Robert Plant was very pleasant to me. Most of his band mates were otherwise "occupied". Grant promised to guide me through the night.

On arrival at Pittsburgh airport there was a convoy of a dozen stretch limousines, complete with police outriders, ready to transport us to the stadium. Sitting in limo No 6 with sirens blaring and traffic being held up for us, I had the sense of what it must be like to be the US President for a few moments. It was surreal, and explains to a minor degree why some pop stars eventually lose their grip on reality.

The baseball stadium was engulfed in fans, many without tickets. Grant, a large gentleman who brooked no dissent, announced to the concert producers that his group would not be ascending the stage with its humongous hundred foot high sound system until he had counted the take in cash. And for this reason, the start was delayed for fifty-three minutes while Grant personally checked the $120,000 in cash that had been promised.

I asked to go on stage, in the wings, with the group to get a true sense of the music and the occasion. Big mistake. I had no idea how noisy the acoustics would be, how much I disliked the music, or how impossible it was for me to leave the stage at any point. My relationship with modern music was tenuous to say the least. I could identify with the *Beatles* and *The Carpenters* but my true love was in the classical field. I was more Mozart than *Manic Street Preachers*.

Vast 55 gallon drums of water (44 imperial gallons) had been placed between those in the front 6,000 expensive seats and the remainder. But the fans from the cheaper seats soon rolled those over and flooded forward. It was mayhem, and Led Zeppelin loved it. The concert lasted for three hours twenty-five minutes and included a half time drum solo by Bonham of twenty minutes which allowed the other group members a break.

At around midnight, relief was at hand and Led Zeppelin took their final bow. It was clear that the fans had adored the concert and that I was in a small minority of dissenters. However I was there to record the occasion, not to be a music critic, and I duly filed a middle page spread documenting all the excesses and the triumphs.

Somehow I knew that this would not be the end of the story. A few days later I learned that the reception clerk at New York's Drake hotel, where *Led Zeppelin* were staying, had disappeared with a huge stash of cash. Peter Grant had placed the takings in the safe at the Drake.

The clerk had evidently decided that the life changing amount of cash was enough for him to risk bettering his circumstances. By the time I returned to London six weeks later the clerk had still not been located by police. It was estimated that he had taken up to $500,000, worth twenty times that amount today.

My return to London proved to be something of an anti-climax. I was placed for several weeks on the night news desk, a sedentary post handing out jobs to other reporters. I regarded myself as an outside man and not an administrator, but you had to do what you were told. Hence my restless feet, and an enquiry to leave the *Express* to join the blossoming *Daily Mail*.

10

Biggs, books & builders

In the autumn of 1973 and prior to the Biggs tsunami, Brian Vine purchased another racehorse called *Overall*. Formerly trained in Ireland, this 'flying machine', as Vine described him, was shared by the same partnership of Vine, Wynn-Morgan, and me, and trained by the ever successful Les Kennard in Somerset. An outing on the flat at Sandown Park was followed by his first hurdle race at Devon and Exeter in which he finished a promising third. A second win for me as an owner clearly beckoned.

Tina and I decided to take a two week holiday in Tenerife, with baby Georgia, leaving the older girls with my mother in Betchworth. On the Thursday before we returned to London, *Overall* was entered at Ludlow. I had left £50 with Vine to place a bet, however as luck would have it, Vine was despatched to New York, thereby missing the fun at the Shropshire venue. In those pre mobile phone days I was blissfully unaware of this salient fact until I read the *Observer* the following Sunday as our British Caledonian flight made its four hour journey back to Gatwick.

Award-winning sports writer Hughie McIlvanney's entire piece was devoted to being a surrogate owner for the day at bucolic Ludlow, mixing with Squire Jorrocks and his pals. Two of *Overall's* owners were abroad and he had made the ultimate sacrifice by stepping in to represent them. There were detailed descriptions of the firm going, in the car park, on the track, and on the terraces, which would suit *Overall*. Even more painful, as it turned out, was the fact that Hughie had hit the bookies for six, hoovering up all the 3-1, leaving the "peasantry" to make do with the evens that was the starting price.

Despite the paucity of phone connections, I managed to find out that *Overall* had won, but I had no idea at what starting price. Champagne was called for and a lavish party was held at our hotel in Puerto de la Cruz. By the time I read the McIlvanney masterpiece I realised I had seriously overspent.

I had got to know McIlvanney quite well during his twelve month transfer from the *Observer* to the *Daily Express* the previous year. His first assignment was the 1972 Derby which was won by Lester Piggott aboard *Roberto* who had beaten *Rheingold* in a pulsating finish.

I was the news reporter on duty to cover matters outside the actual racing at Epsom that day. Little did I know I would have a secondary role – that of persuading the *Express's* big new signing to file his copy on time. Hughie was used to a Sunday deadline and having a whole seven days to cogitate before filing his finely crafted words of wisdom.

By 8.45pm on that Wednesday evening the *Express* had not heard from their man. I had the sports editor and the news editor shouting in my ear to get him to file. Relaying this intelligence to the Sports Writer of the Year did not improve Hughie's temper. "Tell them to fuck off" was the polite version of what he said to me.

Hughie's copy never made the first edition. He found over the next few weeks that he couldn't face a daily deadline with equanimity. The discipline of compromise simply wasn't in his DNA and he would not send his copy to the paper unless it met his exacting standards, which meant he needed more than one day to think about it.

Unsurprisingly both parties realised that his transfer to the *Express* was a mistake. Hughie had probably done it for the money – the *Express* had deeper pockets than the *Observer*. But he was much happier on the *Observer* and this concession to his state of mind won the day and he returned to his natural home within a year.

Overall won four hurdle races and was thought good enough to be entered in the Gloucester hurdle – the Supreme novice hurdle – at the 1974 Cheltenham festival. I was in Brazil en route to Australia where I would stay with Charmian Biggs to debrief her for my upcoming Biggs book.

Overall was unplaced in his race, but Kennard, who generally kept his opinions to himself, let on to Messrs Vine and Wynne-Morgan that he gave *Highland Abbe* a big shout in the Stayers hurdle. The duo scooped up all the 20-1 and the exciting hurdler duly won at odds of 14-1. Up in Brasilia where I was visiting Biggs in the foreigners' prison, I was blissfully ignorant of this coup.

On my return from Brazil in mid February, I was aware of an undercurrent of unease at the office. I bumped into editor Iain McColl making a rare visit to that noted Fleet Street hostelry, the City Golf Club. He was looking shifty and rather ashamed at the outcome of my Brazilian venture. He had authorised a bonus for Bill Lovelace and me of £25 each, a rather modest reward for a story that had lifted circulation above four million again, not to mention the profitable sale of Bill's pictures around the world which had netted a six figure sum.

Later I confronted him in his office, pointing out yet again that Biggs would have given himself up to the British consul in Rio and come back to serve the remainder of his prison term had McColl let me proceed as I had originally planned. He was unmoved, claiming that he had abided by legal advice. As he was on the back foot, I was able to negotiate a year's sabbatical to write a book about Biggs.

I had been in touch with Curtis Brown, the literary agents representing Frederick Forsyth whose first novel, *The Day of The*

Jackal, I had enjoyed so much. Peter Grose, the managing director, agreed to look after me and, after only a week or so, he had negotiated a handsome advance with Hart-Davis, MacGibbon for the UK and Commonwealth rights. He then set about selling the rights to a dozen other countries in languages ranging from Portuguese to Finnish and even Japanese.

To celebrate this glorious news, I took my in-laws Kay and Amador Fonseca, plus my mother Hazel Adair and her actor "walker" Neil Hallett (my step father Ronnie Marriott had died too young in 1972), to the *Savoy* River Room. Dana, a recent winner of the Eurovision Song contest, was singing in cabaret that evening.

Flushed with success over my book deal, I summoned the sommelier, looked down his wine list and ordered a bottle of the 1963 Fonseca port, regarded as the finest port vintage since the war. After an excessively long wait a decanted bottle of this delicious Portuguese product was offered for my opinion.

At this point I turned to the sommelier who was perspiring a little and said, "You're a lucky chap. Mr Fonseca is at the end of the table and he will taste the port for us."

Amador poked his long Iberian nose into the glass, took a serious sip, and washed it around his palate. He turned to the ever-perspiring sommelier and said; "That was delicious but I'm sorry to report that this is not Fonseca '63 of which I have plenty at home."

Full of confusion, the poor sommelier left with the decanted port and returned to the cellars. After another twenty minute pause he returned with a bottle of port, undecanted. He said, "I'm terribly sorry sir; there was an error in the cellars with the previous bottle and we would like you to have this bottle of '63 port free of charge."

"What is it?" I asked. "It's a Mackenzie port," said the sommelier and the whole table burst out laughing. "Sorry, what have I said," continued the hapless fellow before I put him at his ease by announcing that my name was Mackenzie. Relief all round. I have kept the bill for this great evening and the cost was no more than £60, or £10 a head. I also kept the bill for a follow-up dinner with four close friends at the *Connaught* and again the bill was £60 in total. A similar meal in 2020 at the *Savoy* and the Connaught would have cost fifteen times as much.

I flew back to Brazil on March 1, determined to see Biggs in the Brasilia jail he was sharing with other foreigners such as the fraudulent art dealer Fernand Legros, who would later become a godfather to Biggs's Brazilian son Michael. I flew to the Brazilian capital and was granted access with his lawyer Jose Pertence who made Biggs aware of all the legal ramifications of his situation.

I asked Biggs to spend his days writing down everything he could remember about both his childhood and his days as a felon. Although he was a retired crook at the time of the Great Train Robbery, he had led an active criminal life since the war having been dishonourably discharged from the RAF during his national service for theft. It was clear that he was no angel, even though Charmian believed he was a reformed character by the time they married in 1960.

Then it was off to Melbourne to stay with Charmian and her two boys for three weeks while I debriefed her on life with the Great Train Robber on my trusted tape recorder. Charmian, who would go on to become a university lecturer in later life, was no fool. Furthermore, she could recall every detail of their mercurial relationship from the day they first met on a commuter train from Reigate to London Bridge in 1958 to the day in 1974 when she learned of his capture in Brazil by Slipper of the Yard.

Her skill at evading the watching police following Biggs's escape from Wandsworth prison on July 8, 1965, until her own flight from the country in June a year later was astonishing. She and her sister Rosalind had taken Nicky and Chris, now owning passports with the surname Brent (to avoid them being bullied at school) on a trial holiday flight to Gran Canaria, primarily to see if they were followed by the law. Having established they had successfully avoided discovery Charmian made plans for a permanent exit to Australia a month later.

In June 1966, they set out by car – driven by a gang member who had helped Ronnie eleven months earlier – to drive to Brussels for a flight which would end in Darwin, capital of the Northern Territory, where they would book into the *Koala* motel. Charmian had already acquired a new set of identities for her and the boys in the name of Furminger with passports to match. Biggs was due to meet them at the motel when their life together could recommence.

As with so much of Biggs's life it was the minutiae that let him down. The construction of the *Koala* motel had not been completed and it was still a building site. He had seen an advertisement for the establishment in a magazine while working as a carpenter in Sydney. Luckily, he was watching from the sidelines of the airport as the drama of Charmian seeking another hotel unfolded. Once she was on her way, he caught up with her and their life together began again.

In October 1969, the Australian police were closing in on their home in Dandenong, thanks to a magazine article about the arrest in Britain of Great Train Robber Bruce Reynolds alongside Biggs's photo which suggested he might be in Australia. Again, with the help of ex-pat Brits Jess and Mike Haynes who hosted him for a few weeks, Biggs remained one step ahead of the police. Charmian was arrested but was steadfast in her refusal to reveal her husband's whereabouts.

Eventually Biggs adopted the Haynes identity, altering his passport photograph and booking a passage to Panama on the *SS Ellinis*. From Panama he intended to make his way to Brazil which, he had learned, had no extradition arrangements with the UK. On February 5 1970, he set sail from Melbourne to begin the next episode of his extraordinary life on the run.

It was almost four years after his arrival in Rio that he had run out of ideas and money. There had been an awful moment in February 1971 when Charmian wrote a letter to tell him of the "worst news in the world" – the death in a car accident of their eldest son Nicky at the age of ten. She had begged him not to give himself up and set about trying to provide another passport "Day of the Jackal-style" by using the identity of a child who had died young and hoping the authorities wouldn't check up.

Biggs was distraught at the news. Nicky, their first-born, had been a special child, intelligent, loyal and hard working at school. But Ronnie took on board Charmian's supplications and decided to carry on with his lotus-eating existence in one of the most beautiful cities in the world, until he met Constantine Benckendorf in July of 1973 when the idea of surrendering himself to Scotland Yard first took root.

I returned to Brazil via Angola's capital Luanda, where I was fortunate to avoid the incipient Angolan revolution with the sounds of gunshots everywhere. Biggs was due to be released around May 2 and there was still some doubt about whether he would be permitted to remain in Brazil or face expulsion back to Britain.

The Fleet Street massif had assembled again with every national paper represented, not to mention the *BBC's* John Humphreys and *ITN's* Michael Brunson. Ralph Champion, the urbane New York bureau chief of *Mirror* newspapers said, "I must get down to Rio; I've never been to Brazil." One of his colleagues remarked to him, "There's an awful lot of copy in Brazil!"

Brasilia airport had never witnessed anything like the scramble for seats on the internal *Cruzeiro do Sul* Boeing 727 that transported us back to the magical city of Rio de Janeiro. It was only in 1956 that Brazil's capital had been changed from Rio, ostensibly to open up the vast interior of the fifth largest country in the world. Sadly, despite its modernist architecture, Brasilia never lived up to the hopes and aspirations of its architect creator Oscar Niemeyer. Brazilian politicians still had to be bribed with weekend exeats to Rio to persuade them to attend mid week parliamentary sessions in the new capital.

Once on board the aircraft, Biggs was accompanied by two Brazilian *federales* police officers. I was able to smuggle a piece of paper to him with the address of our rented Gastao Bahiana apartment where he would be lodging for the foreseeable future. Unfortunately, before the police would release him to the outside world in Rio, he had to inform them where he was living. It didn't take long for this intelligence to be acquired by my rivals.

This time I had a little muscle with me in the form of experienced reporters Ivor Key, the *Express* New York bureau chief, and Mike O'Flaherty who had flown out from the London office. With their help I was able to keep Biggs at arms length from the opposition – the apartment was literally invaded and the front door attacked by manic reporters, including Brazilians.

Charmian flew in from Melbourne with Chris and Farley in a bid to win back her husband. Biggs was between a rock and a hard place though as part of the conditions of his release were that he would protect and support Raimunda de Castro, the woman who was expecting his child in August.

Tensions rose and although Biggs was thrilled to reunite with his two sons, Charmian could not understand why he had to go home every night to Raimunda's bed and not to hers in the hotel. Within a few days she realised that the man she had loved for sixteen years was no longer hers and she reluctantly conceded that his freedom was totally dependent upon his staying with the pregnant girl from Maranhao.

Charmian flew back to Australia via London so that she could see her parents, acquire some of the train robbery money, and show her boys the city where their father grew up. It was a bitter pill to realise her marriage was over. But she was more than ever determined to finish her degree and begin work as an academic in Melbourne.

I began to chronicle the Biggs biography – *Ronald Biggs, The Most Wanted Man* – but it became clear to me that a busy household with three small children was not the optimum work space for a would-be author. I accepted an offer from sister-in-law Jose Fonseca to use a spare room at the Fulham Rd offices of *Models One* to pound away on my typewriter and deliver 100,000 words by the beginning of October. The book was not due for publication until September 1975 but the publishers needed the words at least ten months ahead so that it could be edited and checked for legal problems. I was able to deliver the book on time.

While I was at Jose's offices, she asked me to deliver a package to one of her models, Ingrid Boulting. When I asked what it was – I didn't want to carry anything illegal– she announced, "It's a present from John Barry. It's a Picasso." Gulping and nervous I handed over the package in person to a delighted model.

In late 1974 I decided not to return to the *Daily Express*. I was looking for other book projects and I still felt wounded by what I perceived as betrayal by the paper. Iain McColl was no longer editor, his role having been taken over by Alastair Burnett who had sacrificed his career at *ITN* to return to Fleet Street. My letter of resignation was addressed to him, and although he made a cursory attempt to persuade me to stay, we both knew that wasn't going to happen.

Meanwhile on the racing front, *Overall* won his fourth race – this time at Wincanton – and we were looking forward to a profitable season with him. A few weeks later I bumped into the amateur rider Richard Smith in the unlikely environs of *Tramp*, the fashionable Jermyn Street discotheque. Richard had ridden *Overall* a couple of times and rode out for Les Kennard. When I said I was looking forward to the horse running in a couple of weeks' time, he shot me a puzzled look.

Overall, it transpired, had been injured at Wincanton and was in a field recovering from a firing operation, where the foreleg tendons are treated to make them stronger. He wouldn't be running for at least ten months, which was news to his three London owners. Although in touch with Kennard this piece of vital intelligence had not been transmitted to us and we were still paying full training fees.

I have never been in the habit of removing horses from trainers. In my fifty-two years of owning I have done it only once: Les Kennard no longer trained *Overall* by the start of 1975. The five-year-old was picked up by Jim Old's horsebox and transferred to the pretty village of Ashmore in Dorset where "young Old", as Nigel Dempster was later to christen him, was beginning his training career.

Jim was known as the Duckpond Genius, after Ashmore's most notable feature. He used jockey Bob Champion when he had a runner primed for victory. And in the early stages of his career he was remarkably successful. He never trained a winner for me but it hasn't stopped us remaining firm friends.

Overall couldn't run until late in 1975 when he was entered in a seller at Windsor. Sadly he broke his fetlock at the second last hurdle and Jim asked our permission to have the horse shot.

Vine's wife Beverly, who was at Windsor with Brian and her mother Betty, was inconsolable, telling Brian that we should not consider shooting such a lovely animal, even if it was the kindest thing to do. "Horses can't talk," she wailed. "It's not as if they're human and could argue for themselves."

"Oh, so it's all right to kill humans is it?" barked Brian. Beverly was by now in floods of tears. "It's better than killing horses anyway," she said. "All right," said Vine. "Betty, you go and stand by the wall over there and I will direct the vet to shoot you instead."

I was in fits of inappropriate laughter, which lightened the moment and we all repaired to the bar to salute poor *Overall*. A large scotch whisky awaited the trainer for whom this was a first racecourse fatality. It's a sad fact that some racehorses do meet their Waterloo on the racecourse; even more are killed through their own stupidity in fields and paddocks. Happily, the percentages are falling as equine welfare improves.

I had three more horses with Jim over the next few seasons, but neither *Burbling Brook, Superfluous*, nor *Chatty Corner* troubled the judge. I would have to await the introduction of David Gandolfo to restore my racing fortunes – but not for another four years.

By the summer of 1975 Tina and I had resolved to upgrade our somewhat rackety Edwardian house rather than sell it and move to Chelsea across the river from Battersea. Tina found a builder and we agreed a £12,000 makeover. This may seem modest by modern standards but it represented four times my annual *Daily Express* salary and nearly double the original cost of the house six years earlier.

Then I made one of the many errors of judgement of my life by advancing the builder, a name-dropping public schoolboy with persuasive confidence, half the agreed sum to get started while I was away in Brazil. Within four weeks I learned from Tina that the wretched Old Harrovian had gone bust and it appeared he had used most of my money to complete work on another client's house. Our house had no roof and no builders, unless I took on his work force myself. And after my return from Brazil that's what happened.

Having delivered the biography to Biggs, by now a hands-on father to baby Mikezinho, eleven months old, I went up country to see my father Gordon. He had acquired, with his business partner Peter Richardson, a farm in the Mato Grosso which mostly grew coffee. It was very basic and the farm house totally lacked amenities such as electricity. A tiny generator was powered by a Heath Robinson contraption that somehow enabled water to be pumped from the river up to the main residence.

I loved the isolation and freedom, although the weather took a surprising turn with overnight frost – unheard of in that part of Brazil – producing temperatures of minus seven degrees celsius. The whole of the coffee crop failed, with the bushes a horrible black colour, visibly demonstrating their overnight destruction.

Knowing I had lost £6,000 to a corrupt builder this was a golden opportunity to get my money back. I knew that the price of coffee would likely inflate by 600 per cent after the largest producer in the world's crop had failed. But there was no telephone within a hundred kilometres. My frustration grew that I could take no action to help myself out of my predicament despite a golden opportunity to do so.

Coffee prices inflated hugely over the next few weeks but I had missed the moment.

I returned to Battersea, furious about the building situation and resentful that a golden financial opportunity had been denied me by third world circumstances. The Old Harrovian's work force, numbering five, wanted £100 a week each in cash to carry on. It was either that or find another builder to solve the problem already exacerbated by the removal of the roof and other vital parts of the infrastructure. I would have to become a builder despite my complete lack of experience and knowhow.

To make matters worse I was about to embark on a nationwide promotion of my book, with appearances on local radio, the *Tonight* television show, the Jimmy Young radio show, and even Southern television where my inquisitor was an old *Daily Express* colleague Christopher Wilson. The latter, now a successful author, was robust in his questioning despite our friendship. I became aware over the next few days that Mr Biggs was not a popular fellow among the public at large.

Then I learned that Tony Delano of *the Daily Mirror* had written a book which he cleverly titled *Slip Up* about the media circus surrounding Biggs's discovery and arrest. The book's theme was that a bungling policeman coupled with an inexperienced journalist had cocked up a great story. It was a case of William Boot, the naïve reporter hero of Evelyn Waugh's 1938 masterpiece *Scoop*, in competition with the Keystone cops.

There was no question *Slip Up* was a very entertaining read – as long as you were not the subject of all the mirth. It painted the Fleet Street rivalries in an amusing and unflattering light. What really irritated me was that Delano insisted that I was little more than a gossip writer lucky to be in the right place at the right time to execute one of the scoops of the century.

There was little concession to the fact that I had probably covered more foreign stories than any other *Express* man over the previous two years. Nor that I spoke Portuguese and knew

Brazil well. He was determined to paint me as a naïve abroad, like the aforementioned Boot, rather than someone who delivered a spectacular scoop to the *Express* under the most trying of circumstances with little help from an out of depth editor.

The book, serialised in the *Sunday Times*, was later made into a television movie, written in 1986 by none other than my brilliant *Daily Mail* colleague Keith Waterhouse. I had to take legal action to protect my reputation, reluctant as I was to do so. The actor who played me, Nicholas Le Prevost, had actually taken me to lunch to discuss the project, so his portrayal of me as a limp-wristed jejeune was deeply disappointing. I can only assume he was acting under orders.

Jack Slipper also took action against the programme. But whereas I was paying my own legal costs, he was backed by Jimmy (later Sir James) Goldsmith who was battling *Private Eye* on a monthly basis for their portrayal of his efforts to buy into Fleet Street through *Now* magazine.

My legal expenses began to get out of hand as meeting after meeting at my solicitor's offices, followed by counsel's opinion, ate into my meagre reserves. Rather than risk my house and everything I had earned, I eventually withdrew from the action after the legal fees already incurred exceeded a five figure sum. Slipper, inured from any financial penalties, went on to win his legal action for libel against the *BBC*. The result is that the programme has never been repeated and he received substantial damages.

It was an expensive and draining experience. Libel laws have since changed and favour the litigant to a greater degree. It was against the grain for me to even initiate proceedings – it's not a good look for a journalist to rely on the law to protect his reputation. In my defence this was a dramatic portrayal of me that, even according to my "enemies", was so radically unfair that I let my heart rule my head.

The building works on our Battersea house dragged on until well into 1976. Luckily for us it was a very dry summer as the roof was still under repair. There was little or no incentive for my builders to hurry themselves along as they would be out of a job once they had completed. Talk about Hobson's choice.

By the end of June, the house makeover was completed and we began to entertain again after a lapse of eighteen months or more. Among our regular Sunday lunch guests was the *Naked Civil Servant* author Quentin Crisp who usually came along accompanied by our mutual friend Peter York, the style guru who created the Sloane Ranger phenomenon.

Crisp was very mannered and great fun. He addressed everyone as Mr This or Mrs That, never Colin or Tina. He didn't particularly like children and so, to my utter shame, we banished our three gorgeous daughters to their playroom in the upper reaches of the house while he was enjoying roast lamb in our dining room. What were we thinking?

But he was entertaining. It was as if Oscar Wilde had wafted into our house from a century before. Sat next to our friend Iwona Whitaker, wife of royal reporter James, he learned she was Polish. "Poland is not a country," he opined. "It's a state of mind." Iwona didn't find this observation quite as funny as the rest of us.

He would pontificate about the plusses of doing without a cleaning lady for his flat across the Thames in fashionable Beaufort St. "I can promise you Mr Mackenzie," he volunteered. "After three years without a cleaner the flat looks no worse and the dust is just the same. Save your money."

We entertained about once a month and among our other guests were actor Terence Stamp and his girlfriend Carol Edge. Terence was very modest and quiet, seemingly unaware of the effect his good looks had on our other female guests. At the time he had rooms in Albany, the smart apartment block off Piccadilly.

James Dearden, who wrote the seminal movie *Fatal Attraction*, was another regular guest with his partner Jennie Marriott, ex-wife of the *Small Faces* band member Stevie Marriott. James was the son of film director Basil Dearden, responsible for many of the great post war British movies. We never imagined James's great idea would become such a significant and iconic film, starring Michael Douglas and Glenn Close.

Tina's sister Jose had also been living with us for a while until she married her first husband, property man and boulevardier David Olivestone. Olive, as he was known to all his friends, was a convivial regular at *Tramp* and *Annabel's*. He had wooed Jose with a certain intensity which involved bricks being thrown through our front window at one point.

That wasn't the only down side of having my sister-in-law living with us either. Jose herself was wonderfully generous to our daughters and a lovely person to have around. But some of her model clients telephoned her at all times of the night, with the phone erupting at 3am with the likes of Jerry Hall calling to say she couldn't get a cab and could Jose assist. I was more than thrilled when she married Olivestone and moved to Belgravia.

At the beginning of 1977 I began research for a war novel that my mother Hazel and I would write entitled *Blitz Over Balaclava Street*. I spent hours at the newspaper library in Collingwood North London gleaning little anecdotes to provide ballast to the main story line of an illicit wartime romance which I suspected had more than a little relevance to my mother's own experience.

By the summer of 1977 we were ready to put our researches on paper for a novel by "Clare Nicol" – Clare being the name my mother would have christened a daughter had she had one and Nicol being an anagram of Colin. Our publishers, *Granada*, wanted a woman author's name on a wartime romantic novel.

At this precise moment our friends Theo and Helen Gobat, who had been our neighbours prior to moving to St Lucia, said they would like to return to Battersea for the summer. Would we like to swap houses for eight weeks? Yes, we would.

So began a glorious idyll in St Lucia where we stayed in the Gobats' glamorous hilltop house. We had to wait in a nearby hotel for two days until the Gobats were ready to fly to London, and I caught a bug which gave me violent diarrhoea. Tina drove me to the hospital in Castries, the capital; where the Irish-born doctor John Christie was holding his surgery. There was a huge queue of mostly pregnant women, which we ungallantly but necessarily overtook. The doctor was Irish charm itself and announced that a few antibiotics would do the trick. He also said that he would have to accompany us as it would involve several different chemists and a formula which he would have to mix himself.

I immediately said we could do it ourselves and that he must attend to his other patients. But he insisted, adding that his waiting patients wouldn't mind because it was like a social club for them.

I made a fast recovery – albeit losing 15lbs weight in a couple of days – and proceeded to my typewriter. My mother wrote in long hand, which I typed up and married into my efforts. After three weeks we invited Dr Christie and his wife to supper as a thank you for his prompt and efficient efforts on my behalf.

"To be sure, it was no problem," said the man from County Limerick. "I took one look at your palm, saw your lifeline, and realised you'll live beyond ninety."

Blitz Over Balaclava Street was published in early 1978. It sold quite well but broke no records. What I had learned was that I was no novelist, the process demanding a very different discipline and mindset from journalism. John Le Carré and Freddie Forsyth can rest easy in their Guccis as I will be one of many millions presenting little threat to their talent or their sales.

I was due to play bridge at the Chiswick home of my good friends James and Iwona Whitaker one October evening in 1978 when news broke that Cardinal Karol Joseph Wojtila had been elected the new Pope. As both Iwona and our other bridge player Janek Murzynowski were Polish there was little or no prospect of an evening debating whether to bid three no trumps.

Janek, a six foot six mini cab driver who had defected to this country in the 1960s as an international basketball player, was particularly enthused. He was a brilliant bridge player whose English was so limited when he arrived in London that he was forced to make a living at the Portland Club playing cards as a hired partner.

Janek also claimed a connection to the new Pope who was born the same year as his mother and had been a neighbour in his native Krakow, where he would later become Archbishop and then Cardinal. As a priest he had regularly preached at the extraordinary 'underground cathedral' in the salt mines outside Krakow, nowadays a wedding venue and tourist attraction.

"I'll call my mother in Krakow and see what she thinks," Janek announced to us. So began an extraordinary conversation which Iwona was able to translate for me. It turned out that His Holiness had been quite a lad in his younger days. He was the Polish equivalent of a Hell's Angel before the war, roaring around Krakow on his motor cycle., and much admired by women although he kept them at arm's length.

The much-loved Cardinal's mother had died when he was only nine, and his father in 1941 just after his twenty-first birthday. It was the latter's shock death that influenced his decision to give up the wild life and enter a seminary in 1942. I gleaned a few more details and then rang the *Daily Express* night news desk who were more than happy for me to file a news feature along these lines.

As I worked on my piece, the rest of the Whitaker household broke out the champagne to celebrate this huge deal for a nation that had suffered so much in the two world wars. Janek had an amusing catch phrase that was repeated by his admirers long after this loveable Pole died far too young. When his partner overbid his hand, he would say in a deep Polish accent, "He who wish to drown – let him." In other words, do not under any circumstances get into a bidding war if you haven't got the cards to justify it.

Iwona, who could not dry her tears all night, met her hero a few years later, and there is a lovely photograph of the Pope greeting her which hangs in their Chiswick home.

By 1979 it was becoming clear that life as a freelance author neither suited me nor was it lucrative enough to sustain a growing family. Because of the house building fiasco, I had also acquired an unwanted mortgage. I'd also acquired a share in two jumpers trained by David Gandolfo and owned by my Oxford pal Grahame Amey. I enlisted another friend, Stephen Freud, and we became part owners of *Kirkstone Pass* and *All Right Jack* who were ready to go to war in the autumn of that year. Stephen was the elder of three brothers who were the grandsons of the eminent father of psychotherapy. His younger brothers Lucian, the artist, and Clement, the MP and raconteur, were far more famous but no more amusing. Stephen had inherited the generous genes from a family who appeared to be constantly at war with each other – indeed the three brothers barely and rarely spoke to one another.

Stephen and I decided to go and see *Kirkstone Pass's* first hurdle race in person at Carlisle, a course much favoured by Gandy whose father had owned a hotel in the Lake District. Indeed the horse was named after a famous landmark which is often mentioned in weather reports as impassable when snow falls.

Kirkstone Pass had had two runs as a bumper horse the previous season and had since grown and matured. According to the trainer, who said he was far from useless, he had needed that experience badly. Recovering from the 365-mile drive, Stephen and I opened our wallets and secured as much of the 14-1 as we could find.

Our jockey was the inexperienced Paul Barton, who claimed 7lbs at this early stage of his career, and he was told to produce the five-year-old at the final hurdle and go and win his race if he could. Amazingly all went well until the final hurdle by which time *Kirkstone Pass* had drawn four lengths clear of his fourteen rivals who included an odds-on shot trained by the northern maestro Arthur Stephenson.

Our horse hit the final obstacle and jinked to one side dislodging the poor jockey in slow motion as he was unseated. It happens all the time, but when it's your own horse it is doubly painful. Still, we were able to dream on the long journey home that we had bought into a decent animal who would give us some fun.

Kirkstone Pass did fulfil most of his potential, winning four hurdle races and three chases. He was a little clumsy but he was very game, and genuine, which is a key factor. *All Right Jack* was a different character. He had more talent in one fetlock than KP but was reluctant to reveal it unless it suited him. He did win three races eventually, but only when he felt like it and never when the Mackenzie wages were risked.

11.

Dempster, Lucan & marriage blues

By the end of 1979 it was time to return to Fleet Street and the semblances of a regular income. Catherine was approaching her eleventh birthday which meant abandoning her state primary school, the Oratory in Chelsea, for the fee-paying Ursuline convent in Wimbledon. Tara would follow a year later, and Georgia two years after her although by then we had discarded the Ursuline convent for More House, a Catholic girls school in Pont Street which was easier for them to access.

Nigel Dempster had left the Hickey column at the end of 1970 when the numbers were culled from a dozen to half that number by editor Derek Marks. The old broadsheet *Daily Mail* was about to merge with the tabloid *Daily Sketch* whose editor David English was to take over as boss. It was the night of the long knives – rather like a Cabinet reshuffle with *Sketch* journalists in the ascendancy when hard choices had to be made.

English had been foreign editor of the *Daily Express* until appointed to the *Sketch* towards the end of 1969, so he was keen to recruit some of the people he knew from those days especially as *The Express* was running a voluntary redundancy programme. When the new *Daily Mail* launched, they used the American syndicated column of Susie Knickerbocker for the first few weeks as the gossip column, although it soon became apparent that her stories didn't resonate with the British public. English appointed Paul Callan, who had been running the Londoner's Diary on the *Evening Standard*, as diary editor with the intention of making Jeremy Deedes, son of *Telegraph* editor and Tory MP Bill Deedes, as his deputy. But at the last moment Deedes decided to stay on the *Standard* where he became boss of the

Londoner's Diary, so there was an opening for Nigel Dempster to be Callan's deputy, which he accepted.

During the summer of 1973, Dempster was sent by English to New York to drum up good gossip stories. As previously mentioned, he wrote that the marriage of Richard Burton and Elizabeth Taylor was over. By the autumn of 1973 he returned to London to be told that Callan was leaving and that the *Mail's* gossip column was his with his own by-line.

Very quickly Dempster established himself as the premier gossip writer of his era. One of his scoops was to announce that prime minister Harold Wilson would be stepping down in 1976 as premier. Roundly criticised by other newspapers, Nigel proved to be right a few weeks later when Wilson announced he had been diagnosed with Alzheimers and would be unable to continue in politics.

Nigel was very competitive and often rubbished stories printed by his rivals, the principal one being the Hickey column. By the autumn of 1979 I had joined his band of gossips – there were four of us – with Nigel having the option to take off four months of the year to freelance and expand his broadcasting opportunities. But within weeks I asked to take a four week furlough to pursue a story that would rival my Biggs scoop for audacity should I pull it off. I had long suspected that Lord Lucan, who was alleged to have killed his children's nanny Sandra Rivett in November 1974 and then committed suicide, was in fact still alive. Discovering him would be another huge story.

Earlier that summer, *ITN* had claimed to have found Lucan on a West Indian island. Their reporter said they were hoping to be able to talk to him a few hours later on their six o'clock edition.

We were giving a lunch party to which we had invited Tony and Jenny Little. Jenny was the half-sister of John Aspinall, owner of the Clermont Club and a close friend of Lucan's. Lucan was an inveterate gambler and had frequently worked for Aspinall as a house player at the Clermont where the likes of the late Lord Derby were systematically parted from their inherited fortunes. Tony Little was a partner in *Osborne & Little*, the fabric designers. Sir Peter Osborne, father of the Chancellor George Osborne, was Jenny's brother and the other partner in the business.

Informing Jenny that Lucan was about to be produced by *ITN* for their six o'clock bulletin produced a hilarious laugh from our guest. I assumed she must either know he was dead or alternatively that he was in a completely different part of the world. After lunch we watched *ITN* and learnt that Lucan would not be appearing as they couldn't find him after all. "I told you so," said a triumphant Jenny.

A few weeks later Tina and I went to their Chelsea flat for a return match. I had a small cutting from that day's *Sunday Times* in which reporter Peter Hawthorne wrote that a businessman commuting from Botswana to Johannesburg was thought possibly to be the missing Lord. This time Jenny went white, said nothing and quickly changed the subject.

You know something you're not telling me, I thought. But there was no way she was going to reveal anything at her lunch party so I changed the subject for the time being.

I made a phone call to South Africa to an old friend who was an officer in the South African RAF intelligence unit. He told me that he might be able to access police files on some flimsy pretext just to see if there was any evidence of Lucan's presence in the country. A week later he called me with the astonishing revelation that there was indeed a Lucan file but that he couldn't access it without further authorisation.

Meanwhile, and by pure coincidence, a group of tourists claimed to have seen a person resembling Lord Lucan while they were on a white water raft on the Zambezi river. Smidgens of clues were beginning to mount up. I was prepared to take a chance and fly to Johannesburg to see if I could pull off my second world scoop of the decade.

The great difference between Biggs and Lucan was that the former was willing to be found. The latter wasn't. All of Lucan's close friends, including my old sparring partner Dan Meinerzhagen and Charles Benson (by now The Scout, racing correspondent of the *Daily Express*), were adamant he had fallen on his sword. Dempster, a good friend of Benson, went along with the party line and told me not to waste my own money in pursuit of a nonsense.

In the end the story remained a pipedream. But I am convinced I was on the right trail, especially after a barman in Laurenco Marques, the capital of Mozambique, agreed that he regularly saw the man whose photo I was holding that I knew as Lucan. He claimed that Lucan came to his bar every three months or so to pick up money forwarded to his bank in Laurenco Marques from England via the Seychelles.

After four weeks I was resigned to failure. I returned to London, poorer but still hopeful that this story would one day materialise. After my retirement in 2010 I wrote to Bill Shand-Kydd, Lucan's brother-in-law and the man who raised the Lucan children, to ask if he would see me with regard to doing the definitive book on the Lucan saga.

Bill, a former amateur jockey tragically confined to an iron lung as the result of a riding injury, wrote back to say that his wife Christine, sister of Lady Lucan, would not allow the children to be upset by any further revelations. Sadly Bill, the bravest of the brave, who did a parachute jump in his iron lung for charity, died three years ago and his secrets were buried with him. I haven't revealed everything I learned in South Africa, principally because, like Scotland Yard, I believe the story still has legs, although Lucan would now be eighty-two.

By January 1980 I was part of the Dempster team. We played squash in the RAC Club at lunch time when not taking out contacts to the *Savoy* and other nearby hostelries in pursuit of good stories. Nigel was very sporting, could be very generous, but also had a mean side to him.

A couple of months after my arrival, Helen Minsky joined the column. Rather than work on current stories she was tasked with one objective – to rubbish Dempster's predecessor Paul Callan who had joined the *Daily Mirror* and was also appearing regularly on *LBC* as a chat show host with Janet Street-Porter.

Callan, who had married American journalist Steffi Field in 1973, was affable and prone to wearing an Old Etonian bow tie. This pale blue and black confection became his trademark, together with quite a posh accent. However Dempster was convinced Callan had been no nearer Eton than Ronnie Biggs had.

Poor Minsky, a very competent and hardworking member of the team, was not allowed to do any other story for weeks. She dug and she dug – and in those pre-internet days it was not so easy to locate facts and figures. She could find no evidence that Callan had been at Eton from the college records so it was now a matter of finding out where Callan had actually been educated and this would take longer.

In the end it was a piece of luck. It turned out that a relative of hers had been at school with Callan in north London – at Woodbury Down secondary modern school. Minsky had secured her future on the column with this piece of intelligence which duly led the Dempster page. It's hard to imagine that more than a handful of people could possibly have been interested, but Dempster felt he had crushed another of his potential rivals. Callan's Old Etonian bow tie was rarely, if ever, given another public outing.

It must be said that Callan's unmasking had no effect on his career which far outlasted poor Nigel's. The latter died in 2007 after suffering the debilitating and progressive supranuclear palsy, an enhanced version of motor neurone disease. There weren't too many Etonians on the *Mirror,* or on the *Daily Express* where Callan subsequently worked, and his colleagues admired his self-styled panache, thick skin, and broad back.

Set against this desire to demean his rivals though, Nigel could be extraordinarily generous. A Kent policeman lost his life in a terrorist incident later that year and Nigel immediately wrote out a cheque to his widow. I had a quick look when his back was turned and saw the figure of £3,000, equivalent to a year's salary for the average working man in 1980.

The *Mail's* proprietor, Lord Rothermere, one day described Nigel's column as "old, cold, roast potatoes". This was not very encouraging for his new recruits, let alone for Nigel who was writing a biography of Princess Margaret to whom he had become quite close. The Princess occasionally telephoned the column to get hold of Nigel and often asked if there were any good parties that night. Another regular caller was Lord Rothermere's estranged wife who was affectionately known as Bubbles. She was also an avid party goer.

The calls from Kensington Palace became rarer after the publication of *Princess Margaret – a Life Unfulfilled.* She was extremely disappointed with the title and slightly less so with its contents. It's a lesson well learned that it's hard to please all of the people all of the time.

I soldiered on, writing as many good stories as I could on a daily basis. One little story about Gregory Peck's daughter Cecilia, who was attending college in London, remains with me simply because on the day of publication the Oscar winning actor telephoned from Paris to thank me for the article. That doesn't happen to a gossip writer every day.

In the early 1980s I also had a regular lunchtime squash game with my namesake Kelvin Mackenzie (no relation) who had taken over from Larry Lamb as editor of the *Sun*. We used to meet at *Cannon's* club by Cannon Street station for a forty minute workout.

One day, Kelvin, who was surprisingly skilled and fit, stopped in mid rally and started panting. Concerned for his health I asked him if he was all right and he said, "Colin, do you know the four most dangerous words in journalism?" to which I demurred. "Well I can tell you what they are. Exclusive by Harry Arnold."

Harry was the *Sun's* royal reporter, and in the increasingly ferocious circulation war royal reporters strained their talent dry to get scoops. Evidently Harry had gone too far – again – and the Buckingham Palace press office was complaining.

The Dempster column had its fair share of complaints and legal actions. By their very nature gossip columns are trying to inform the public about something they don't already know. In those pre-internet and tweet days all the material had to be sourced from contacts and interviews. Nigel was remarkably sanguine about complaints and told the *Daily Mail* lawyer one day, "Writs are the Oscars of our trade."

In 1982 Nigel and I decided to try and win the *Daily Express* Triumph hurdle at Cheltenham – nothing like winning money and bragging rights from your old employer. Having sung Jim Old's praises I felt it incumbent upon me to visit him in his new quarters at Dundry, south of Bristol, to locate the animal that was to bring us untold riches. Jim had trained *Cima* to be runner-up in the 1982 renewal – 'young Old' could clearly train.

Martin Pipe once said the Triumph hurdle was harder to win than the Derby, but what did he know? So down to Dundry where Jim paraded *Superfluous* for our delectation. "I stole him from Sir Mark Prescott for £8,000," he announced. "He won a nice race at Ayr three months ago and got a little jarred up. He'll be fine after a rest."

The deal was done. Nigel would have fifty per cent while I and two friends, Chris Morgan and Stephen Freud, would split the other half. To this day I feel guilty about it but the two of them remained friends throughout the next two years of misery as *Superfluous* lived up to his name. Talk about fool's gold.

His first appearance was in the Freshman's Hurdle at Newbury in November at the Hennessy meeting. We didn't want the horse to break his rivals' hearts at humble Huntingdon or lowly Leicester. Dempster and I were an appalling sight in the front of Newbury's grandstand, all puffed up with nowhere to go.

It took little more than four minutes for the chimera to collapse and our dreams to disintegrate. *Superfluous* managed a distant seventh of seven. "Must have needed it more than I thought," were the trainer's words of wisdom.

Fast forward two years to a sunny Kempton in September. The only money *Superfluous* has ever earned was when the entry fee for the Triumph Hurdle was returned to us because he was balloted out of the race as not good enough. In a total of sixteen races, *Superfluous* never beat another horse home.

Jim decided to run him back on the flat, and the Diary supernag who habitually ran in the colours of Nigel's second wife Lady Camilla Dempster, was equipped with blinkers and spurs affixed to jockey Willie Carson's riding boots. He set off last and stubbornly refused to pass any of his dozen rivals.

Nigel was hiding well out of public view – there's only so much humiliation a chap can take – in the members' restaurant behind the grandstand. I was in the stands where I spied a rather sheepish looking Sir Mark Prescott, the Newmarket trainer from whom we had "stolen" the bay gelding for £8,000.

"Mark, come and say hello to Nigel Dempster who'd love to meet you," I ventured. And I could see Sir Mark weighing up the pros and cons of this endeavour, balancing the possibility that the diarist would further investigate the love life of Newmarket's most eligible bachelor against the possibility of pacifying one of Jim's owners. "Okay," he said.

In the restaurant, Nigel waved a bottle of Krug at Stephen and Chris and a bottle of the finest malt whisky at Jim. Quick as a flash Sir Mark took in the scene and shouted "Good god, Jim! What the hell is he going to buy you when this horse beats one home?"

The Diary supernag never got the chance to answer that question. After seventeen runs, the penny dropped that *Superfluous*, charming and good looking as he was, just didn't fancy going very fast, let alone beating a rival. He was given away by Jim to go hunting while his owners tried to explain to their partners quite what had happened.

My wife Tina was not very receptive to the notion of *Superfluous* from day one. Sadly, she and I had not been getting on well for a while. She complained of my interest in matters equine, my propensity to imagine the horse I had backed was always going to win, and my general lethargy in matters domestic. I confess that compared with my six sons-in-law (I later acquired three stepdaughters), I was not an assiduous hands-on father. 'An unreconstructed male' was the polite version of what Tina said.

For my part I resented the fact that my lively wife was envious of her sister Jose's jet set lifestyle. We had three gorgeous daughters, a lovely house with a huge garden, and a good life. I had been away a lot while forging my career on the *Daily Express* but now Tina was frequently off to the south of France to complete her first novel *Memory and Desire* which she was writing with two American girl friends.

The crunch came in September 1983 when after a noisy one-sided row, we agreed to part and immediately put our lovely home up for sale. Local estate agents valued the house from £110,000 to £150,000. Foreseeing a sticky financial future, I put an advertisement in the *Sunday Times* for £165,000 o.n.o. Then I flew to Paris to attend that year's Prix de L'Arc de Triomphe won by *All Along*.

Back from Paris late that Sunday evening I was astonished to learn that Tina had been knocked over in the rush to buy our house for £165,000. How much do estate agents really know, I wondered.

The pressure was on to find somewhere for Tina and the girls to live and for me to be not too far away. She settled on a three bedroom, two storey maisonette in Brechin Place, just off Gloucester Road. I found a short lease on a flat in The Little Boltons, half a mile away, a place the girls could come to revise for their exams when they needed peace and quiet.

Separation was painful, both emotionally and financially. Christmas 1983 was a lonely experience as Tina took the girls with her to her parents' home in Wales. I had tried to be as generous to them all as I could be. There was no legal agreement and I didn't want our modest assets to be engorged by the legal profession. The result was that I was living on thin air and expenses. I felt guilty about what had happened and not a little sheepish. Now I really had to work hard to improve the Mackenzie finances.

Life in Fleet Street continued oblivious to my personal heartache. Our regular watering hole *El Vino's* had undergone its own legal shenanigans in 1982 when Sheila Gray, a photographer on the communist (as it was proud to be called then) *Morning Star*, sued the celebrated bar for refusing to allow her to purchase a drink. *El Vino's* also had a dress code which disallowed trouser suits on women.

Among other famous women hacks to join the action were Mary Kenny, Anna Coote, and Sandy Fawkes. In the end, *El Vino's* argument that they were acting on behalf of women in allowing only men to purchase drinks failed in the High Court. Not only that but the dress code was amended, to the relief of Ian Wooldridge's wife Sarah.

She recalled, "I was sitting in the back bar where women were confined while Ian was getting me and a friend from New York a drink. The owner of *El Vino's,* Christopher Mitchell, asked Ian if I was the girl wearing a trouser suit and he said yes. Either I had to get out of the bar or change my apparel, so I borrowed my girlfriend's mink coat, took off my trousers and sat back down showing my legs. And that made Mr Mitchell happy."

Nigel and I were shocked by the news that a colleague on the rival Hickey column had been killed by the IRA when they bombed *Harrods* in December 1983. Philip Geddes was a young man of twenty-four with his life and career ahead of him and this was a real tragedy. Three policemen and three civilians were killed and ninety injured. The war of words between the Hickey and Dempster columns was put on hold. Hickey editor Christopher Wilson graciously invited Nigel and me to read lessons at Philip's well attended funeral.

One of the bigger stories I initiated while on the Dempster column made headlines around the world. I had learned that Robert Sangster was about to leave his second wife Sue – known in the racing world as "the Sheila" because of her antipodean origins – in favour of Mick Jagger's girlfriend Jerry Hall.

The popular Sangster was racing in Australia when we contacted him. He begged that we delay publication of the story, which he confirmed, so that he could get his flight from Melbourne to Los Angeles the following day. He was en route to Kentucky for the thoroughbred sales.

This was a small price to pay for a story that would resonate at Group One level. The heady mix of horseflesh, wealth, pop, and glamour is the stuff of gossip. Was Jerry encouraging this romance to make Mick jealous and was Robert serious in his pursuit of one of the most beautiful women in the world?

We published as Robert was taking off from Melbourne with his faithful lieutenant Charles Benson, the scout of the *Daily Express*. It was more than amusing to see Benson described as Sangster's minder in the *Express's* sister paper the *Daily Star* two days later when they were photographed after landing in Los Angeles. Benson was not named.

The romance of racing's best-known face and the Texan model lasted little more than three furlongs, with Jerry having achieved her aim of making Mick jealous, while Sangster had acquired his longed-for break from Susan, ex-wife of Australian politician Andrew Peacock and mother of Newmarket-based trainer Jane Chapple-Hyam.

Terry Wogan once memorably described Royal Ascot as "50,000 people in search of Nigel Dempster". Nigel's fame went far further than the pages of the *Daily Mail* by the mid 1980s. One of the more extraordinary facts I had learned about the person *Private Eye* ridiculed as "The Greatest Living Englishman" was that his elder sister Pam was a senior figure at the Foreign Office and had been a successful spy. The thought of this quiet, respected, and brave lady having the King of Gossips as her sibling boggled my brain.

In the autumn of 1985, actor Peter Bowles was researching the lead in *Lytton's Diary*, a television sitcom based on the life of Fleet Street's leading gossip writer. He spent some time at the *Mail* talking to people like me about Nigel's modus operandi. He even guest edited the Dempster column shortly after I left at the end of that year.

Just after the Royal Ascot of 1985 I was to receive a phone call from Brough Scott that would take me on another path in my eclectic career. Would I like to join his new venture, a brand new racing paper called *The Racing Post?* Is the Pope Polish, I replied.

It would be a giant gamble. There are no guarantees in journalism and Fleet Street history is embellished with gallant failures in the publishing business. But Brough assured me that Dubai's Crown Prince Sheik Mohammed, the proprietor and mentor of this new paper, had properly funded the venture. He also explained that the creation of a rival to the *Sporting Life* had been occasioned by the threat by the latter's publisher, Robert Maxwell, boss of Mirror Newspapers, to close the paper which had been created in 1859 when it numbered Charles Dickens among its avid readers.

Main photo, LtoR: Slipper, Biggs, Jones, plain clothes Brazilian policeman

LtoR: Bill Lovelace, author, Biggs, Mike O'Flaherty

LtoR: John Humphreys, Raimunda, author

'Hi Colin, Perhaps not the best set that have been taken, but certainly as good as those found on the Monopoly box and the sauce bottle! Convinced?! R.A. Biggs'

Gordon & Hazel, wedding day, October 1940

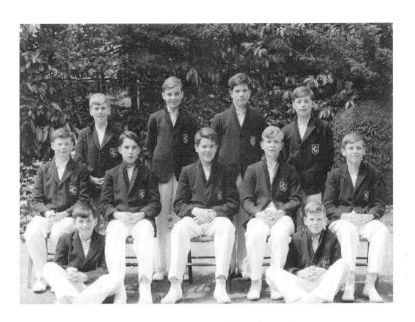

Lambrook, Captain of cricket, 1955

Malvern prefects, author centre front
Michael Manson (best man), directly above

Author at Oxford (with broken nose)

Jose, Carol, Maria, author, Tina

Linda & Colin, wedding day, April 1993

Mackenzie teenagers, Georgia, Tara, Cate

Step-daughters, Kate, Alex, Helen

Miss Peru 1967

Author, not very rock'n'roll in suit & tie, with Robert Plant

Biggles Mackenzie in Spitfire

Stephen Freud, Grahame Amey, author, All Right Jack

Grahame Amey, Welsh Oak, author

1981 Grand National winner Aldaniti with overweight jockey

Fleet Street ridden by Marcus Foley

Three greys: trainer David Elsworth, Desert Orchid, author

Mike Dillon, Hayley Turner, author, Henry Ponsonby, Georgina Bell, receiving the Mallard Cup 2008

Joy Hawken on Welsh Oak in retirement

Author with triple gold cup winner Best Mate

Author with David Gandolfo, trainer of the month award

Lord Daresbury, author

Jockey Michael Kinane, Rock of Gibraltar, Sir Alex Ferguson

Trueshan with winning jockey Hollie Doyle after his Champions Day win 2020

Colin Mackenzie

Retired

128

MEDIA 2020

Royal trainer Ian Balding, author, HM The Queen

12.

Racing Post

Racing is the Great Triviality as the wise old Phil Bull, founder of *Timeform*, once remarked. Whether or not it is more frivolous than men kicking a football or athletes pounding a tennis ball back and forth is for others to debate. All I knew was that when Brough Scott made that call to my office in Carmelite Street I was thrilled to dream of combining my job and my hobby.

At this point, I hadn't read Jamie Lambie's wonderfully thorough history of the *Sporting Life* and its 139 year sojourn as the punters' pal and guide book, which ended in 1998 when it merged with the *Racing Post*.

Lambie discovered that HL Dillon, the first Paris correspondent of the *Life,* who had previously covered the Crimean war with some distinction as a roving reporter, was killed after only a few months in the job in 1862. He had written in very uncomplimentary terms about an amateur rider called Ludovic, Duke de Gramont-Caderousse, following which the French aristocrat challenged him to a sword duel. Foolishly Dillon accepted and breathed his last in the forest of St Germain near Maisons-Laffitte racecourse just outside Paris.

Had I possessed this piece of form I might have thought twice about joining the *Racing Post*. Yet here I am, some thirty-four years later, still able to chronicle the painful birth but ultimate survival of Britain's newest national newspaper. It combined the modern technology of computers, colour, and tabloid shape in one hit, despite the prevailing conservatism of its readership – the middle-aged, middle market, middle income, racing enthusiast.

Brough, whom I had known slightly when we were contemporaries at Oxford, was and is an extraordinary enthusiast for the sport he embraced as a teenage point-to-point rider. He went on to a perfectly respectable career as a professional jump jockey with over a hundred winners before graduating to a career in the media. He firstly wrote for the *Evening Standard* and then the *Times*, the *Sunday Times* and the *Telegraph*. He became the front man for *ITV* racing in the 1970s and developed into a consummate performer in front of the camera.

Perhaps Brough's greatest achievement was to inherit Lord Oaksey's role as president of the Injured Jockeys' Fund for which he received the MBE. He has nurtured that vital organisation, overseeing the creation of three wonderful centres in Lambourn, Malton, and Newmarket, where jockeys can seek rehabilitation following injury. The IJF also financially supports many former jockeys and grooms who have fallen on hard times. In 2020, aged seventy-seven, he ceded his job to younger hands. He is the classic example of the adage that if you want something done always ask a busy man.

In 1984 there were strong rumours that Robert Maxwell wanted to cull the *Sporting Life* from his Mirror Group stable of newspapers. Although alone in its field, since the *Sporting Chronicle* had died a year earlier, it was failing to make a profit. Cap'n Bob, as Maxwell was not so affectionately known, may have been a regular in London's racier casinos but he remained no fan of the turf.

Against this background, with the very real possibility that punters and the racing industry would be left without a specialist daily newspaper, Brough decided to propose to Sheik Mohammed al Maktoum, a coming force in ownership, that he finance a new newspaper. The Sheik had already tested the water by evincing interest in *Pacemaker*, racing's magazine for the owners and breeders. But Brough alerted him to the fact that his principal rival to the champion owner title, Robert Sangster, had a financial interest in that publication. The Sheik agreed that it would be like buying someone else's wife.

By 1985 Maxwell was threatening almost weekly to shut down the *Sporting Life*. He was also taking on the print unions who for decades had had a hold on the throats of national newspapers on a nightly basis. His chief rival Rupert Murdoch, by now the owner of the *Sun*, *The News of the World* and the *Times*, was engaged in a similar battle.

Brough, who was also a director of the Newmarket-based International Racing Bureau which facilitated international travel to and from the UK for the breeding and racing industries, consulted his colleagues who all agreed that if the *Life* went under, racing would be "fucked".

With a grant of £20,000 from Sangster, Prince Khaled Abdullah, and John Leat – Sheik Mohammed's homme d'affaires – Brough investigated the possibility of setting up a brand new title for racing buffs. He quickly realised the venture would cost many millions – or in Arab parlance, the purchase of one bad yearling.

In 1983, at the Keeneland sales, Sheik Hamdan al Maktoum, the second eldest of Sheik Rashid's four racing-mad children, had paid a then world record $10.2 million to buy *Snaafi Dancer*. He was sent to Classic winning trainer John Dunlop to be trained at his Arundel stables for the top races.

It is a sad fact that Dunlop realised early on that *Snaafi Dancer* could not "get out of his own way" – in other words he was too slow to risk being beaten because defeat would cause his value to dissipate. *Snaafi Dancer* never ran in public and was sent to stud where he proved to be largely infertile. Some horses are just born losers.

In this context, Brough argued, putting up £5 million to set up a new newspaper, was relatively good value. Whether it could hold its own in the ultra competitive world of Fleet Street was another matter. This was the gamble, and Sheik Mohammed needed to know in advance that the paper would not be the Maktoums' poodle.

In other words, there was little upside for the Sheik whose principal ambition was to sell Dubai to the world as a tourist destination and airline hub. But it would be seen as a generous and almost philanthropic act by the racing community.

Nearly one and a half million British citizens bet on the horses on a daily basis in 1985, and including those employed in betting shops, racing accounted for 90,000 jobs and an important place in the nation's economy.

In April 1985, Brough was invited out to Dubai to see the Sheik and to put his proposal for a new newspaper. The Sheik was being advised by Leat, whose father had been Sheik Rashid's chauffeur, and by Colonel Dick Warden, an ex-spy and SAS man. The Sheik himself had spent time being trained at the Mons army academy and liked the military.

At a *majlis* – a tented meeting where the Sheik would sit like a medieval baron to hear complaints and resolve disputes between his Bedouin people – Brough waited earnestly to put his proposals. And after the *majlis* was completed he had his moment. The Sheik had already done his homework and made up his mind. It was green for go.

Now it was a question of hiring suitable staff, appointing an editor, finding office space and a data base, and locating printers. It was the latter that was to prove the most difficult element of the equation, because Cap'n Bob Maxwell immediately blacklisted the title with the print unions he was still talking to, threatening to withdraw his own vastly bigger business if they agreed to print the nascent *Racing Post*. In the end, Sir Gordon Brunton, a former *Times* boss, was appointed chairman, with other directors drawn from the IRB. Notably, the *Voice of Racing* commentator Sir Peter O'Sullevan also agreed to be a director. Graham Rock, late of the *Sporting Chronicle* and currently working in Hong Kong, was appointed editor. *Trainers' Record*, owned by Peter Jones (later Chairman of the Tote), would provide the necessary data base.

Five Fleet Street veterans – George Ennor of the *Sporting Life*, Howard Wright of the *Daily Telegraph*, Tim Richards of the *Mirror*, Tony Morris, bloodstock editor of the *Sporting Life*, and myself from the *Mail* were hired with a proposed starting date of January 1 1986.

This turned out to be hugely optimistic, although I turned up for work in the new offices in Raynes Park, Wimbledon, eyes akimbo and ready to work. Our launch date was soon put back to the Grand National meeting in April.

Thereafter, Rock recruited avidly from his former contacts at the *Sporting Chronicle* and from *Timeform*, the weekly form guide and bible for many punters. We had many excellent form pundits but what the paper lacked was good design and production staff. And this deficiency was to bite us in the circulation backside on our launch.

We had located a printer in Warrington prepared to produce the paper which had to be faxed up north on a nightly basis. Photographs were printed and processed in Burgess Hill in Sussex. If this seemed a little Heath Robinson, it was. Poor Graham Rock spent most of his time chauffeuring material around rather than editing the paper.

The Grand National, won by *West Tip* and Richard Dunwoody, came and went, and the first day of publication became April 15, the start of Newmarket's Craven meeting. I produced a diary column for practice sake. Top weight in the race was the Czech horse *Essex* and the enthusiastic Prague press were at Aintree in force. They were so keen that every fence attendant, every coffee dispenser, and every racing official was being interviewed by two hard working Czech hacks.

Watching this attention to duty in some amazement I said to Brough, "We ought to hire these chaps – I've never seen anyone working harder." To which Brough replied, "Then we could advertise 'The Czech's in the Post!'"

Our front page headline on launch day at Newmarket's Craven meeting was "We're Off" and the main tipster Adrian Cook went for Sheik Mohammed's *Sonic Lady* to win the Nell Gwyn Stakes. A lovely picture of the filly dominated the page.

It should have been a perfect day as *Sonic Lady* duly trotted up. The trouble was that no one in Newmarket could locate the paper. Production hiccups had rendered the launch a near total disaster. And the plain fact was that we were under prepared. We had never produced a dummy copy of the paper which might have thrown up logistical problems which would beset us during the opening months. Sheik Mohammed, in particular, was displeased and it was pure luck that he had been distracted by the victory of his favourite filly that afternoon.

It was a chastening experience for the whole staff who had worked tirelessly in the weeks leading up to the launch. It hadn't helped that the *Sporting Life* had been re-energised by editor Monty Court, an old Fleet Street hand who was determined to see off this annoying tsetse fly of a rival. He even got Maxwell to pronounce the words, "If the Maktoums want to take me on, they'll find me as appetising as eating concrete."

It was the stated ambition of the *Racing Post* to be the dominant racing paper within a couple of years. We had colour and the tabloid shape which would eventually encompass most of Fleet Street.

However, we underestimated the determination of the *Sporting Life* staff and the innate conservatism of racing folk more used to the form guides in that rival paper and content with its output. This was going to be dog eat dog – especially after the *Life* lowered its price from £1 to 50p and then to 25p which was our launch price. It was economic suicide and it hurt both publications.

This was gladiatorial, and in the end, it took a poor decision by *Life* in 1997, eleven years later, before the *Post* would outsell the *Life*. And that decision was to print a special betting shop edition of the paper. This elevated the *Post's* circulation when 10,000 betting shops took a couple of copies each. The bell tolled for the *Life*.

By 1998 Sheik Mohammed tired of owning the *Post* and agreed to a merger with the *Life*, as long as the *Post* retained its title and most of its staff. The *Mirror Group* would be responsible for redundancy payments and the *Sporting Life* would become an on-line facility for racing aficionados. In effect the *Post* had won the battle, which had turned into a war, but it was a close-run thing which cost two billionaires a fortune.

I realised how unprepared the *Racing Post* was to report the Sport of Kings very early on. I went to Towcester on the bank holiday in May 1986 when there were fourteen meetings. Unlike most outside men, I did not have a computer, so I filed my copy by telephone to our ladies who normally took down greyhound results. I had to spell the names of every horse I mentioned. I was so concerned about the situation that I thought I had better pop in to the Raynes Park office to check on my copy later that evening and was shocked to read Colin Mackenzie from 'Toaster'. Imagine the satirical response that we would have received from our rivals had that survived to the morning edition.

In 1986 I had a diary column which published three times weekly. And I very soon discovered that the pool in which racing people swim is small and very sensitive. Whereas I had been used to covering social events that would embrace most of the population, racing had a relatively small cast of characters about whom to write. Not only was that a hazard but I soon learned that the racing fraternity, with a few notable exceptions, lacked a sense of humour about themselves. So when I described Michael Dickinson's newly acquired Wiltshire yard as Stalag Manton (because lads were denied access to socialise in nearby Marlborough), we were told by the trainer that we would not be welcome at the yard to do previews.

I managed to upset Nicky Henderson and his wife Diana by revealing that one of their guests had lost his false teeth overnight while staying with them in Lambourn at their Windsor House stables. Under the headline of "The Mystery of the Missing Molars" I described how the senior starter, Sir John Guise, had mislaid his teeth on the journey back to the stables from an Italian restaurant in the village.

This was the Monday before the start of the 1987 Cheltenham Festival and Sir John was on his way from Market Rasen to the Cotswolds via the Henderson yard. Arising on the Tuesday morning, Sir John could not find the infamous teeth, at which point Henderson summoned his staff and asked them to retrace Sir John's steps from the night before and locate the molars, albeit it had started snowing and they were on their hands and knees.

The poor lads were in the snow for quite a while before giving up the unequal struggle, only for Sir John to discover the offending teeth underneath his bed where they had fallen. He continued his journey west to the most important meeting of the year.

This was too good a diary item to ignore and it appeared on the Wednesday of Cheltenham, to the evident merriment of those in the Turf Club tent who were teasing Sir John. I was at the weighing room waiting to talk to a jockey or two when a furious Diana Henderson came up and berated me loudly and for quite a while. I apologised but pointed out that Sir John hadn't minded the story and that the Hendersons had been perfect hosts throughout.

It was Mrs Henderson's misfortune to be drawn next to me at a charity dinner for the Bob Champion Cancer Trust in Cheltenham that same night – she was very civil and bore her burden with grace.

Later that year, *Aldaniti*, the horse on which Bob Champion won the 1981 Grand National, was used to raise money for his Cancer Trust. Readers were invited to bid in excess of £1,000 to have the privilege of riding *Aldaniti* for a mile. Bob was and remains a good friend so I offered the ride to any of my readers who would double the amount I had raised to take the ride, which was £1,600.

To my amazement I got a reply from Canada where assistant trainer Reade Baker telephoned to say he would offer £3,200 if I stopped the bidding there and then. He would fly over from Toronto and take the ride with the opportunity of meeting his hero Bob Champion – and this he did. I rode the great chaser for 100 yards and then Baker mounted him for the remainder of the mile.

In total, *Aldaniti's* marathon walk raised £829,000 for the charity which builds hospital wings for children suffering from testicular cancer, the disease which almost felled Bob in 1979. To date Bob has raised a total of £15 million plus for his charity, with a new wing in the Royal Marsden hospital being the ultimate achievement.

By mid summer 1987 there was a revolution at the *Post* with Graham Rock paying with his job for the failure to make inroads into the circulation of the *Sporting Life*. He was replaced as editor by Michael Harris, the long-time boss of *Pacemaker*. I, in turn, replaced Howard Wright who was news editor, with the idea of bringing a sharper news edge to the paper. Howard took over the very important industry side of reporting.

My diary column was eventually and rightly reduced to one day a week. Although readers enjoyed my slightly irreverent style, it was counterproductive to upset too many key players in the sport. The paper had been perceived as too tabloid, not so much in content as in design, and this was amended with new design staff brought in.

We made several new appointments with Simon Crisford becoming our Newmarket correspondent. Simon had worked for Sir Mark Prescott and John Dunlop as an assistant trainer and was a good judge of a gallop. It helped enormously that he was popular in Newmarket, and Henry Cecil in particular liked him and frequently off-loaded some of his fancy shirts to bolster Simon's scanty wardrobe.

I discovered that in our results department there lurked some talented writers, notably Paul Hayward, who went on to win awards for his writing on the *Telegraph, Guardian* and *Mail*, and Jim McGrath who would become the successor to Sir Peter O'Sullevan as the *BBC's* commentator of choice. Jim had worked in Hong Kong with Graham Rock who had promised him a job. Jim later graduated to become the *Daily Telegraph's* racing correspondent.

I was responsible for sourcing the best sports photographer in the land, Edward Whitaker, elder son of my old pal, royal reporter

James Whitaker. Edward had graduated from Sheffield college where he had done a course in journalism. He couldn't wait to get started. Edward has since won the Racing Photographer of the Year award a record nine times and National Newspaper Photographer of the Year award twice. His imaginative and ground breaking photography has featured in many books.

The hardest worker of all was the popular Tim Richards who may have lived in North Yorkshire but was a ubiquitous presence on southern racecourses. Tim kept everyone on their toes and I was well aware that I had to be manning the news desk early whenever Tim was in America covering the Breeders Cup. Even though Kentucky was five hours behind the UK, Tim would call from his 5am jog to get his orders for the day. Woe betide any executive arriving too late to receive his call!

In the autumn of 1986, I attended a dinner party in Ealing given by my good friends public relations chief Peter Cunard and his wife Sue. Across the table sat an attractive dark-haired girl called Linda, possessor of a gentle and beguiling smile. It turned out she played bridge and also had three daughters. Would I like to partner her in a bridge four the following week?

I was semi involved at the time; being a bachelor again, albeit 40 plus, was no disadvantage to an active social life. As they say in racing parlance, I was having a rare run of luck and it took me a few weeks to disentangle myself in order to pursue the newly divorced Linda Sharman.

We met in her house to play bridge with a couple she had met in Singapore, where her children had been born in the late 1970s. Her ex-husband John Sharman had a little in common with me as he was also an Oxford PPE graduate. Furthermore, he had shared rooms in University College with Bill Clinton.

The bridge, even by my modest standards, was rather Singapore kitchen – win your winners and hope. So I endeavoured to assist in a few post mortems after the hands were played. Evidently my "charity" went unappreciated as after I left, the couple from Singapore advised Linda to have nothing more to do with this arrogant oaf. Luckily for me Linda is made of stern stuff behind her charming and delicate exterior.

Even though I had to wait another few weeks to finally free myself from outside interests she was more than happy to come on a first date which included the premiere of a thriller at the Savoy Theatre, followed by dinner at *Silks* restaurant and a few dances in *Tramp* nightclub.

Linda had parked her car outside my Little Boltons flat and I was quick to assure her that it might resemble a smart address but I was but a humble hack and remarkably impecunious. I didn't want the relationship to get off on the wrong foot having over egged the pudding on my first date. I suppose my case for poverty was weakened further when I suggested we go and see *Kirkstone Pass* run in his final chase at Towcester a couple of Saturdays later. I explained that mine was a small share in the beast and not to read too much into my ownership.

Towcester was shrouded in fog that wintry afternoon and racing was in serious doubt until it lifted after two hours. Trainer David Gandolfo, colloquially known as the Wizard of Wantage, was introducing us to the joys of brandy and port. It was very nippy, but by the time of KP's race we were feeling little pain. To cap a great day *Kirkstone Pass* won his final race. The prize money was modest but there was a huge silver trophy which I was allowed to keep for a year.

My romance with Linda proceeded at a gentle trot so that our six daughters could get to know one another, mine on average being eight years older than Linda's. Alex, then ten, and twins Helen and Kate, eight, would become a very important part of my life. They very quickly and generously accepted me as their mother's new man, and along with my daughters Catherine, Tara and Georgia, were as thrilled as we were when Linda and I married in 1993.

I have always been an optimist, and having in effect six daughters was a big positive as far as I was concerned. When one of my friends queried my mental health, I quoted Churchill at him, "A pessimist sees the difficulty in every opportunity – the optimist sees an opportunity in every difficulty."

Once *Kirkstone Pass* retired, Grahame Amey offered Stephen Freud and me a share in his promising novice hurdler *Welsh Oak* who was a half brother of the 1979 Welsh Grand National winner *Peter Scot* and a full brother of Gandy's talented *Warner For Leisure*.

Welsh Oak would prove to be the best horse I have ever had a share in, not so much talent wise but economically, as he paid for himself in prize money for six consecutive seasons which is very rare for any racehorse.

In total, *Welsh Oak* won sixteen races and among his other efforts he was runner-up at Cheltenham's December meeting in the valuable Kennedy Construction Gold Cup, beaten in a course record time by Gordon Richards' *Clever Folly* with the brilliant *Barnbrook Again 20l* back in third place. That prize money alone paid for a year's training fees.

Welsh Oak also had the distinction of winning the Portlane handicap chase at Kempton in 1988. This was the race in which Princess Anne made her National Hunt riding debut on *Cnoc Na Cuille* on whom she would later win.

I was marooned in a friend's box that winter's day, and rather annoyingly from my perspective, the in-house television director stayed with Princess Anne throughout the race. It was only because I could hear the commentary in the windowless box that I realised *Welsh Oak* had won.

He was a lovely grey horse who went whiter with age. He particularly liked two and a half miles at Kempton and won the same Boxing Day chase there two years running. On one of these occasions he beat his brother, to the dismay of his owner Terry Warner who had had a small private bet with me on the result.

If only all my investments had been that clever. *Welsh Oak* enjoyed a wonderful retirement hunting with the equine artist Joy Hawken who featured him in some of her Christmas cards for the Injured Jockeys Fund.

Back at the *Racing Post* we were making slow but significant inroads into the *Life's* circulation by the summer of 1987. One great help was that the *Life* was posting its content for the following day on its new website, presumably in the hope that it would whet readers' appetites to buy the paper. What it did achieve was alerting us to any story we had missed. It was six months before they realised what was going on.

One small problem arose when Anthony Stroud, who was buying much of Sheik Mohammed's horseflesh at the time and was effectively his racing manager, clearly preferred to talk to the *Sporting Life* and not to the Sheik's own paper *The Racing Post*.

It was time for action, and Brough and I took him to a restaurant in Soho to encourage him to realise on which side his bread should be buttered. In his defence I don't think he had fully realised what he was doing and happily for all he mended his ways.

Competition between the *Life* and the *Post* got quite personal. Within five years Maxwell would be dead and his empire in need of serious government aid. One story I wrote seemed to infuriate the *Life's* editor, Monty Court, for whom I always retained maximum respect.

The flamboyant businessman and punter Terry Ramsden had been warned off Newmarket Heath as the result of owing Ladbrokes in excess of £1 million. This meant that he could no longer go racing on any British racecourse.

At the time Ramsden owned a large number of horses with the likes of Jenny Pitman and Rod Simpson and sponsored many races through his Glen International company. I discovered that several racecourses, including Sandown Park, had not been paid the sponsorship money his company had put up for big races.

Monty seemed to think it was unconscionable to expose a man who had been so generous with donations to racing charities. However, as luck would have it, Terry Ramsden telephoned me to discuss his problems and how they had developed. It made a very good piece and silenced the *Life's* criticism.

In essence Terry was a gambler who had overstretched himself; he had had a bad run of luck and Ladbrokes in particular had been unforgiving.

Gradually the *Racing Post* developed into a very readable and visually satisfying product. And while there was intense competition with the *Life,* the price remained low, enabling racing professionals to afford both papers. It was costing Sheik Mohammed serious millions to subsidise, but he could be proud of what Michael Harris and his team were producing.

In September 1988, the *Daily Mail's* Captain Heath, Jim Stanford, the author of many a fine scoop, indicated he would like to retire. Jim was a great man for filing copy on the hoof, holding the phone to his ear while he composed his prose in his head. He was not suited to the new era of computers, especially as his lunchtime gin and tonics were not good galloping companions for modern technology.

On one occasion the racing press were invited to Dalham Hall to see a parade of Maktoum stallions. Champagne was on offer but Jim always faxed his acceptances forward with the rider that he would prefer a Gordon's gin and tonic – and go light on the tonic.

On this occasion it was raining heavily so the guests moved into the great dining hall which had a huge plate glass window through which the horses could be viewed. Jim suddenly spotted one of his favourite stallions being led round by a groom who was drenched. Anxious to please the lad, Jim determined to go tell him how wonderful the horse had been in his racing career, so he marched straight through the enormous plate glass window, scattering shards of glass everywhere as he fell.

He got up, dusted himself down and turned to his astonished hosts and uttered these immortal words – "You'd think these fucking people could afford a fucking door." There was never a dull moment with Jim around.

My old colleagues enquired if I would be interested in taking over Jim's role on the paper. Even the editor, Sir David English, who had refused to allow me a by-line on the Dempster column when Nigel was away because of our history with the Biggs story, was back on side. He invited me for an interview and said he would be thrilled to have me back, albeit I had to take a small pay cut because my *Racing Post* salary "would put the whole Daily Mail Sports Department out of kilter". "You'll make it up on expenses," was his cry.

It was an offer I couldn't refuse, especially as I felt I had served my apprenticeship as a racing correspondent. So, for the third time in my career I resigned from a secure job to go elsewhere.

13.

Daily Mail & marriage

By the beginning of 1989, the *Daily Mail* was on the cusp of outselling its old rival the *Daily Express*. Sir David English had spotted the big growth market – women readers – and had introduced the successful *Femail* section of the paper. Even the advertising for the paper – 'Start Your Day with your Daily Mail' – was suggestive and the paper's circulation was flying.

1989 was a big year for racing too. There was *Desert Orchid* winning the Cheltenham Gold Cup, *Nashwan* winning the 2,000 Guineas and Derby, and *Aliysa* winning the Oaks only to be disqualified for failing a dope test. The latter incident would have major ramifications for British racing with *Aliysa's* owner, the Aga Khan, eventually withdrawing his horses from their UK-based trainers to concentrate his cavalry in France and Ireland.

At end of the year, the *Daily Mail* moved home – from Carmelite Street where it had been headquartered for more than a hundred years to High Street Kensington where it would occupy a five storey office based around a huge internal atrium behind the department store Barkers of Kensington.

By March 1989, *Desert Orchid* was a rival to *Red Rum* in racing's affections. The three times Grand National winner was still a celebrity, opening pubs and attending big social events.

The grey *Dessie* was a charismatic do or die front runner who had captured the public imagination with two wins in the King George VI chase at Kempton on Boxing Day together with many other weight defying triumphs. However, like many racehorses he had a preference for going right-handed. Cheltenham with its roller coaster left-handed track didn't suit him at all. Nor did he particularly enjoy soft or heavy going. And on that March day the rain rendered the going so intractable that principal owners Richard Burridge and his father Jimmy were exhorted to pull the ten-year-old out of the race.

Trainer David Elsworth, who had announced that *Dessie* was a definite runner, was doing his best to avoid *Dessie's* concerned connections. But eventually Richard caught up with his trainer to ask the inevitable question. "If you want to pull him out then pull him out," Elsie told the principal owner. "I just think you're making a big mistake. I understand your concern for the horse, but he's the best qualified to run in these conditions and next year he might have a leg or something."

That settled matters. The Burridges were rightly concerned for their horse who by now had become public property. A fatal injury would have been devastating not only for connections but for the sport as a whole. On the other hand, really heavy ground causes horses to go slower and any fall is mitigated by softer landing at a slower speed. Janice Coyle, *Dessie's* faithful groom, marched him round the paddock and the almost white grey sparkled in the gloom.

Despite everyone's misgivings, *Dessie* was 5-2 favourite in a field of thirteen top chasers. Leading rider Simon Sherwood, unbeaten on the grey in seven previous outings, was nervous but confident in his mount. Instead of pulling into a clear lead which had often been his run style, *Dessie* was happy to sit alongside four or five rivals in the early part of the race. He jumped brilliantly and appeared to be enjoying himself.

By the time *Dessie* and *Ten Plus* approached the third to last downhill fence they had pulled a few lengths clear of their rivals. As they leapt that fence, *Ten Plus* was a little too low and came crashing down, leaving our hero in the lead. *Yahoo* hove onto the scene, ridden by Tom Morgan. He sneaked up *Dessie's* inside and was clearly going the better as they jumped the second last fence. All at once *Dessie* came off the bridle and seemed dog tired.

As they approached the final fence *Yahoo* clung to the inside while *Dessie* was drifting right, losing a length or two. After the last, *Dessie* again drifted, first right and then left to eyeball *Yahoo*. It was as if a heavyweight boxing champion was looking for a last ditch knockout punch. *Dessie* was running on raw courage and telling his two years younger rival, "This is my race – get out of the way." He pricked his ears and urged on by Sherwood ran to the finishing line as Peter O'Sullevan's memorable commentary rang out all over the racecourse, "He's beginning to get up, he's beginning to get up. *Desert Orchid* wins the Gold Cup." And with that Sherwood punched the air in delight as the grey went on to a one and a half length victory. The huge 60,000 crowd went berserk as the country's favourite horse jig-jogged back to the winner's enclosure.

This was a fabulous result and a story that would invade non-racing sections of the *Daily Mail* and other daily papers. I was at my desk in Cheltenham's press room until well after 10pm that day filling feature pages, back pages, racing pages, and news pages. They all wanted a part of a story that transcended sport.

For the newly appointed racing correspondent it was a breakthrough moment. And it was pure luck for me that heavyweight writers such as Ian Wooldridge were not on duty at Cheltenham that day – I had the field to myself. Woollers was quite a racing fan – he admired jump jockeys as the bravest of all sportsmen and he was plotting a way to avoid the 1990 World Cup because he so despised cheating footballers. Indeed, he had researched a holiday in Bhutan because there were no televisions in that Himalayan hideaway to interrupt his soccer-free reverie.

Raw emotion had characterised Gold Cup day and it would soon be replicated at Newmarket in the 2,000 Guineas. To the shock of many in racing, Major Dick Hern had been sacked by the Queen as her principal trainer. Based at the yard she had purchased in 1982 at West Ilsley, Hern was going to have to re-locate his training operation and lose his principal patron.

The Royal racing manager, the Earl of Carnarvon, bore the brunt of the blame echoing round racing's inner circle. What seemed manifestly unfair was Hern was now confined to a wheelchair as the result of a hunting accident. And yet it did not seem to have impaired his skill as a trainer. Carnarvon's defence was that he thought Hern was going to retire because of a heart problem and that the Earl of Huntingdon would be a suitable replacement.

Word trickled out into Newbury's press room one day in February that Hern's three-year-old colt *Nashwan* had done a fantastic gallop that morning under Willie Carson, the stable's retained jockey. At the time he was thought to be a Derby prospect, but now appeared to be quick enough to take in the one mile 2,000 Guineas classic en route to Epsom.

For once we hacks took note and backed the colt at 33-1 for the Guineas and 100-1 to complete the double in the Derby. In my case it was not a life changing amount, but one or two people, including a bookmakers' representative, certainly upgraded their residences after the Derby double was landed.

When *Nashwan*, owned by Dubai's Sheik Hamdan al Maktoum, surged past *Exbourne* and *Danehill* to land the 2,000 Guineas there was a tangible roar at racing's headquarters. The normally royalist racing crowd understood the significance of what had just happened and *Nashwan* was roared and cheered into the winners' enclosure.

The taciturn Hern, who was never very communicative with the press, smiled and was charm itself. He had let his horse do the talking. And for once he was happy to talk to the Fourth Estate who had been so supportive of him following his sacking. Royal jockey Willie Carson was so shocked Hern had had his marching orders he refused to speak to Lord Carnarvon thereafter.

There was an even bigger roar at Epsom a month later when *Nashwan* blasted clear of *Terimon* and *Cacoethes* as a very popular 5-4 Derby favourite. Poignantly, Hern was invited up to the Royal Box following the race to share a cup of tea with the Queen who was gracious enough to offer sincere congratulations. There was no reprieve however and he had to vacate West Ilsley at the end of 1989.

The one hack who could and did talk to Hern on a regular basis was Old Etonian Mikey Seely of *The Times*. Seely, who bravely battled alcoholism for most of his adult life before eventually succumbing to cancer, was very popular in the press room. So much so that one day at the York Ebor meeting when he had gone AWOL due to an excess of gin, his colleagues got together and filed his report to the *Times* for which he received a surprising herogram the following day.

I'd received intelligence that Hern was going to be bankrolled by *Nashwan's* owner Sheik Hamdan in future and that he had found him a suitable place to train at the Kingwood House stud, a mile north of the M4 motorway and in sight of the telecommunications tower at the Membury service station. I knew the Major would be reluctant to speak to me on the phone so I asked Seely if he could confirm the story with Hern. A few minutes later I received a return call from the Seely household in Arnold, Nottinghamshire, to the effect that I was a hundred per cent right and the move would be made within weeks. A shared scoop is better than no scoop I reasoned, and both papers carried the story the following day.

The Derby meeting of 1989 threw up a second major story when *Aliysa*, winner of the Oaks from *Snow Bride*, failed a post-race dope test. The Michael Stoute trained filly, owned by the Aga Khan, was disqualified and placed last.

The Aga Khan was incandescent with rage and challenged the ruling in the High Court. But British justice decided it could not interfere in a domestic racing matter. He also had his filly's blood tests examined by French laboratories but to no beneficial effect.

By December he had got nowhere with his various appeals and held a press conference in the Savoy and announced he would pull out of British racing, removing all his horses from Stoute, Luca Cumani and Fulke Johnson Houghton. It was a major blow to British racing as the Aga was a big player. The beneficiaries would be his Irish and French trainers.

In a year that was full of drama, another significant event took place that September when All Weather racing was launched at Lingfield Park. Nine races at distances ranging from five furlongs to a mile and a half were run in front of what was a modest crowd of interested spectators. It was the future.

Today there are six All Weather racecourses in the UK with Kempton, Wolverhampton, Southwell, Chelmsford, and Newcastle added to Lingfield. There are three different surfaces: the original polytrack at Lingfield, Chelmsford and Kempton, being accompanied by fibresand at Southwell, and Michael Dickinson's invention, Tapeta, at Wolverhampton and Newcastle There are even floodlights at all, except Lingfield, and the courses have more than proved their worth even though spectator numbers continue to disappoint.

The 1990 Cheltenham Gold Cup was famous for the fact that a 100-1 outsider, *Norton's Coin*, trained by Cyrill Griffiths, a Welsh permit holder, beat his eleven rivals with *Desert Orchid* only third. He was ridden with great dash by Graham McCourt whose great pal was the *Racing Post's* Lambourn correspondent Neil Morrice. As the horse passed the winning post in front, Morrice hurled his binoculars in the air with delight and they landed on an outraged Clement Freud. As Morrice exited the press room, Freud launched a physical attack on his nearest neighbour who he perceived to be responsible. This poor innocent had to say it was nothing to do with him as Freud continued simmering with rage. Morrice had backed a 100-1 winner and was feeling no pain.

It was a year for the amateur as Marcus Armytage, later to become the *Daily Telegraph* racing correspondent, won the Grand National on *Mr Frisk* with the pair following up in the Whitbread Gold Cup three weeks later. The elderly American owner Mrs Duffey, dressed rather like a bag lady, stood next to *BBC* television host Des Lynam who was trying to edge her out of the picture until the penny dropped. The elegant Lynam recovered his equilibrium with consummate haste.

The summer was dominated by a charming filly called *Salsabil* who not only won the 1,000 Guineas and Oaks but went to The Curragh and obliterated the best colts in the Irish Derby. It is rare indeed for a filly to take on the colts in the Classics. To win as she did marked her out as very special and one of jockey Willie Carson's all-time favourites.

Paul Cole announced his presence at racing's high table with the St Leger victory of *Snurge,* while his flashy chestnut *Generous,* who had been second in the Coventry Stakes at Royal Ascot, took the Dewhurst as a 50-1 shot.

In October, the office supplied me with a mobile phone the size of a brick, attached to the facia of my Ford Mondeo. I was on my way home to London when the phone burst into life and paid for itself with one call. Did I know that Lester Piggott, who had retired from riding five years before and had since served one year of a three year prison sentence for defrauding the Inland Revenue, had re-applied for his riding licence?

I called his old weighing room colleagues Joe Mercer, Jimmy Lindley, and Pat Eddery to get their reaction. After all, "the maestro hisself" as Lindley used to call him on *BBC* television was rising fifty-five and could hardly be expected to compete with the best overnight. And yet he was hoping to ride for Vincent O'Brien, reprising their old partnership, in the Breeders Cup in America. The phone was buzzing as I parked alongside the A303. I filed a thousand words as fast as I could to copy takers. Thank God for the mobile as trying to contact the ten jockeys I spoke to would have been nigh impossible from a public phone box.

Piggott was given his licence and I was off to the most dramatic and exciting race meeting I have ever attended at Belmont Park, New York, which was staging the Breeders Cup, the Olympics of the thoroughbred world.

For starters, *Dayjur*, who had won the Prix de L'Abbaye at Longchamp the previous month, was thought to be the British banker in the Sprint. Trained to the minute by Dick Hern he looked magnificent in the parade ring. But in the race Willie Carson had brought him to win, he jumped a shadow fifty yards from the finishing line. He didn't recover in time and it cost the colt certain victory which went to the US champion *Safely Kept*.

Then we watched enthralled as two talented fillies, *Bayakoa* and *Go For Wand*, pulled ten lengths clear of their field in the Distaff. Just as both jockeys went for everything, *Go For Wand's* off foreleg snapped leaving the winner to come home alone in front of a shocked crowd of 140,000 fans. It was a sobering moment for all and hard to watch.

The Turf Mile, in which Piggott was to ride *Royal Academy*, was tailor made to showcase his magic. As the pair went to post the US commentator told the crowd, "Here's England's Lester Piggott just three weeks out of jail". In fact Piggott had been released on parole after only one year and had been out on bail for the intervening two years.

Despite his lack of match practice Lester's innate judgement of pace and timing came to the fore as he produced *Royal Academy* to perfection inside the final furlong to beat *Itsallgreektome* by a head. It was an extraordinary feat by an extraordinary man.

At the press conference afterwards, Lester was his usual taciturn and laconic self, replying to the locals with one word answers in his unique accent which had been dulled by deafness. "What the fuck language is this guy talking?" an American colleague asked me as Piggott made to leave. "I'll translate," I replied as Piggott was dragged back unwillingly to finish the conference. Lester loved public adulation but was never comfortable with the press.

A call from Ascot came just after Christmas inviting Linda and me to lunch with the Trustees. On the Saturday morning came another call begging us to be in situ by 11.30am as Queen Elizabeth the Queen Mother was a lunch guest of Her Majesty's Representative Lord Hartington. The future Mrs Mackenzie located her best bib and tucker and we were off.

Prior to lunch, Stoker Hartington came up to us and said the Queen Mum would love to say hello and would we join her and her Gin and Dubonnet for a pre-prandial conversation. As we arrived, she was doing her best Geoffrey Boycott impression. A *Channel Four* racing executive was seeking her backing for the channel to take over coverage of Ascot from the *BBC* (which they achieved a decade later). She was far too experienced – at ninety years old – to let slip anything that might have seemed helpful to the hapless executive, blocking his every entreaty with consummate skill. Then she spoke to us. I was amazed at her acuity, complaining about the cost of keeping so many horses in training while clearly enjoying the experience of owning and following her horses. She even asked Linda to sit down because she had a crick in her neck looking up at my five foot nine girlfriend. We had more than ten minutes discussing the world of racing and the Queen Mother was charm personified.

Early in 1991, *Daily Mail* staff received a memo from the editor Sir David English enquiring if we knew anyone in Saudi Arabia. The bid to oust Saddam Hussein from Kuwait was under way with Allied forces mustering in the North East province in preparation for retaking this important oil producer on the Persian Gulf. Rather foolishly I admitted to an acquaintance with Prince Fahd Salman, a member of the Saudi Royal Family and the Vice Governor of this province. The Prince was Paul Cole's principal patron and had bought the magnificent Whatcombe stables on his behalf five years earlier. He was the proud owner of forty horses in the yard including Derby hopeful *Generous*, the flashy chestnut who had surprised everyone with victory in the Dewhurst Stakes three months earlier.

Nervously I phoned the Prince, a nephew of Prince Khaled Abdullah. I knew him to be gregarious and quite a joker, but would he answer questions to do with military operations? It was clear from despatches that the presence of Allied forces in the holy land was not appreciated by the Muslim community around the world. Amazingly Prince Fahd himself answered my initial call and deftly parried my questions about the progress of the military preparations. All he wanted to know was – how was *Generous*, had he been galloping and was he thriving? Having spoken earlier to his trainer I could assure the Prince that the colt still had four legs but that he hadn't done much work yet. I made a further half dozen calls before the invasion launched on January 31, but Prince Fahd remained non-committal about military manoeuvres and diverted the conversation to *Generous*.

As I knew he was speaking on a daily basis with Paul and with his racing manager Anthony Penfold I told him there was nothing I could usefully add to what they had told him. But his enthusiasm was infectious and I felt a call to my bookie was needed. A little 33-1 was on offer – thank you very much.

Happily for Prince Fahd and the Allies, Kuwait was returned to its people in short order leaving the Prince to ask yet more questions about *Generous* who was being prepared for the 2,000 Guineas en route to the Derby. As a result, his odds had shortened to 20-1. "How is he working, Colin?" was his last query. "I don't know, sir. Paul knows far better than I." "Yes, but I want your unbiased opinion," he insisted. "He's going well," I replied.

Come the big day and *Generous* could finish no closer than a staying on fourth in the 2,000 Guineas despite the best efforts of jockey Richard Quinn. The Prince was inconsolable in the Newmarket unsaddling enclosure until I went over and repeated that old canard, "Fourth in the Guineas, first in the Derby".

Unknown to me, *Generous* had been held up in his work immediately prior to the Guineas with a minor bruise to his foot. He was a gallop short before Newmarket, and very unfairly in my opinion, Richard Quinn was blamed for the defeat and forfeited the Derby ride to young up and coming Alan Munro who would be retained as the Prince's own jockey.

In late May, Paul Cole took *Generous* for a private gallop at Newbury with regular work rider Tommy Jennings on board. He worked with some really good horses entered at Royal Ascot and treated them like selling platers. "He's really come to himself now," Jennings told Cole. This was music to my ears as I located my bookmaker's phone number to press my cause at 14-1.

Munro enlisted the help of Lester Piggott's father Keith to go over tactics at Epsom. He was serving a four day riding ban so had plenty of time to study tapes of Lester's many Derby triumphs. Munro had won on all four of his rides for the Prince prior to Derby day and was full of confidence, even if the public sympathy was for Richard Quinn.

The race itself could not have gone better for *Generous* as he followed the strong pace set by *Mystiko* who had beaten him in the 2,000 Guineas. As *Mystiko's* suspect stamina gave way after Tattenham Corner, Munro engaged the after burner and *Generous* surged to a five length lead which he maintained to the finishing post. It started a magical summer for the Cole horses and *Generous* went on to win the Irish Derby and the King George and Queen Elizabeth Stakes at Ascot.

Sadly, Prince Fahd, who was such a fun person to be around, died from heart failure at forty-six. It was a blow to his family and to Paul Cole, the Master of Whatcombe, who lost a major patron and a man who owned Classic winners in England, Ireland, Italy, and Germany. These owners are hard to replace.

Breeders Cup 1991 was notable for the extraordinary performance of *Arazi* who won the Juvenile Colts as if he had been dropped into the race at halfway. It was like watching a 1930s movie of *Seabiscuit* with improbable acceleration being over emphasised. He was owned by Allen Paulson who had sold a half share to Sheik Mohammed just before the race. Between them they decided to operate on *Arazi's* knees following the race to remove bone chips. The horse was never the same afterwards.

My colleague and good friend Jonathan Powell, covering the Breeders Cup for the *Sunday Express* (having previously worked for *The People, The News of the World,* and *the Sunday Times*) decided we deserved some rest and recuperation in Florida afterwards, so we booked a week's holiday at the *Ritz Carlton Naples* on the Gulf of Mexico to play tennis. I'd known Jonathan since 1970 and he had been instrumental in assisting my journey towards the racing press rooms.

Imagine our dismay after booking into the hotel to discover that merchant bankers Goldman Sachs were holding a conference at the hotel and had booked all eight tennis courts for a tournament for their employees. Hard as we tried, we couldn't get a court for two days. Grumpily wondering whether to give the beach an outing, I turned on *Sky* news in my bedroom. It was leading on the story that Robert Maxwell had been found dead, drowned off the Canary Islands, having fallen from his yacht the night before. In the back of my mind a little bird told me that Goldman Sachs had recently bailed out the ailing *Mirror Group* of newspapers.

Jonathan and I decided to "invade" the tennis courts, dropping the hint that the highly paid bankers might like to know the latest news. The courts emptied as the full implication of our news became apparent. They had work to do, while Jonathan and I could continue to pretend we were Pete Sampras.

In the Canaries, John Jackson of the *Daily Mirror* was helping to identify the body of his one-time boss. Later he would accompany Maxwell's widow Betty to Israel where the Maxwell family had paid for a burial plot on the Mount of Olives. John can confirm that conspiracy mongers are off the pace in alleging the Bouncing Czech and father of nine could still be alive.

I had a nice little exclusive to launch the 1991 Cheltenham Festival when I learned that Irish owner trainer Noel Furlong had had to pay a visit to HM Customs and Excise before his *Destriero* could be allowed to run in the opening Supreme novice hurdle. Furlong was Britain's second largest carpet manufacturer and operated out of Belfast and Dublin. It was the former venue that was causing him pain.

Having settled a £500,000 VAT bill twenty-four hours earlier, Furlong planned to win the first race of the meeting with the once raced *Destriero* on whom he had placed a £300,000 bet at odds of 6-1 or greater. He had acquired the stake money when landing a huge coup with his Champion hurdle hope *The Illiad* in the Ladbroke hurdle at Leopardstown the previous Christmas where *Destriero* had also won his debut hurdle. He netted at least £1.5 million. He thought *Destriero* was a certainty but was less sure of *The Illiad* who was to run in the Champion Hurdle seventy-five minutes later. He backed *The Illiad* at 14-1 and placed a double on the two horses. Had *The Illiad* won he would have walked away with £5.5 million. However *The Illiad* was dehydrated, ran no sort of race, and finished last of twenty-one.

Furlong watched both races from JP McManus's box. *Destriero* dotted up by four lengths from the future champion hurdler *Granville Again* at odds of 6-1. Furlong was understandably thrilled and said, "I hadn't paid half a million to the VAT people just to go to Cheltenham. I thought he was a certainty." Be that as it may, *Destriero* won only one more race in his career. Furlong, meanwhile, showed another side of his punting skills when he won the $1 million World Poker Championships in Las Vegas in 1999.

The Queen and the Queen Mother were at Newbury's Spring meeting which heralded the start of the racecourse's 1992 flat season. They were officially opening the new Berkshire grandstand. I was in the fifth floor press room with its marvellous panoramic view over the track when the racecourse chairman Lord Carnarvon decided to risk taking the Queen into the lion's den. Her Majesty's racing press were probably amongst the most loyal and friendly she could ever hope to encounter, hence her racing manager's confidence.

I had borrowed the services of a young student called Toby because I was temporarily off the road and I had been late arriving at Doncaster's first ever Sunday race meeting the previous autumn. My new black Mazda sports car had been clocked at 110mph on the M1 as I tried to make up time. Linda called the vehicle my menoporsche.

So I sat Toby down with a *Racing Post,* £10 pocket money, and my best tips, while I beavered away on my laptop. Suddenly there was a brief knock on the outside door and in marched the Queen with Carnarvon in hot pursuit. She walked straight to the front of the box to admire the view. And then she turned to the youthful looking Toby and said, "Who do you work for?" The student was a little nonplussed, not to say unprepared, and stammered, "I'm Colin Mackenzie's driver." Her Majesty's eyebrows nearly hit the ceiling as she absorbed the shock of learning that racing correspondents could afford chauffeurs. Luckily, before she could debrief me, she was interrupted by Tony Stafford of the *Daily Telegraph* who proceeded to berate the Queen that her racing manager was rubbish and that he could do a better job. It didn't take long before Her Majesty was swiftly ushered out by Henry Carnarvon who was doubting the wisdom of his impetuous decision to show her the press room.

At the Guineas meeting in Newmarket we were to witness an exciting and newsworthy race. Lester Piggott, now fifty-six, still had a few aces to play and he astonished the thoroughbred world with the thirtieth Classic win of his extraordinary career when guiding the 6-1 shot *Rodrigo de Triano* to victory in the season's first Classic. The colt, trained by ex-stable lad Peter Chapple-Hyam for Robert Sangster, glided over the lush turf to win effortlessly. He was good enough to go on to land the Juddmonte International at York and the Champion Stakes at Newmarket to give his veteran jockey an age-defying Group One treble.

Five hours later *Arazi* proved to be a huge flop as he finished out of the money at Churchill Downs. As previously mentioned, he had undergone surgery for bone chips in his knees the previous autumn, against trainer Francois Boutin's wishes, it seemed. He was never again that ground devouring colt he had seemed in the

Juvenile Colts. It was a shame as we hacks like to see a great horse in action.

Rodrigo de Triano's trainer Peter Chapple-Hyam was scarcely able to pinch himself as *Dr Devious* won the Epsom Derby for the American Craig family. The colt had made the trip across the Atlantic to take part in *Arazi's* Kentucky Derby on dirt, a very unconventional prep race for our Derby. And yet he had won the Blue Riband of racing.

A curious postscript to this victory is that the American owners disputed the winning percentages automatically deducted by Weatherbys and given to the successful trainer Chapple-Hyam and jockey John Reid. Somehow they managed to intercept the money due to the Manton-based pair. And the matter wasn't resolved for several months until the Jockey Club stepped in and reinforced the British rules which insist on set percentages.

The summer proved to be a bonanza for popular Newmarket-based owner Bill Gredley whose *User Friendly* won the Oaks, the Yorkshire Oaks, and the St Leger. This gave veteran trainer Clive Brittain and much travelled jockey George Duffield a fine treble of Group One victories too.

Alan Munro, who had won the Derby the year before on *Generous*, was much in demand as a talented rider. He won the Spitfire handicap at Glorious Goodwood which carried the bonus of a flight in the iconic aircraft from Duxford airfield east of Newmarket. The *Daily Mail's* racing correspondent was invited to record proceedings.

After Munro finished his fifteen minute tour of Essex and Suffolk I asked if there was any possibility I could have a little joyride too. "Why not" said the pilot, introducing me to an air suit with parachute attached. This was a modified Spitfire with the pilot sitting in the single-seat cockpit behind the passenger. It was *Boy's Own* stuff for a man who adored listening to the roar of the powerful Merlin engines as they flew over Barton-on-Sea during late 1945.

As we took off, I could sense the adrenalin surge in my body which was pressed in tight – those wartime pilots must have been slim chaps, I thought. Within five minutes, though, my thoughts were elsewhere as the pilot told me that ground control had noticed that one of the wheels of our undercarriage had failed to retract. Panic stations! "Had I ever used a parachute before," was the immediate query. "No, I hadn't and what's more this wasn't part of the guided tour," I replied. "Well," said my new best friend. "I'll have to do some manoeuvres to get the wheel back in place. Breathe deeply and don't be sick!"

Ten minutes later we made a successful landing, although I thought I saw a fire engine beetling down beside the runway. Talk about a roller coaster thrill of a ride. Short of a mount in the Grand National – which was never going to happen to someone like me for whom a beach donkey would represent a challenge – this was excitement and terror distilled in its purest state.

For Piggott, the year would end in disaster when his mount *Mr Brooks*, winner of that summer's July Cup, slipped and fell in the Breeders Cup Sprint at Gulfstream Park, Florida. When horses, especially sprinters, fall on the flat it is usually bad news for the jockey. This was dirt and Piggott had to be hospitalised.

Tim Miles, an experienced reporter I'd known on the *Mail*, had moved to Florida and covered the Piggott story, discovering that his mistress Anna Ludlow, rather than his wife Susan, was a regular visitor to his hospital bed. He filed the story to all the popular papers in Britain except the *Mail* with which he'd fallen out.

I knew of Ludlow's presence at the Piggott bedside but thought it prudent not to write it for Piggott's benefit. Big mistake – all it meant was that the *Mail* did not have the story and I got a large roasting from the new editor Paul Dacre on my return. Sir David English had been made chairman of the *Mail's* parent company Associated Newspapers earlier that year with Dacre promoted to editor, a position he finally left in 2018.

On Maundy Thursday 1993, Linda and I married at Ealing Town Hall register office, witnessed by our six lovely daughters and six other family members. We had a small reception at our house followed by a two night honeymoon at the Dorchester hotel which was almost empty that Easter weekend following a change of ownership. We even got upgraded to the Oliver Messel suite (his and hers bathrooms no less) which was delightful.

Linda had known nothing of the world of racing when we met. By the time we married she had come to embrace this extraordinary sport and its unique vocabulary, such as "lie up" when I wanted her to walk faster with me. Lots of my colleagues and other racing folk were entertained to supper in our new Ealing house which was always a welcoming haven after a long day. She even enjoyed having the occasional punt, especially on the Grand National where we were bound a week later.

Poor old 'Captain Cock-up' – for that was the nickname of the Grand National starter Captain Keith Brown after the 1993 race was declared void following two false starts. *Esha Ness*, trained by the Queen of Aintree Jenny Pitman, and jockey John White actually completed the course as "winners" (along with six other finishers) despite the best effort of stewards to stop the runners. As the nation's showpiece race it was a disaster, broadcast to 600 million television viewers worldwide. It made a mockery of British racing and the poor Captain paid the price with his instant retirement.

At a subsequent enquiry headed by Deputy Senior Steward and High Court Judge Sir Michael Connell QC a portion of blame was attached to Keith Brown for whom the Grand National was his final race as a starter. However, disgracefully in my opinion, the majority of the blame was allotted to the lone flag man Ken Evans who claimed, quite rightly, that Brown's false start flag failed to unfurl on the second occasion when the starting tape was caught around jockey Richard Dunwoody's neck.

The cock-up was almost certainly caused largely by a group of fifteen animal rights activists who sought to stop the race from happening. Bookmakers had to return more than £75 million in bets – by far the largest amount wagered on any race during the calendar.

Andrew Parker Bowles, former husband of the Duchess of Cornwall, chaired a subsequent working party which made several recommendations about the starting procedure. As he said, "In 7,000 races a year the flag procedure has failed only three times. One of these was in the Grand National and it won't happen again." It hasn't happened again, but the race was abandoned in 1997 when an IRA threat was lodged with local police. The race took place two days later on a Monday.

After two hundred and forty years in charge of horseracing, the Jockey Club finally ceded authority to the newly formed British Horseracing Board in 1993. There had been rumblings about elitism and nepotism at the Jockey Club, and the Home Affairs select committee, headed by Tory MP Sir John Wheeler, determined that racing should be more accountable and more democratic.

Nevertheless, Lord Hartington, now the Duke of Devonshire, who was senior steward of the Jockey Club, was elected Chairman of the BHB to ensure continuity of purpose and to provide the necessary expertise and leadership. An Oxford graduate, Stoker Hartington was much respected in the industry within which he owned and had bred several good horses. His father owned and bred the brilliant filly *Park Top*, runner-up in the 1969 Prix de L'Arc de Triomphe.

One of the areas that was considerably beefed up and given more power was security. Ex-army officer Roger Buffham was recruited in 1992 by the Jockey Club (who retained responsibility for day to day racecourse matters) to root out bent jockeys and trainers and to discover if there was endemic corruption in racing. In particular he had been tipped off through his confidential phone line "Raceguard" that horses were being doped and prevented from winning.

The nature of his job made Buffham unpopular. While there were certainly corruption issues to be found it was nonsense to suppose all jockeys and trainers were wrong 'uns. Having won an MBE while in charge of bomb disposal in Northern Ireland between 1977 and 1981 there was little doubting Buffham's courage and determination. But his assertions that racing was institutionally corrupt and that the "regulators lacked the moral courage and resolve to deal with racing's ills" won him few friends, especially in high places.

On the racing front there were many significant victories, not least the filly *Urban Sea's* great win in the Arc. She went on to be a very successful brood mare, producing the ultra stallions and Derby winners *Galileo* and *Sea of Stars*. Down under, Dermot Weld led the way for northern hemisphere-trained horses when *Vintage Crop*, winner of the Irish St Leger, went on to win the Melbourne Cup. This hugely valuable handicap would thereafter attract multiple entries from Japan and Europe.

By 1994 my friend Grahame Amey left the Gandolfo fold to breed and race his own horses on the flat. Stephen Freud and I hitched our ownership wagon to another of Gandy's successful owners, Timmy Whitley, whose father Claude had been chairman and clerk of the course at Newton Abbot and whose brewery company, together with the Greenall family, had sponsored the Greenall Whitley chase at Haydock for many years.

We leased a quarter share each in the mare *Garrylough* and over the next three years she won seven races, was runner-up seven times, and gave us huge fun. The highlight of her career was winning the 1996 Mares Chase Final at Uttoxeter in a common canter.

I felt a little guilty about this as handicapper Christopher Mordaunt, surely the most charming man in racing, had raised her 15lbs for winning a modest race at Fakenham. I telephoned Christopher and pleaded that *Garrylough* had beaten nothing and he promised to look again at the race. In the month between the two races Christopher dropped *Garrylough* 5lb each week back to her Fakenham mark for which I was very grateful. To reward Christopher by winning this prestigious Final by fifteen lengths was a little ungrateful and Christopher took appropriate action – with a rueful smile.

Stephen and I had several nice horses in partnership with Timmy, contributing to the thirty-nine winners Gandy trained for us in total. The Wizard of Wantage looked after us well and he did his level best to mitigate expensive training fees by getting us into decent horses who could pay their way.

The 1994 2,000 Guineas was won by *Mister Baileys*, significant for the fact that it launched winning trainer Mark Johnston on an upward curve in his promising career. By 2019 "Braveheart" Johnston, born in Scotland but training at Middleham, North Yorkshire, had broken all training records when he overtook Richard Hannon senior as the most winning trainer in history in November 2019 with 4,193 successes. He also overtook Martin Pipe's record of 243 winners in a season when he landed his

245th winner that month. He has recorded an astonishing twenty-five consecutive seasons with over a hundred winners.

One of Pipe's greatest days was when Richard Dunwoody brought *Minnehoma* home in the 1994 Grand National. The horse was owned by the comedian Freddie Starr, famous for eating a hamster sandwich, as *The Sun* reported. The comedian denied the story although it had a beneficial effect on his career. Even though Dunwoody and Pipe never had the warmest relationship – unlike Pipe's friendships with Peter Scudamore and AP McCoy – this was a great achievement and a second National victory for the jockey who won on *West Tip* in 1986.

Martin Pipe, who enjoyed the most extraordinarily successful training career considering his background was working in his father's betting shops as a board man, was one of the more difficult people to deal with. Understandably perhaps, he felt people were suspicious of him because of his high success rate and revolutionary training methods. He believed in interval training for racehorses and he utilised regular blood tests which disclosed the wellbeing of his string.

Oddly enough it took a programme called the Cook Report, fronted by the New Zealand-born journalist in 1991, to render the shy and taciturn Pipe a more popular figure within racing's establishment. The television programme sought to paint Pipe as a doper, a ruthless trainer of horses, and a man who would send a horse to the knackers if it wasn't good enough to justify keeping in training. None of this was proven.

By then most of his rivals accepted that his training methods, mostly learned from books, had outpaced their own. His horses were simply fitter, faster, and ran from the front where there was minimal danger of being brought down or falling. So it was troubling to the racing press that the fifteen-times champion trainer was still so difficult to deal with and contact. The kinder members of the press room put this down to reticence. Others thought he enjoyed being difficult.

In the summer of 1994 Roger Buffham was concerned that a number of racehorses had been blood doped with EPO, the same drug that was illegal in athletics and cycling because it elevated haemoglobin levels. He orchestrated dawn raids on several top yards, including Pipe's Nicholashayne stables near Wellington in Somerset. Pipe was deeply unamused by this but consented to his horses being tested – and the tests all came back negative.

During that summer and early autumn, a number of Pipe's horses were tested at the racecourse where they had just run, to which he strongly objected. He ended up being fined by the Jockey Club for his failure to comply with the rules of racing. A Jockey Club employee told me, "In essence he spit his dummy out and became very defensive, which was a great shame. He took on a siege mentality when in truth it was a marvellous opportunity for him to be statesmanlike and to show the world that he had nothing to hide."

It was a surprise to most of us when one Saturday morning in 2006 Pipe telephoned *Channel Four* racing to let them know he was retiring and handing the business over to his son David. He was only sixty-one but was suffering from a muscle-wasting disease which could claim his life at any time. Happily, Pipe is still with us and seems a much happier, more relaxed fellow, content that his achievements were recognised by the Queen with a CBE. He has the honour of a race at the Cheltenham Festival named after him.

Two doping incidents did occur in 1997 at Exeter where Charlie Egerton's *Avanti Express* was pulled up and at Plumpton where Josh Gifford's *Lively Knight* was tampered with. These two incidents, with the alleged dopers caught on CCTV in the racecourse stables, were to form part of an intriguing but ultimately failed court case in Southwark three years later. Roger Buffham, the former military intelligence officer, was good at collecting evidence but deficient when it came to providing proof that would convict.

Cheltenham 1995 provided trainer Kim Bailey with a wonderful showcase of his talents when he added the Champion Hurdle and the Gold Cup to his Grand National triumph five years earlier with *Mr Frisk.* The victories of *Alderbrook* and *Master Oats*, both partnered by Norman Williamson, were the first such double since 1950 when the legendary Vincent O'Brien and Aubrey Brabazon combined to win both races with *Hatton's Grace* and *Cottage Rake.*

Bailey was in tears after *Alderbrook*, in only the third hurdle race of his life, having beat *Large Action* and *Danoli* by five lengths and two lengths. This was an out and out flat horse who had won the Group Two Prix Dollar under Paul Eddery for Newmarket trainer Julie Cecil the previous autumn. *Danoli,* touted as the new *Arkle* when winning at Cheltenham the year before, didn't quite live up to the expectations of his charming and humble trainer Tom Foley who wore the expectations of Ireland on his shoulders. In 1994 he was Ireland's big hope and Foley was bodily lifted into the winner's enclosure by visiting turfistes. This time he had to settle for third place but his arrival in the hallowed unsaddling enclosure still merited a huge Irish roar.

I got a nice little exclusive when Richard Dunwoody announced at the end of May that he would be parting from Martin Pipe as stable jockey. He intended riding for Edward O'Grady and going freelance. By leaving Pipe he realised he would no longer be champion jockey. Tipped to replace him was the promising David Bridgewater – and that's what happened. Dunwoody, surely the most stylish jump jockey of his generation, had never jelled with Pipe – as personalities they were chalk and cheese.

This, rather than promised riches, was what guided Dunwoody's decision.

Racing was stunned in September 1995 when Lester Piggott finally decided to hang up his riding boots, two months short of his sixtieth birthday. By now a grandfather, he had ridden in Dubai that Spring but had taken no rides since. To say he was a flawed genius would tell only half the story. He wasn't good with money – hence his three year prison sentence for defrauding the Inland Revenue – but his genius on a horse elevated his world standing to that of Arnold Palmer in golf, Pele and Bobby Charlton in football, and Muhammad Ali in boxing.

To some extent, this news, released on the day when his heir apparent Frankie Dettori rode his thousandth domestic winner on St Leger victor *Classic Cliché,* threatened to sour relations with the rest of the weighing room. But every jockey revered him and Dettori said, "The name Piggott tells the whole story. I have been in Britain only ten years and I never saw the best of him. But I lost my 5lb and my 3lb claim on one of his horses (when he briefly trained) and he never stopped ringing me to tell me how to ride them." Ladbrokes Mike Dillon said, "He brought the Derby to life every year whether he rode Pegasus or the pack horse. Whenever he won, we lost – but he was great for the game." He won the Derby on nine occasions, earning the soubriquet 'the Housewives Favourite'.

In February 1996, Walter Swinburn, whose career had withstood various crises, suffered an appalling fall at Sha Tin racecourse when his mount *Liffey River* careered out of control into some running rails. His injuries included a broken left shoulder, three fractures to his left collar bone, multiple fractures to his ribs, and badly bruised lungs. The career of the man who rode *Lammtarra* to a wonderful Derby victory only eight months earlier seemed at risk.

Two weeks later I got an interview with the jockey known as The Choirboy (for his angelic and youthful looks) by phoning the Prince of Wales hospital. He had been watching the Hong Kong Derby on television and revealed that his competitive juices were intact, even if he wouldn't be riding again for two months. (In fact it was six months.) Because of his accident, no debutant (*Liffey River* had never run before) would be allowed to race in blinkers, which had apparently caused his antics.

Swinburn, surely the most talented natural rider of his generation, had been inundated with cards and phone calls. Even Lester Piggott had bitten the bullet and telephoned from Newmarket. "It's been very uplifting hearing from so many friends," Swinburn told me. "Steve Cauthen called my mother, Cash Asmussen faxed me from the States, while Gerald Mosse, Mick Kinane, and Alan Munro came to see me in hospital."

Poor troubled Walter had many riding successes left in him but always struggled with his weight and with alcohol and epilepsy brought on by the *Sha Tin* fall. Later he trained from his father-in-law Peter Harris's racing stables in Hertfordshire. He even became a guest columnist on the *Daily Mail*. It was a real tragedy when his body was found beneath the Belgravia flat where he had been living alone in December 2016. Racing looks after its own well but somehow Walter slipped through the net.

At Leopardstown, *Collier Bay,* trained by Jim Old, won the 1996 Irish Champion Hurdle under Jamie Osborne with the ever popular *Danoli* half a length back in third place having recovered from a serious leg injury. All the cheers were reserved for Tom Foley's *Irish folk hero* who was promptly promoted to 3-1 joint favourite for the Cheltenham highlight alongside *Alderbrook*.

But Old would have the last laugh at Cheltenham when his pride and joy got first run on *Alderbrook* to win by two and a half lengths, with *Danoli* only fourth, a further seven lengths back.

But the main story concerned winning jockey Graham Bradley who would have ridden *Alderbrook* but for missing a key gallop on the 1995 winner because he had overslept.

Jamie Osborne had elected to ride *Mysilv* and a furious Kim Bailey told Bradley that Richard Dunwoody would now ride *Alderbrook* because of his carelessness – apparently caused by getting drunk at Dean Gallagher's birthday party the night before. Bradley who had won the Gold Cup thirteen years earlier on *Bregawn* (when winning trainer Michael Dickinson had the first five home), said that the winning feeling was every bit as good. He even pointed to his watch as he entered the winner's enclosure at Cheltenham in a thank you for his luck.

The first running of the Dubai World Cup, the world's most valuable race, took place in March with the Breeders Cup Classic hero *Cigar* living up to his unbeaten record. Being on dirt, this was always going to attract US horses with the Europeans largely contesting races on fast grass at Nad al Sheba.

The world's racing press were guests of Sheik Mohammed who was footing the hotel and other bills. It was not the Fourth Estate's finest hour as sports editors (and others) pocketed bottles of Perrier-Jouet champagne to put in their luggage before flying home business class on *Emirates*. Clement Freud famously wrote about all the goodies on offer, which included gold watches, and the headline on his piece in *The Times* was "The Mother of All Freebies," referencing the earlier Gulf war which was called the Mother of All Wars. Understandably our Bedouin hosts were hurt and puzzled by what had gone on and the freebies in future years came to a rapid halt. It was not a moment to be proud of, although I exclude myself and most of my colleagues from the more egregious excesses.

Henry Cecil and Sheik Mohammed had a spectacular falling-out towards the end of 1995 over what the Sheik perceived to be the interference of Cecil's second wife Natalie in the training of his horses. He removed his entire string, including the talented 2,000 Guineas hope *Mark of Esteem*, and transferred them to his Godolphin operation. Cecil's "mistake", if that was what it was, was to back his wife publicly after she had complained on behalf of the lads who looked after the Sheik's good horses that it was deflating and disappointing to see these horses go elsewhere. In 1995 Cecil had lost *Moonshell* (Oaks winner), *Vettori* (winner of the French 2,000 Guineas), and *Classic Cliché* (the St Leger winner). With those horses in his team Cecil would have been champion trainer for the eleventh time.

Cecil told me, "I must thank him (the Sheik) for kicking me up the butt and giving me renewed ambition. I have lost a stone and a half in weight, I haven't smoked for sixteen months, and I haven't had a drink for two years. In fact this whole business has given me a new lease of life. The yard is buzzing and frankly it's quite exciting. The adrenalin is coursing again and I have had wonderful support from my other owners so that no lads have had to be made redundant."

The town of Newmarket had watched these machinations with mounting interest. As always it would be the horses who answered the questions of who was right. But the ever-popular Cecil would be the main beneficiary of the cheers if one of his team downed one from Godolphin. Cecil had always been a popular ratepayer in racing's headquarters. He would take time out to talk to tourists up on the gallops, identifying his stars and often inviting them back to Warren Place to show them his roses.

The opening Guineas meeting could be called a score draw after Godolphin's *Mark of Esteem* lived up to his billing in the 2,000 Guineas while Cecil's *Bosra Sham* responded with a brilliant victory in the 1,000 Guineas. Frankie Dettori, who rode *Mark of Esteem,* received an eight-day riding ban for overuse of the whip. This was a topic that would be revisited on many occasions over the next two decades as horse welfare advanced to the top of racing's political agenda.

Frankie Dettori created history at Ascot in September, going through the card with seven consecutive winners, costing the bookmaking industry a minimum £40 million. The Sardinian was dynamite that afternoon and won on horses that did not represent good investments at all and had little right to succeed; especially his final ride *Fujiyama Crest* who was easily available at 12-1 in the morning skirmishes. Punter Darren Yates won £550,000 and the combined odds were 25,091-1.

Fujiyama Crest's trainer Michael Stoute thought Dettori would be too tired to motivate his lazy horse over Ascot's stiff two miles. But Dettori told the trainer it would be his fault if the gelding failed to win because "I am on fire". Bookmakers like Gary Wiltshire laid *Fujiyama Crest* for fortunes in the belief that his starting price of 2-1 was false and unrealistic. He paid for doubting Dettori by nearly going out of business.

Two weeks later Dettori was back at Ascot with another seven rides. This time bookies were taking few chances. Ladbrokes and Hills, the two principal players in the country, were refusing to take multiple bets on the jockey's mounts. Hills' odds compiler Mike Bellamy was quoted as saying, "It's like asking a fellow who's had his house robbed what price he'll give to have it robbed again a fortnight later."

There is a now a statue of Frankie at his favourite racecourse, although it would take the jockey's nearest and dearest to recognise the figure. Frankie remains racing's greatest asset, a jewel who can promote the sport. He acquired the charisma of Lester and is a very nice guy who can laugh at himself.

At the 1996 Breeders Cup, *Pilsudski* added to Michael Stoute's impressive record at the meeting when he trotted up in the turf. But it was another half-forgotten trainer who caught the eye of the British press hounds. For Michael Dickinson, the brilliant jump trainer whose career had faltered when becoming Robert Sangster's private trainer at Manton, had prepared *Da Hoss* to the minute to win the Turf Mile.

Dickinson had moved to America following his split with Sangster in 1986 and was training at Fair Hills, Maryland. He had fewer than fifty horses and even though he was competitive he refused to countenance the use of American drugs Bute and Lasix to assist his horses. So it was a huge achievement to win at this level. And *Da Hoss* who suffered intermittent injuries throughout his career would duplicate his victory in the 1998 Breeders Cup Turf Mile.

Dickinson, who invented the All Weather surface Tapeta, which is kinder to horses than other products, is a regular at the Cheltenham Festival every year. He misses little, follows the form, and it is a foolish punter who fails to listen to his views on the outcome of the biggest races. Middle age has conferred on him a calm that may have been missing in his younger days.

We tend to forget what a potent enemy the IRA was in the years prior to the Good Friday agreement which was concluded in 1998. The year before, it had a devastating effect on the Grand National meeting when a known code was relayed to Merseyside police which meant the big Saturday meeting had to be abandoned as the horses were in the parade ring.

The public was told to disperse to the infield while cars were marooned in the racecourse car parks unable to be used, although the ever-astute Sir Peter O'Sullevan made a rapid exit in his Jaguar having seen what was about to happen. It was to be Peter's final call in the race he had commentated on from 1948 onwards when it was radio. It was first televised in 1960. On his retirement following *Benny The Dip's* Derby he was knighted.

One of the funnier sights was watching the red jacketed Tote girls forming circles of a dozen in the infield while the thirteenth had a wee on her haunches in the middle. Human ingenuity knew no bounds. As mobile phones were neutered by police it was difficult for people to catch up with friends and relatives. In other words, the IRA had caused chaos. Some of my Sunday paper colleagues were utilising private homes of Aintree folk to file copy as the press room had to be abandoned.

After much discussion, the race was rescheduled for the following Monday as a stand-alone race. The Princess Royal, together with Prime Minister John Major, not a known race fan, decided to support the sport by being present. It was in these circumstances that *Lord Gyllene*, owned by Sir Stanley Clarke, trained by Steve Brookshaw and ridden by Tony Dobbin, raced to a famous victory. I still have a race programme for that day which will make a couple of quid one day when valued by the *Antiques Road Show* – I hope.

The dead heat of *Ya Malak* and *Coastal Bluff* in the Nunthorpe Stakes at York was significant for the fact that the former's jockey Alex Greaves, later to marry trainer David Nicholls, was the first female jockey to win a UK race at Group One level. Alex paved the way for other talented women such as Hayley Turner and Hollie Doyle.

1998 was a key year for the sport with a revolution at the BHB intertwined with shocking revelations about corruption in racing. Peter Savill, the former Ampleforth College Head Boy and Cayman Islands resident, had for some months been making adverse noises about BHB chairman Lord Wakeham's failure to provide a long-term financial plan for the sport.

Savill was convinced that a more robust arrangement with the bookmaking fraternity, coupled with effective lobbying of government would reap beneficial results for the sport which, he claimed, was grossly underfunded. Indeed the cost of owning and running racehorses was inflating far faster than the cost of living and the UK was at a disadvantage with Ireland and France whose participants could reclaim VAT costs.

Wakeham, a former Tory minister who had replaced Lord Hartington as BHB Chairman, had his hands full with around six other jobs which diverted his attention. Savill's campaign to have him defenestrated was swift. Before the year was out the new BHB Chairman was *Celtic Swing's* owner. Whether this punchy, aggressive gentleman could unite racing and take on the world would be the great talking point for the next few years.

Far more dangerous for the sport were the arrests of trainers, jockeys, and alleged dopers who had been identified by the Jockey Club's security chief Roger Buffham. His allegations of endemic corruption were beginning to bear fruit, even if only half of his assertions were true. But he was not a popular figure even with his employers and, as we shall see later, he was eventually dismissed from the Jockey Club in surprising circumstances with a string of investigations under his belt that eventually bore little fruit.

Istabraq won the first of his three consecutive Champion Hurdles in 1998 and he could well have made it four on the bounce had a foot and mouth epidemic not caused the 2001 Festival to be abandoned. This was the horse Charlie Swan had been entreated to ride with "balls of steel" the previous year when winning the Sun Alliance hurdle for owner JP McManus and trainer Aiden O'Brien.

He was to join the legends such as *See You Then, Persian War* and *Hatton's Grace* as triple winners of this great race and gave his enthusiastic owner much fun and kudos. JP, as McManus was universally known in racing, was a formidable punter who loved nothing better than a huge wager on one of his horses. But

Istabraq transcended a bet, JP was truly proud to own a horse that would acquire legendary status prior to his retirement to his Martinstown stud in County Limerick.

Earth Summit, bred by Jim Old, won the Grand National for Nigel Twiston-Davies and the Summit Partnership headed by Aintree press supremo Nigel Payne. He beat the gallant *Suny Bay* who was giving him 23lbs and established the Gloucestershire trainer as a coming force in National Hunt racing.

Curiously Jim Old is now his assistant having handed in his training licence four years ago. *Suny Bay's* defeat caused his trainer Charlie Brooks to bring to a close a short, and at times controversial training career.

Charlie, an Old Etonian who had a try out for Watford as a goalkeeper, is a decent tennis player – by far the best in the racing orbit. Unfortunately a knee injury has curtailed even social tennis for this likeable fellow who may have been gifted a silver spoon at birth but never relied upon it. He trained for Nigel Dempster for a while and gave a charming address at the latter's 2007 memorial service in St Bride's Fleet Street.

There were echoes of the *Daily Sketch-Daily Mail* 1971 merger when publication of the *Sporting Life* ceased on May 12 1998. So many people were made redundant including two of my hard-working friends and colleagues, Geoff Lester of the *Life* and Tim Richards of the *Post.* The *Life's* editor Tom Clarke took a lot of unfair flak for the merger. In effect it was out of his hands and he did his best for the existing staff.

Alan Byrne, the *Racing Post* editor, had some difficult choices to make but in the end it came down to money. Lester and Richards were well paid, long serving members of staff. It made economic sense for them to be let go. For Lester who had started out as a sixteen year old tea boy on the *Life* in 1964 and had known no other employer, it was a bitter pill to swallow. We were all at the

Dubai World Cup meeting in March when he was told one moment he was in the new combined paper and the next day was told he was out. It was devastating to the popular reporter known to his colleagues as "Barrow" because of his cockney accent.

I will never forget the day when Charlie Brooks rode his own horse *Observe* to victory in the Foxhunters chase at Cheltenham and entered the winner's enclosure shouting "Where's Lester?" Most of us thought he was comparing himself to the world's greatest flat jockey Mr Piggott. In fact he was looking for my friend Geoff who had been less than complimentary about his riding style in his race preview in the *Life*.

Geoff made a good living working for Satellite Information Systems, the short-lived racing paper *The Sportsman,* and for the *Racing Channel* in subsequent years. But it was a cruel way to end the career of a man who lived, ate, and breathed the *Sporting Life* for which he was proud to be the Senior Reporter.

Tim Richards had been on the *Racing Post* from day one in April 1986. He was marginally less shocked to lose his job than Geoff. And he very quickly picked up work on *Horse & Hound, The Weekender, The Sunday Times, Pacemaker,* and *Owner & Breeder* magazine. Talented Tim was never going to be out of work but as the new millennium progresses the world of the freelancer becomes more and more financially hazardous.

In 1999 The Queen decided to sell her *West Ilsley* stables where the introduction of Lord Huntingdon to replace Dick Hern had not really worked. Huntingdon – the old joke was that he was a much better trainer than William Hastings-Bass even though they were one and the same person – could not fill all the hundred and twenty boxes. The terms of the lease meant that he had to refurbish and repaint the yard regularly and the maths didn't add up, so he resigned. He said that he wanted to travel the world while young enough to do so.

In a parable of our times the yard was purchased for in excess of £2 million by none other than Mick Channon, the centre forward who played for England forty-six times and was celebrated for his windmill-like rotation of his right arm whenever he scored a goal. He was born the same week in 1948 as Prince Charles. Would Mick now be tilting at windmills?

The difference was that the birth of Jack and Bet Channon's son Michael was in the two-bedroomed council house in Orcheston, Wiltshire, and instead of the finest champagne and christening cake for the assembled royal dynasties of Europe, their celebration was limited to a pint of stout and a cup of tea. The odds of the Queen and Michael ever meeting were quite long. That Mick should buy the Royal stables fifty years after his birth defied logic and imagination. He had left Amesbury secondary modern school without an O level and although he was a football international he had never earned more than £1,000 a week, having retired before the era of the multi-millionaire players.

With the stables came an eight-bedroomed mansion, a dozen cottages for staff and three hundred acres of rolling Berkshire Downs. Mick told me, "As soon as I saw the house and stables, I had to have it. It's so warm and welcoming; it's a bit unique being so private. I feel very fortunate to be buying it. It's far too much for me and not enough for Her Majesty – that's the best way I can put it. I've met the Queen on a few occasions. My wife Jill and I were fortunate enough to be invited to lunch at Windsor Castle and to drive by carriage up the Ascot straight at the Royal meeting in 1996."

Mick has made a great success of training at West Ilsley and although he hasn't added to the stable's tally of twenty-six Classic winners (including Derby winners *Troy, Henbit,* and *Nashwan*), he came close and retains a yard full of potential. His colt *Youmzain* was three times runner-up in the prestigious Prix de L'Arc de Triomphe at Longchamp from 2007-9.

Jenny Pitman used the amphitheatre that is Cheltenham to announce her retirement as a trainer. She handed over to her former jockey son Mark. It takes quite a moment for the launch of the great three-day jumping festival to be upstaged but the former stable girl from Hoby, Leicestershire, managed it with a tearful announcement to the crowd.

Some feared that the thyroid cancer she had suffered a year before had returned but she assured those present this was not the case. She wanted to travel the world with her husband and partner David Stait and to try her hand at writing novels. She's achieved both ambitions. The Queen of Aintree who also won the Cheltenham Gold Cup with *Burrough Hill Lad* in 1984 and *Garrison Savannah* in 1991 brought to an end a remarkable career in which she had broken records as a woman trainer.

I got wind of her announcement at the Kempton meeting four days earlier and tackled Mark Pitman about it. He said nothing and ran for cover with his mobile phone firmly attached to his ear. That evening I received a phone call from an irate Jenny threatening me with a libel action if I went into print because it wasn't true. It nearly cost me my job, as sports editor Bryan Cooney, who liked to bully his staff, was unforgiving at my failure to land this scoop.

See More Business, so unlucky in 1998 when forced out of the race by the injured *Cyborgo*, causing a major spat between Paul Nicholls and the latter's trainer Martin Pipe, made amends with a game victory over *Go Ballistic* in the Gold Cup. This gave Nicholls, the rising star of the training ranks, a brilliant Cheltenham treble initiated by *Flagship Uberalles* in the Arkle chase and *Call Equiname* in the Queen Mother Champion chase.

It had been owner Paul Barber's childhood ambition to milk a thousand cows and own the winner of the Cheltenham Gold Cup. He had long since achieved the first of those goals, but the Blue

Riband of chasing was his principal joy. Barber owned the Ditcheat yard where Nicholls was starting to make a big name for himself, so it was doubly satisfying.

Barber, a big cheese manufacturer, told me, "I was devastated last year with the horse being taken out of the race in the most extraordinary manner. For Nicholls to get him back is quite fantastic."

Sports editor Bryan Cooney who had come to the *Daily Mail* from the *Sun*, loved signing up big sports names and for this reason I was to "ghost" a column for Kieren Fallon, by now champion jockey and the retained rider for Henry Cecil. Fallon was in his third season riding for the Master of Warren Place and the idea was to write daily at the big meetings and once a week during the quieter times.

We began rather badly when Fallon told me that three of Cecil's fancied runners would need their races at the big Craven meeting. Trouble emerged when all three won and the jockey thought it was a bit of a joke to mislead our readers. I read him the riot act and the relationship went downhill from there.

I arranged to meet Fallon outside the weighing room at a particular time and he kept me waiting, claiming a need to be in the sauna to lose weight. As he was being paid handsomely for his views, I was increasingly exasperated at his intransigence. Meanwhile he won the 1,000 Guineas on *Wince*, the Oaks on *Ramruma,* and the Derby on *Oath* – all for Henry Cecil.

I stayed as loyal to Fallon as I could in the face of these successes, all the while wishing I had had the same deal as Brough Scott did with Lester Piggott in 1970 when writing for the *Evening Standard.* Brough was having a terrible time locating Piggott for his views when one day the maestro told him, "Why don't you just make it up – you know what I think."

All hell broke loose during the Glorious Goodwood meeting when Fallon was summarily sacked by Henry Cecil. The great jockey had switched off his mobile phone so I couldn't reach him. Luckily, I got hold of the charming Cecil who confirmed that Fallon would no longer be stable jockey. He didn't elaborate further but it became apparent later on that he mistakenly thought Fallon was having an affair with his wife Natalie.

On the Thursday of Glorious Goodwood, Fallon remained pretty unavailable to his new paymasters, calling the whole press pack parasites. And that from the man who was being handsomely rewarded every day he spoke to me! We recovered some equilibrium later on and by September that year Fallon had been signed up as Sir Michael Stoute's retained rider.

It was an object lesson in dealing with a high profile sportsman. Maybe I was the wrong person to be speaking to Fallon, although I tried to help him with sponsorship negotiations and other matters when he was at the Jockey Club dealing with a disciplinary matter. Revenge is a dish best served cold, they say, and it would be another eight years before I was able to score a winning goal against the six times champion jockey.

In December, Fallon issued a High Court writ against Henry Cecil claiming that, following his sacking in July that year, he had not been paid the remainder of his retainer (believed to be £12,000) or his stallion share for winning the Derby on *Oath*. He was also claiming for two fines of £1,000 and £1,500 when *Oath* broke the parade at Epsom and at Royal Ascot. Eventually the matter was settled out of court with the jockey believed to have accepted £250,000.

The millennium ended on a controversial note when yet again the IRA chose a big racing occasion to promote their evil. Within minutes of *See More Business* landing his second King George

VI chase at Kempton Park's Boxing Day meeting, a coded telephone call caused the meeting to be abandoned.

Instead of celebrating Paul Nicholls' chaser's seventeen lengths win (the greatest distance since *Mill House's* 20l demolition in 1963), the 20,000-strong crowd were urged to leave the Sunbury racecourse in an orderly fashion. Stewards had taken a calculated gamble to let the big race be run even though a man with an Ulster accent representing an IRA splinter group had earlier rung the track with his threat.

There was deep frustration, not least from the Irish-born winning jockey Mick Fitzgerald whose celebrations were cruelly cut short. He was unbeaten on the winner. His boss Nicky Henderson, Kempton's greatest supporter, said, "Everyone here is trying to put on a show and it's been wrecked with one irresponsible phone call."

14.

The doping scandals

The name Brian Wright would come to haunt those in charge of racing's integrity and security. From 1985 onwards it became clear that his fingerprints were all over racing's biggest doping and corruption scandals and his influence would extend, like the tributaries of a poisonous blood stream, to every corner of the sport.

To the weighing room – especially to jump jockeys – he was known as "Uncle" or "The Milkman" because he always delivered – money, presents, holidays abroad, and cocaine to his customers. He entertained in *Annabel's* and *Tramp,* the two most fashionable nightclubs in London. One jockey was so grateful that he thought he'd buy his round and was shocked to learn that the pink fizz he had been guzzling was £150 a bottle.

Wright always had cash on him and he loved to splash it around. He was popular with jockeys and with one notable exception (Dermot Browne) he maintained friendships with most of the top jump jockeys. He relied upon inside information gleaned from jockeys and claimed a lot of success as a punter, but it was increasingly difficult to get his bets on because bookies were running scared.

A more likely scenario is that he was not nearly as adept as he claimed which is why he suborned Dermot Browne into doping at least twenty-three horses to lose – often in high profile races. He had them injected with acetylpromazine (ACP), a drug used to tranquilise horses in transit or when they are going out to grass for a summer break. It caused racehorses to be drowsy and fail to give their running.

Browne claims, in Richard Griffiths' excellent book *Racing in the Dock*, that he was frogmarched from Goodwood with a gun to his head by members of Wright's gang to a swanky West London hotel where Wright offered him £10,000 to start doping horses. He claims he had little option as he was trying desperately to get his nascent training operation going in Lambourn.

Dermot, son of the much-respected Irish trainer Liam Browne, had been a decent amateur rider for Tony and Michael Dickinson in Yorkshire. He was champion amateur rider twice in the 81/82 and 82/83 jump seasons. He was part of Michael's team of magnificent five (the first five home in the 1983 Cheltenham Gold Cup), finishing fifth on *Ashley House*. Famously the race was won by Graham Bradley on *Bregawn*.

Browne had also been the subject of much anger among punters when he rode *Browne's Gazette*, 4-6 favourite for the 1985 Champion Hurdle. The horse darted around and was facing backwards when the starter let them go. It was a hopeless task to win the race after he lost nearly twenty lengths, but many believed Dermot had been bribed to lose the race. A subsequent Jockey Club enquiry cleared him of blame however.

But he had weight worries and once Michael Dickinson decided to train on the flat at Manton in Wiltshire in 1986, the 5 foot 11 Browne followed him down to base himself in Lambourn, jump racing's headquarters. Graham Bradley, another Dickinson graduate, also moved to Lambourn.

And that's when his troubles began. He was not getting enough rides to sustain a decent income while his reputation was such that many trainers refused to trust him. So he took out a licence to train. To do this successfully a trainer probably needs a minimum of twenty horses just to break even and cover overheads. Browne never had this many horses.

He entered the clutches of Brian Wright and his cronies after a fateful visit to Glorious Goodwood in August 1990 when he was threatened with a gun as he poked his nose into a box where one of Peter Walwyn's horses was being doped to lose. His intention was to seek a lift for a friend back to Lambourn in the Walwyn horsebox. As a licensed trainer he was entitled to be in the racecourse stables; the people in that box were not and Browne was escorted out at gunpoint by one member of the gang and taken to London.

He arrived at the swish Halcyon hotel in Holland Park and was frogmarched to a table in the foyer where he recognised Brian Wright – and that saved his life. Wright immediately indicated to his cronies that they were mates. Browne had provided information to Wright in the previous years as a jockey and he had "stopped" several horses from winning for reward.

Wright, it seemed, was now moving into doping horses because he was fed up with getting erroneous information from jockeys. In other words, some of those he backed to lose were winning while some he was advised to back weren't doing the job. Browne knew that backing horses with ten plus rivals was the road to Carey Street, but apparently Wright had been doing that recently.

He invited Browne to be his officer in charge of doping for a fee of £10,000. And Browne, desperately short of cash to build up his stable and find new owners, agreed. First "victim" was the Peter Walwyn trained *Hateel* in the Glorious Stakes which boasted only four runners. Wright determined that taking out the favourite or second favourite in a field of four would render backing the winner that much easier. Laying the doped horse to lose on the newly emerging Betfair betting exchange would be even easier. But that carried the risk of identifying the punter.

Hateel finished a lifeless third with the second favourite, backed by Wright, winning. Walwyn had his horse tested the following day but nothing showed up and he thought he had just run a lifeless race as did jockey Willie Carson. Wright then went to work, using Browne as his doper, alongside a member of his gang named Alfred who was merely a witness to the needle Browne used to inject his victim.

Absaar, owned like *Hateel* by Sheik Hamdan al Maktoum but trained by Alec Stewart in Newmarket, was the next victim at Windsor in a three horse race in which the Queen owned the odds-on favourite *Once Upon A Time* who duly won by fifteen lengths. Poor *Absaar* looked and ran desperately. But again the dopers got away with it as a post-race test revealed nothing.

Then it was the James Fanshawe trained *Stylish Senor* at Kempton who still managed to finish second to Wright's bet *Sea Level* despite being doped with ACP. Worryingly for Browne, the horse was immediately led off to the testing box for a urine sample. Again nothing came of it. Bookies at Kempton reported that *Sea Level* had been "backed off the boards".

Paul Cole's *Pink Bells* was the next target to be injected with the yellowy green liquid that apparently masked the ACP. Wright's selection *Sandford Springs* duly won the race with poor *Pink Bells* beaten twenty-five lengths in a sprint. Newbury, which was Browne's local racecourse, was the scene of the doping of the Dick Hern trained *Ijtihaad* in the prestigious Geoffrey Freer Stakes. The poor animal finished last of five, fully twenty lengths behind the fourth horse. This was a staying race and indicated to Browne and his fellow gang members that the drug was even more effective over a long trip.

Then *Berillon* was doped at Windsor finishing tenth of thirteen runners behind the 13-8 favourite *Baylis* who had been backed by Wright. *Tyrone Bridge* was doped in the prestigious Lonsdale

Stakes at York, although it's entirely possible that *Chelsea Girl* who won this at 12-1 was not the subject of Wright's financial backing. This may have been one that got away, proving that horses are not machines.

Just seven lined up for the Roses Stakes at York the following day. Second favourite *Silken Sailed* got the treatment allowing hot favourite *Mujadil* to streak home, backed by Wright. The next day *Dayjur's* big rival *Argentum* was doped, exaggerating the distance by which Dick Hern's hot favourite coasted home.

At Ripon there was system failure when Browne doped the wrong horse when he discovered that the Barry Hills-trained *Cameo Performance* who he had doped was not the *Laxey Bay* he should have injected. The problem was that *Cameo Performance* had already won the Virginia Stakes at Newcastle the night before and was merely hitching a lift back to Lambourn in the same horsebox. Wright's fingers were burned.

To try to make up for his error Browne then doped a further four horses at Ripon. You have to wonder where racecourse security was and how any horse managed to finish a race. Then it was Thirsk where *Kasayid*, the 10-11 favourite was the target, leaving Wright's selection *Pipatina*, the 11-8 second favourite, to sluice home by twenty-one lengths. Browne and Wright were not only messing with individual races they were damaging the form book and the whole integrity of racing. It would be another three years before Roger Buffham, the much-maligned head of security, got the go-ahead to introduce CCTV into racecourse stables.

By now Browne reckoned he was owed in excess of £30,000 by Wright. He had even asked Wright to back *Waki Gold*, 4-6 favourite for a five runner race at Redcar, after he had doped the second and third favourites to lose. *Waki Gold* stormed home, providing winning trainer Paul Kelleway with a false form line which made him ambitious enough to fly him to Italy next time out for a listed race. Inevitably the horse finished nowhere as his form was, in reality, moderate. The trouble was Browne never received his money from Wright and the near perfect system was starting to unravel.

But at Leicester a few days later he was able to dope *Claret*, the 4-7 favourite for the Kegworth Stakes in which Henry Cecil had entered *Peter Davies* for his debut. The latter was a 5-1 shot having drifted markedly in the betting, a move which didn't quite accord with Brian Wright's modus operandi. Perhaps he was now betting with the illegal bookmakers so that his investments didn't show up, thought Browne. And he may have been correct.

Then came the St Leger meeting at Doncaster when the Jockey Club's suspicions were raised following a positive dope test from Barry Hills' *Norwich*, 11-4 joint favourite for the Kiveton Park Stakes. *Norwich* had won five races on the bounce already, most recently the Hungerford Stakes at Newbury. Most racegoers in the grandstands thought he would be a warm favourite for the Kiveton Park. *Norwich* finished fourth and Hills was unhappy enough to contact Jockey Club security. The sedative ACP was later to be found in his urine sample.

The following day, *Channel 4's* John McCririck said that the betting "smells down here" as *Bravefoot*, previously unbeaten favourite for the Champagne Stakes, drifted from odds-on to 11-8 against. Not only had Browne doped the horse but some of Wright's cronies had already half completed the job earlier. Because they weren't sure whether or not the horse had been properly sedated, they asked Browne to inject the horse again. In effect the poor horse had a double dose. Despite the misgivings of his connections *Bravefoot* was allowed to run eventually finishing last of the five runners. It was a disaster for Wright however as his fancy *Arakat*, whose odds had contracted from 7-

1 to 15-8 in a welter of bets was beaten by the 8-1 shot *Bog Trotter* who ruined the day for the plotters.

In all, Browne doped twenty-three horses to lose that summer. The tests on *Norwich* and *Bravefoot* returned positive for ACP and the balloon was truly in orbit. How do we know about the details of these criminal comings and goings? Because Dermot Browne was interviewed by police under caution in Dublin in 2000 at the height of the prosecutions and arrests of jockeys and trainers.

Was he telling the truth? This is always an important variable when dealing with Browne. But Richard Griffiths who interviewed him for his book in 2002 after the dust had settled on various trials (but before Brian Wright was finally arrested in Spain in 2005), believes the majority of his story to be true as it checked out when tested against the memories of jockeys such as Willie Carson and some of the trainers.

One of Browne's major assertions, unrelated to the dopings, was that he had offered jump jockey Jamie Osborne £20,000 to stop horses on behalf of Brian Wright. He claimed that Osborne in fact wanted another £10,000 to stop the last two favourites at the 1985 Cheltenham Festival.

In evidence at the trial of former police officer Bob Harrington at the Old Bailey in January 2000, Osborne admitted that this offer was made. He said in evidence, "I was offered £20,000 when I was nineteen to stop the last two favourites at the Cheltenham Festival. The probable name behind it was Brian Wright. I know where he lives but never met him. I didn't take it and I've never been asked since, on my life. I had a £5,000 overdraft and didn't sleep all night, but I decided in the morning that I was not going to ruin my name to go hooky." When asked by defence counsel Richard Ferguson QC who offered him the money Osborne replied, "A fella called Dermot Browne."

It was after this court exchange that Browne, via Richard Griffiths, contacted Ferguson to confirm the offer and to claim that Osborne wanted another £10,000 to stop the horses. Two years later Browne was sticking to his version of this episode which Osborne had so clearly denied. Osborne did admit, however, that the offer had the finger prints of Brian Wright all over it. He told Ferguson, "There were a lot of stories going around about things that were going on with racing. That man (Wright) was linked to a lot of them."

Later at the trial in 2001 at Winchester of former jump jockey Barrie Wright (no relation of Brian) for dealing cocaine (for which he was found not guilty), Graham Bradley made an extraordinary assertion when giving evidence as a character witness for Barrie. But he was talking about "his good friend" Brian Wright. His words alerted the Jockey Club's security department to a tangible link between Brian Wright and the weighing room.

Bradley, who met the cocaine king through Barrie Wright, said in court, "He was very knowledgeable, very intelligent, very affable. He was a very good-looking guy, just generally helpful, kind, nice, and generous. I couldn't say a bad word about him and anybody I've ever met has said the same. He would always be seen with a large roll of notes – big enough to choke a donkey."

Bradley admitted to regularly exchanging information with Brian Wright and with members of his gang who all had his phone number in their diaries. He admitted to having received some presents from Wright and some flights – especially to Spain where jump jockeys joined him at the Sotogrande golf course. Bradley agreed, "He was expecting privileged information, yes."

As at least eight of the top jump jockeys were at the Sotogrande golf tournament, Bradley must have known that his evidence was dynamite to Roger Buffham and Co who had always maintained there was endemic corruption at the heart of racing. As for Bradley he naively thought he was helping an old friend (Barrie Wright) with this evidence which was given at a time when he had stopped riding. Maybe he hadn't thought of further consequences which would eventually lead to a five year ban from racing.

Much of the evidence given at Barrie Wright's trial was held in camera until after the trial of Brian Wright junior and others was completed at Woolwich in 2002. Their principal defence to the charges of smuggling cocaine was that they were all punters who derived their bundles of cash from betting. Wright junior was sentenced to sixteen years and the whole gang received in excess of two hundred years in prison for drug smuggling.

Brian Wright senior removed himself to Northern Cyprus where there were no extradition arrangements with the UK following the arrest of his son in 1999. In September 2002 at the conclusion of all the trials when evidence could now be revealed, he gave an extraordinary interview to the *News of the World* in which he said, "I ran a huge operation and had a string of jockeys giving me vital information. If I needed a rider to win or lose a race, he did. If I wanted to fix a race, I could."

If only half of what Wright claimed was true there was certainly something rotten at the core of racing over the period 1985 to 2000. One way or another his actions led to the arrests of jockeys Ray Cochrane, Graham Bradley, Barrie Wright, Dean Gallagher, Jamie Osborne, Leighton Aspell, and trainer Charlie Brooks. All were eventually cleared and released, although Gallagher's bail extended to fourteen months causing the rider much hardship.

Wright senior was finally caught and arrested after sneaking back into Spain in 2005. Believed to be the mastermind behind the smuggling and importation of £1 billion worth of drugs he was sentenced to thirty years, the same term as the Great Train Robbers received. He was released in April 2020 on licence and ironically his ban from racecourses expires in 2023 when theoretically he can place his fingerprints on the winning post of the Derby at Epsom again.

There was another doping trial I attended at Southwark Crown Court in 2000. Apart from the professional need to be there, I had been asked about the machinations of the betting and gaming industries by none other than the Judge in the case, Christopher Elwen. He was an acquaintance and neighbour of mine in Ealing and I invited him to dinner with the likes of Wally Pyrah of *Sporting Index* so that he could comprehend more fully the intricacies of betting.

If only the police who gave evidence at Southwark had had the benefit of studying the complexities of gaming, the prosecution case might have had more chance of success. In the end the case collapsed after only two of its expected four weeks had elapsed. The police were made to look foolish by defence counsel who included well known racehorse owners and QCs Jeremy Gompertz and John Kelsey-Fry, not to mention the late commentator Raleigh Gilbert's brother Francis.

The case involved the doping in 1997 of jumpers *Avanti Express* at Exeter and *Lively Knight* at Plumpton. In the dock were five men – Ray Butler, 52, from Cricklewood; Glen Gill, 33, from Fareham; Jason Moore, 30, from Woodford Green; Adam Hodgson, 38, from Slough; and John Matthews, 36, also from Slough.

Prosecution counsel Richard Whittam, a late substitute for a more experienced QC told the jury that ACP was found at Butler's flat together with two syringes and three hypodermic needles. Asked about the syringes Butler said they were used to keep greyhounds quiet in transit from Ireland. He failed to answer the question when it was pointed out the syringes were purchased in Kilburn.

Whittam admitted there was no evidence these syringes had been used on *Avanti Express* or *Lively Knight*, especially as they were found ten months after the doping of the two jumpers. Then the betting habits of the men were analysed and this is where DC Kelly, the police officer leading the case for the prosecution, revealed his ignorance of turf matters and of betting in particular.

Cross-examined by Gill's QC Jeremy Gompertz, Kelly admitted being "a bit green" on the subject. In particular he could not understand why a punter would back against a 1-7 shot (*Lively Knight*). "Do you accept that, as a rational punter, opposing the odds-on favourite is a reasonable thing to do?" Gompertz asked Kelly. "No."

"Do you realise that if you are constantly backing horses at 1-7 to compensate for one loser you have to have seven winners? That's your idea of sensible betting?"

Kelly said, "If the bookmakers made the horse 1-7, they must have thought it was going to win."

Gompertz, who had kept a record of all odds-on shots for a month, had found that a £10 stake on all of them would have yielded a net loss of £96.32. "Automatically backing odds-on shots is the road to perdition, isn't it?" he pointed out to the hapless Kelly. "Possibly," replied Kelly. "But it's not something I would know and that's why I could not understand Mr Gill."

The case was disappearing faster than *Dayjur* up the York straight, and after only six full days of evidence the Judge stepped in to call off the unequal struggle by telling the jury, "Central to the charge of conspiracy is the idea that the defendants were in some way involved in the doping, or arranged for horses to be doped. My conclusion is that there is no evidence from which you can infer that part of the plot took place."

It was a massive setback for the Jockey Club. Lack of police expertise destroyed three years hard work which included a lot of CCTV evidence from both Exeter and Plumpton. The only action they could take in the end was to ban three of the men indefinitely from British racecourses – they were Ray Butler, Adam Hodgson and John Matthews. The case cost the taxpayer over £500,000.

Lastly, we can look at the *Man Mood* case which involved trainer Charlie Brooks and jockey Graham Bradley at Warwick racecourse on November 5 1996 and caused fireworks. The horse started 4-7 favourite in a two horse race (after the paper favourite *Mine's An Ace* was withdrawn). *Man Mood* who had a history of wind problems was pulled up by Bradley with six fences to go after the chaser choked. This left Kim Bailey's *Drumstick* to win as the only finisher.

What got Brooks into trouble was his advice to *Man Mood's* owner Julian Robbins that he place a saver bet of £500 on *Drumstick* on the perfectly logical grounds of balancing his books in a two horse race. After all, he stood to win £4,000 if the horse won which would have been preferable. Even though Brooks was interviewed by the Warwick stewards after the race, revealing *Man Mood's* history of wind problems, and even though his explanation was accepted, he was subsequently arrested. The police clearly did not realise that *Man Mood* ran another fourteen times after this race and never won again.

As for Bradley, he was charged with conspiracy to defraud on April 14 1999 over the *Man Mood* case. Shortly afterwards the Yorkshireman attended a hearing by three Jockey Club stewards at Portman Square. They determined that Bradley should have his licence to ride removed. Meanwhile they would pay him

£29,000 a year, the amount he would have received had he been injured.

Bradley consulted Brian Wright who recommended that he use the legal firm of Law Mooney, and Wright would pick up the bill. Paul Rexstrew of this firm must have done a good job because in less than seven weeks all charges against the jockey were dropped on the grounds of insufficient evidence. It was party time for one of the most popular jockeys in the weighing room who would bow out of racing on his own terms later that year by retiring from the saddle.

What this case had demonstrated was that bookmakers – and William Hill in particular – had traditionally refused to open their ledgers to reveal who had bet on which horse. Without this evidence it was extremely hard for the police – or even the Jockey Club – to prove that a crime had taken place.

Whatever subsequent generations of punters and stewards might think, the arrival of Betfair, the betting exchange, altered all that. The company which now dominates the markets (no racecourse bookie is without his lap top to enlighten him to the realistic Betfair odds of horses these days) agreed to open up its books to inspection. They have willingly and tellingly uncovered corruption – especially when horses are laid to lose. The average punter needs a deal of skill to show a profit by backing winners. It is far easier to back a certain loser if you know the horse has been doped or stopped by the jockey.

It would be naïve of me to suggest that all of racing's ills have been successfully laundered in the current era. Month in and month out there are cases of non-triers. In the vast majority of cases it is because the horse needs the run, is unsuited by the track, and/or prefers different going. But jockeys are not immune to giving a horse an "easy" if the trainer so wishes.

Corruption – on the scale employed by Brian Wright and his associates between 1985 and 2000 – has been largely eradicated. As a part time tennis correspondent in my retirement, I receive regular emails from the Tennis Integrity Unit which reveal that around twelve tennis players every year are banned for corruption. The majority are players in the lower echelons, ranked under 150 in the world. But they have lost matches for reward and are handed bans of eighteen months plus. If that level of corruption existed among jockeys, racing would not be able to continue as a viable sport.

New systems and regulations have done much to end corruption among jockeys. There is better education for apprentices, warning them about associating with the wrong people. CCTV and television cameras, together with more vigilant stewarding and a pro-active press, ensure that "bent" races are relatively rare. Without this, punters would seek their adrenalin rushes elsewhere and the sport which relies so heavily on betting turnover for its survival would die on the vine.

15.

Fergie, Fallon & the final furlongs

Millennium celebrations were completed when our computers survived the entry into the 21st century. Scaremongers – aka geeks – had suggested that the world's ether would not survive this mathematical journey for reasons above my pay grade. But there were no worries.

Sheik Mohammed had taken the potentially ambitious decision to call his finest thoroughbred *Dubai Millennium* to coincide with the dawn of the new century and victory in the world's richest race, the Dubai World Cup. The imposing colt had run in the 1999 Derby at Epsom where, having become coltish in the paddock and disliking the firm going, he manifestly failed to stay the stiff mile and a half distance. It was his only career defeat.

For trainer Saeed Bin Suroor, still proving himself to his boss, it was an important goal to demonstrate that *Dubai Millennium* was a special colt who would light up the sky as dusk enveloped Nad al Sheba on that March evening in 2000. Frankie Dettori was poised to deliver a mind-boggling display of speed and stamina which would be a signature for the nation of Dubai as it entered the 21st century.

The horse didn't disappoint. He shot into a fifteen length lead from the stalls and it appeared from the grandstands that he had taken charge of his jockey. But Dettori had matters in hand and having given him a breather turning out of the far straight, the colt lengthened again to stretch away from two top American colts, *Seeking The Gold* and *Public Purse*. There was no gainsaying the pride on the Sheik's face as he led in his magnificent horse.

It was a huge tragedy for the Sheik's breeding operation when the colt died from grass sickness after only one season at Dalham Hall stud, denying him the chance to prove that he could become a great stallion. Having said that, his one crop produced the 2005 Irish 2,000 Guineas and Prix Jacques Le Marois winner *Dubawi* who has gone on to terrific success as a prepotent stallion.

His performance that night in the Dubai desert matched some of the greatest I have seen in my lifetime – and they include *Sea Bird's* extraordinary win in the 1965 Arc, *Secretariat's* annihilation of his field in the 1973 Belmont Stakes, and *Frankel's* wonderful win in the Juddmonte International in 2012 before an enthralled and knowledgeable York crowd.

Looks Like Trouble won the 2000 Cheltenham Gold Cup outstaying *Florida Pearl* and *Strong Promise* with Richard Johnson providing his future father-in-law Noel Chance with a second such winner in three years. In 1997 Chance won the race with *Mr Mulligan* partnered by the man who was to become Johnson's nemesis, Tony McCoy. Johnson was runner-up in the jump jockey's championship sixteen times before McCoy retired and effectively gifted the title to his younger rival.

For Chance this was a huge achievement. The Irishman established himself in Lambourn, but seldom had more than forty or fifty horses in his yard. Very likeable, he was able to set up touches, especially in bumper races, so that his owners could try and balance the books. It was a shock when he retired far too young in 2013 aged only sixty-one.

I received a shock phone call in the middle of the night on April 23, 2001, to tell me that my father Gordon had been involved in a fatal car accident in his home town of Aracatuba. He was about to celebrate his ninetieth birthday with a tennis tournament in his honour as a founder member of the Aracatuba Clube. Luckily there were no other fatalities as it emerged that my father had inadvertently traversed a red traffic light.

His funeral was held within twenty-four hours, as is the custom in Brazil, with the result that I could not get there. More than two thousand people paid their respects in the Catholic church, even though he himself was not a Roman Catholic. In a unique ceremony three years earlier, he had been given the freedom of Aracatuba as a pioneer of the town. He was much loved and respected by the locals and his sudden death was the front page splash in the town's two newspapers.

It would be another eleven years before I was able to visit Brazil again to see his grave. He was always a loving but distant influence on my life. I adored seeing him whenever he came home on leave and my holidays with him in Brazil were treasured experiences. He was in the UK for my daughter Tara's 1995 wedding to Rupert Lecomber and I had last seen him in 1998 when I took Linda to Brazil for the first time. We played some tennis (he was still a five-times-a-week man at ninety) and visited the magical Pantanal, a wetland the size of France that bordered Bolivia, with wild life such as jaguars, capybaras, and caiman, not to mention jabiru storks with wingspans wider than spitfires.

Another popular Irishman John Oxx was to have his day in the sun when *Sinndar* won the Derby. A fine horse owned by the Aga Khan, *Sinndar* never won by too far. But he had loads of class and scope and won the Irish Derby, and in October the Prix de L'Arc de Triomphe where as usual he was ridden by Johnny Murtagh. Oxx, who would later lose the patronage of the Aga Khan, was generous with his time and I enjoyed going to his yard at The Curragh.

Foot and mouth disease caused the cancellation of the Cheltenham Festival in 2001. It was set to go ahead despite the discovery of the disease in sheep on February 19 in Essex until only five days before the start of racing's annual orgy of top class jumping. But just as hopes were rising a local farmer's sheep strayed onto the hallowed Prestbury Park turf and Supremo Edward Gillespie had to call the meeting off.

I was lucky enough to telephone Edward at 9pm that night just as he made his decision and therefore got the story into the first edition which went to Ireland to alert the ten thousand racing fans that they wouldn't be spending St Patrick's Day in Gloucestershire. It was bad luck for JP McManus who had hoped his *Istabraq* would register a fourth consecutive Champion Hurdle, a feat never achieved since the meeting began in 1922. *Istabraq's* trainer Aidan O'Brien meanwhile had other things on his mind.

In March 2001 the British racing press were invited to what would become an annual pre-season tour of the magnificent Ballydoyle stables in Co Tipperary where Ireland's wunderkind Aidan O'Brien was training for the Coolmore Stud syndicate of John Magnier and Michael Tabor. The third member of the triumvirate, Derrick Smith, would join later.

Aidan, a former champion amateur rider, had trained as an assistant under the astute Jim Bolger, and had held a trainer's licence since 1993. He was appointed the Master of Ballydoyle following the retirement of the great Vincent O'Brien in 1996. The latter, who practically wrote the bible on how to train, would be a hard act to follow. But the self-effacing and ultra modest Aidan somehow managed it.

He always addressed me as Colum and I was grateful he remembered my name until during my retirement season in 2008 some wretched hack finally volunteered to Aidan that my name was Colin. Poor Aidan was unnecessarily embarrassed, as was I, and later I tore into my colleague for being so ungracious.

In 2001 Aidan was nurturing an unusually talented bunch of potential Classic winners. But even he could not control his excitement when he mentioned *Urban Sea's* son *Galileo*. It's out of character for Aidan to go overboard about any horse before the season has commenced but this beautifully bred son of *Sadler's Wells* (out of the Arc winner) couldn't wipe the smile off his face. Those of us who knew him quite well by then realised we were getting a preview of a special colt.

And so it turned out, as *Galileo* beat *Golan* and *Tobougg* in the Epsom Classic. He went on to complete the same mid season treble as *Generous* had a decade earlier by adding the Irish Derby and the King George VI and Queen Elizabeth Stakes at Ascot to his winning roster. In the latter he mastered Godolphin's two years older *Fantastic Light* in a tremendous finish only for the latter to gain his revenge three months later at the Curragh in the Irish Champion Stakes.

Galileo's true worth to his owners would emerge over the next two decades after he sired Derby winner after Derby winner plus many other Group One winners. He has now outstripped his own father, *Sadler's Wells,* as Ireland's pre-eminent stallion of all time. That Aidan had recognised his potential so early on demonstrates what a true horseman he is. *Galileo*, now twenty-two, stands at upwards of 400,000 euros (if you can get a nomination to him for your mare). And he shows little sign of faltering as the dominant stallion of his era. He has been champion sire for eleven of the last twelve years, responsible for no fewer than eighty-four Group One winners.

Red Marauder's slog through the mud at Aintree to post a 33-1 Grand National victory was controversial. For a start it was a record slow time, the only time the race has taken in excess of eleven minutes due to the heavy going. Secondly the Richard Guest ridden winner was one of only four finishers (of which two were remounted). This was quite unacceptable whether you were an animal rights activist or just a plain racing fan.

This race began the serious debate to modify the fences to ensure the race was fairer and less dangerous for the participants. From 2000 to 2012 there had been eleven fatalities in the race but, since 2012, there have been none, which says much for the intervention of the RSPCA and for the amendments that have been made to fences. Becher's Brook in particular caught out some horses because the landing side was more than three feet lower than the take off.

Roger Buffham's sacking as the Jockey Club's security chief surprised few in August 2001. Even among the hierarchy at the Jockey Club – and especially among his thirty colleagues in the security department – he'd have struggled to muster a bus fare home had he needed to borrow cash from them. One of the allegations against him was that he had sexually harassed a female colleague in 1993. She continued to work for him until his sacking, which at the time was seen to undermine her complaint. There was also a complaint about his management style.

On his departure, Buffham claimed to have received £50,000 in compensation together with a full and flattering reference. He returned to his native Lincolnshire where he was able to continue in his role as a Grantham magistrate, having satisfied the Lord Chancellor's office of his probity.

But he harboured a major grudge against his former employers who were forced to the High Court to take out an injunction preventing him from assisting the *BBC's Panorama* team who were making a programme about corruption in racing. He was also helping a rival programme called *Kenyon Confronts* which was on a similar mission to discredit the sport.

According to the Jockey Club, on his departure Buffham had signed a confidentiality agreement which prevented him from assisting these two programmes. This hadn't stopped him from making the producers of these two programmes aware of previous enquiries into corruption and to the fact that the Jockey Club was sitting on its hands.

He agreed to meet his Jockey Club Security successor, Major-General Jeremy Phipps, in the *Tapster's* wine bar, Victoria, to discuss what he had said. Phipps, a former SAS soldier who had taken part in the raid on the Iranian embassy in 1979, was tasked with warning Buffham about assisting the television people. Buffham had his own agenda, which was to get Phipps to admit that there was a conspiracy of silence and inertia among the Jockey Club hierarchy.

Unwisely, ostensibly to gain Buffham's trust, Phipps was indiscreet about his bosses. Buffham was taping every word he said as he downed his wine. In the transcript of the conversation, later broadcast by *Panorama*, Phipps is heard to say of the evidence given by Graham Bradley at the Barrie Wright trial in Southampton Crown Court, "It's dynamite. Brad's gone and shot his fucking mouth off."

Buffham: "It's pretty horrendous stuff, isn't it?"

Phipps: "It is. And all exactly what you said I'm afraid. I had steward David Oldrey in my office this afternoon. I said why the fuck have you done nothing about this before, apart from the odd warning?"

Buffham: "Nothing's happened?"

Phipps: "Nothing's happened. It's actually the backbone (of the Jockey Club) that is not very strong."

When Phipps was interviewed at Newmarket racecourse, the transcript was played to him live on air. Phipps looked as if he had just walked into a minefield. Only after the Jockey Club's press officer John Maxse led him away did he recover his equilibrium. The poor man resigned from his new post three days later. It's little consolation to Phipps that syndicate manager Henry Ponsonby named his useful flat/hurdles/chase winner *Who Dares Wins* (the SAS motto) after him because he is sired by the stallion *Jeremy*.

Buffham said after both programmes had been broadcast, "After almost ten years in horseracing, I say with some sadness and great disappointment that racing is not as straight as the Jockey Club and others would ask the public to believe it is.

"I believe that racing is institutionally corrupt in some respects and I believe that the Jockey Club falls short in regulation, in having the moral courage and resolve to deal with some of these problems."

The main thrust of *Kenyon Confronts*, hosted by Paul Kenyon, was that horses are "stopped" all the time by jockeys and trainers. Three trainers – Ferdy Murphy, Jamie Osborne and David Wintle – were secretly filmed. Wintle had sold *Seattle Alley* to the Kenyon team for £4,000 as he was "a fiddling horse". He was featured being prepared for a gamble having lost two previous races. When asked about this on camera, Wintle was seen fighting with Kenyon who fell to the ground.

Murphy claimed to Kenyon that he had laid one of his horses to lose on Betfair. His explanation later was that he had told one of his owners that the horse concerned wouldn't act on the changed going at Fakenham and that the owner had laid him to lose.

Osborne told Kenyon he was "prepared to cheat" with his horses and had an in-house jockey prepared to assist in that endeavour. Later Osborne claimed he only said these things because he had his salesman's hat on and thought he was gaining an owner. "Every time I steered them away from this, they steered me back. And as soon as they got what they wanted they left. It was a con. It was a sting."

This may well have been the case, but it painted racing in a very poor light. There is little doubt the Jockey Club beefed up its act after this, appointing former senior police officer Paul Scotney to the role as security chief. The belief was that he would be able to use his expertise as an evidence-gatherer to facilitate prosecutions in the future if the need arose.

As for Buffham, who had been characterised as 'Roger Buffoon' and 'Inspector Clouseau' by racing insiders, the outcome of the Southampton, Woolwich, and Brian Wright senior trials were vindication of his allegations about institutional corruption. In hindsight, I plead guilty as a racing correspondent to a certain level of supine acceptance of the status quo. But I don't believe the Jockey Club were complicit, as he alleges. The fact that members of the Jockey Club owned horses didn't mean they were corrupt or accepting of duplicity. Far from it. But they, like me, did not realise how far Brian Wright's insidious tentacles had spread through the sport until after details of these trials were made public.

Meanwhile at Cheltenham, back on the map after the previous year's foot and mouth outbreak, we were witnessing the start of the *Best Mate* era. He won the first of his three successive Gold Cups to the delight of his trainer Henrietta Knight and her husband Terry Biddlecombe, the former roistering champion jockey. Their handling of *Best Mate*, which was subject to some criticism because he was a rare sighting on the racecourse, was immaculate. And they were such an entertaining double act that they provided wonderful copy fodder for me and my colleagues.

Hewn from an aristocratic pedigree (her younger sister Cece is Lord Vestey's wife), Hen was a former teacher at St Mary's Wantage and had graduated to the point-to-point field where she trained successfully before taking out a full trainer's licence in 1989. Terry, from a Midlands farming background, was on his third marriage, having conquered alcoholism. He called her "The Mare" but it was done with great affection and they were gloriously happy until Terry's untimely death in 2014 aged seventy-two. Not long after Terry's sad demise Hen handed in her trainer's licence but she remains much in demand schooling horses and solving problem jumpers.

In November 2005, *Best Mate* was making his seasonal debut in the Haldon Gold Cup. He had added at least two thousand fans to Exeter's regular mid week gate. But tragically it was to be his last hurrah, as jockey Paul Carberry, sensing something was wrong, pulled him up before the second last fence. Best Mate's huge heart had failed him and he died as Hen reached him to comfort him. Terry meanwhile returned to the grandstands and simply said, "He's gone". It was little consolation to the distraught pair that they won the following race with *Racing Demon*. Terry was in tears while the stoical Hen quoted Dick Hern saying, "When you've got livestock you've got deadstock."

Meanwhile at Newmarket there was a minor shock when Coolmore's No 2 fancy *Rock of Gibraltar* won the 2,000 Guineas from stable companion *Hawk Wing* whose jockey Jamie Spencer steered a lone course down the middle of the track. Time would prove that *Rock of Gibraltar*, who went on to win the Irish 2,000 Guineas and landed seven Group One races in a row, was no mean athlete.

Equally interesting was the fact that Manchester United manager Sir Alex Ferguson was registered as the fifty per cent owner of the colt and in whose colours he ran. The remainder of the colt was owned by John Magnier's wife Sue. Fergie was there for most of his juvenile triumphs the year before and proudly led in *Rock of Gibraltar* when he won at Newmarket. *The Rock* was a fabulous horse to own, but did Fergie really own him?

The Manchester United manager was introduced to John Magnier by Ladbrokes public relations chief Mike Dillon. Dillon was a fanatical Reds supporter and season ticket holder and he also had a warm and friendly relationship with the Coolmore team. Prior to *the Rock*, Fergie had been gifted shares in four less successful animals namely *Heritage Hall, Baker Street, Zentzov,* and *Juniper.* He never paid the training fees or shared in the purchase or sales of these animals, all of whom lost value after being raced.

Magnier, together with JP McManus, had invested £28 million in Manchester United shares. To celebrate this and to cement their friendship, Magnier telephoned Sir Alex one day in August 2001 and offered him a share in *the Rock*. He could either have five per cent of the winnings or a breeding right each year. Having consulted Dillon, Sir Alex rang back and stated he would prefer a breeding right. and "would you thank John and Sue for their tremendous generosity."

Sir Alex paid nothing towards the purchase of the colt nor did he contribute to the training fees or other costs such as transport and jockeys' fees. He believed Coolmore were getting a good deal by utilising his image rights in connection with the horse. All went incredibly well with the colt finishing his career as runner-up to Pascal Bary's *Domedriver* in the 2002 Breeders Cup Mile at Arlington Park, Chicago. He had won no fewer than ten of his thirteen starts, almost all at the highest level. On paper he was worth a King's ransom for breeding purposes.

Magnier, conservatively worth £400 million, believes his word is his bond. Few if any in Ireland have ever challenged that notion without regretting it. But towards the end of 2003 Sir Alex, advised by his son Jason who ran the Elite agency which represented some Man U players, started to take a dim view of the fact that he had neither received any prize money nor any income from breeding rights for the horse he was registered as fifty per cent owner of with the Irish Turf Club.

With every passing victory the ownership of *Rock of Gibraltar* assumed greater significance. But there were ambiguities and obfuscation concerning the precise details of the telephone deal. Poor Mike Dillon, who had introduced the two men, was literally between *the Rock* and a hard place. Furthermore, he didn't know precisely what had been said in that fateful telephone call. But he couldn't really sit on the fence without offending one party or the other. On the other hand, Coolmore was more important to his employers and regretably he had to take this on board. Ferguson was not amused.

Coolmore were under no illusions as to why *the Rock's* ownership was registered as 50-50 – without that technicality the colt could not run in Ferguson's scarlet colours. Furthermore, Ferguson had claimed no prize money or breeding rights from the previous four horses he had shared with them. When *the Rock* beat the Group One record of consecutive wins held by the iconic *Mill Reef* in 1971, Ferguson had played the role of adoring owner to the full. And as the Gimcrack Stakes winner he made the traditional speech at the annual York dinner. His words came to haunt him later. He told the black tie audience, "My deepest gratitude to two friends who are not here – John and Sue Magnier. It is because I have been given the privilege of teaming up with them that I am standing before you this evening. Nobody could be blessed with better partners on the Turf. In my business, togetherness is not just a nice concept that you can take or leave according to your taste. If you don't have it, you're nothing. Selfishness, factionalism, cliquishness – all are death to a football team and I believe their influence can be just as destructive for racing."

Alarm bells started to ring at the Coolmore stud in March 2003 when Fergie telephoned to discuss the possibility of setting up a charitable trust for *the Rock's* earnings. But why would you do this if your earnings were only £45,000 a year (the fee for one breeding share in *Rock of Gibraltar*) they wondered. When Sir Alex was reminded that he had only one stallion share he was deeply unhappy.

Through their Cubic Expressions company, Magnier and McManus had raised their shareholding in Manchester United to twenty-three per cent, worth over £160 million. To placate Sir Alex, Magnier telephoned him in April and made an improved offer. Would Sir Alex like two breeding rights in *the Rock*? When that failed, Magnier made one final offer. As *Rock of Gibraltar* was going to shuttle between Coolmore Ireland and Coolmore in Hunter Valley, New South Wales, would Sir Alex like two northern and two southern hemisphere rights which would provide an annual income of £200,000?

When this was declined, Magnier instructed his Dublin lawyers William Fry to prepare for battle. In effect he told Sir Alex, "See you in court".

Not until November 2003 did the Magniers receive Ferguson's writ. By now Jason Ferguson had been joined by his two brothers Darren and Mark. Between them they had allegedly accumulated a war chest of £500,000 to fight the action. They had instructed the Dublin lawyers LK Shields.

At this point Magnier and McManus were increasing their shareholding in Manchester United up to an eventual maximum of 28.89 per cent. They also engaged a firm of private detectives to unravel the murkier transfer dealings at Old Trafford, specifically those that involved the Elite agency. The Irishmen famously asked ninety-nine key questions of the Manchester

United board about various business deals and transfers such as that of Dutchman Jaap Stam.

Sir Alex, who won a record total of thirteen premiership titles for Manchester United before his 2013 retirement, must have been concerned about his own future at the club as the powerful Irishmen took increasing boardroom control of the Man U franchise.

The case never came to court, as most predicted. In mid 2004 there was an out of court settlement leading to speculation that Sir Alex was invited to walk away for a sum of £2.5 million. My understanding is that the eventual figure was somewhat less than that, but we will never know as both parties signed a non-disclosure agreement.

It was an uncomfortable time for Mike Dillon in particular. Relations with Sir Alex, now a regular on racecourses with his own horses, have cooled. But they maintain civility in public and he is still a season ticket holder at Old Trafford. You can live in Buckinghamshire but you can never take the boy out of Manchester, where he was born and bred and where he began his working life in a Ladbrokes betting shop.

Magnier and McManus – the latter having no part of the *Rock of Gibraltar* saga as he concentrates on owning jumpers – made a huge profit when they sold their shares in Manchester United to American billionaire Malcolm Glazer and his family. Their investment returned them a profit in excess of £200 million. You could argue that no one was a winner, but my feeling is that the Irishmen were definitely the financial beneficiaries, even though eighteen year old *Rock of Gibraltar's* stallion fees have now descended from £45,000 to under £5,000 as he has proved to be no *Galileo* in the breeding shed.

Henry Ponsonby is a jovial character who exudes enthusiasm, bonhomie, and joie de vivre. These are admirable qualities when you're trying to sell shares in racehorses, which is a job he has embraced for the past forty-five years. His white colours with scarlet braces and quartered scarlet and white cap are familiar to regular racegoers in Great Britain.

He is very fond of reminding all those within ear range that his kinsman Sir Henry Ponsonby was Queen Victoria's private secretary. And he claims that during visits to Windsor Castle our dear Queen reminisces about Sir Henry; the Old Salopian has graced the castle salons after taking part in amateur races at Sandown Park's military meeting in March, as jockey and owner. Amazingly, as an amateur rider, he actually won the Barclay's Bank hurdle there in 1985 on *Desert Hero* who must have been as well handicapped as his rider was courageous.

In general, Henry syndicates horses to groups of ten to twelve owners, retaining a share for himself. These days he charges around £300 per month per share plus the purchase price which can vary from £20,000 to as much as £50,000. For example, a ten per cent share in the former would cost an owner £2,000. Amazingly one of his early buys – *Affair of State*, a filly costing only £5,000 – won a sales race in Ireland worth 500,000 euros, still the biggest financial win of his and trainer Mick Channon's career.

Over the years, Henry has had remarkable success with his partnerships, winning around four hundred and fifty races in the last four decades. The aforementioned *Who Dares Wins* is the current star of his team which usually numbers around seventeen horses. He was slow to correct the *Racing Post* who assumed the horse's name meant that he had once adorned the ranks of the Special Air Services himself. He did serve his country with distinction and underwent the necessary square bashing at Catterick barracks when a trooper with the 15th/19th Royal Hussars.

I have had shares in half a dozen horses with Henry over the years – you forget the pain of the losers and treasure the wins. The first decent horse I had was *Fleet Street* in whom I had a share along with Brian Vine and Johnno Spence whose father Christopher had been Senior Steward of the Jockey Club.

Fleet Street began his racing career in Germany. He was sourced by Henry's some time girlfriend Fiona Marner and sent to Nicky Henderson to be trained. He made his debut for us in a modest novice hurdle at Stratford in which there was a Martin Pipe odds-on hotshot. Jockey Marcus Foley was told to hold him up and produce him turning into the straight. He won "doing handsprings," as winning owners like to boast. Maybe we had a good one, we thought.

Next time out he was ridden by Henderson's No 1 jockey Mick Fitzgerald at Newbury in a much better race and carrying a 7lb penalty. Although he ran on strongly, he could manage no better than third place. And so to Taunton in another novice hurdle after Christmas where he beat seventeen others including runner-up *Made In Japan* who went on to win the Triumph hurdle at Cheltenham's Festival meeting two months later.

Fleet Street was rejected by Mick Fitzgerald in favour of a stable companion, so Andrew Tinkler took the ride in the opening Supreme novice hurdle of Cheltenham 2004. The game *Fleet Street* was always prominent among the nineteen runners but was overtaken by *Brave Inca* and *War of Attrition* at the second last hurdle. These two went on to fight out a terrific finish with the former prevailing by a neck. And there, seven lengths back, was our gorgeous chestnut with the splash of white on his face keeping on gamely for third place at 20-1.

I was in the paddock reporting on the race and was ignorant of his placing as the television cameras zoomed in on the first two – so third place, when it was announced, was a wonderful and chest expanding surprise. As *Brave Inca* went on to win the next two Champion hurdles and *War of Attrition* the Gold Cup this was a classy race to savour. *Fleet Street* was the first English-trained horse home.

At Aintree three weeks later, *Fleet Street* again finished third, this time to *Royal Shakespeare*, but injured a foreleg when staying on in his usual game fashion. Unknown to us at the time, this injury, exacerbated by the equine version of MRSA, would keep *Fleet Street* off the track for two and a half years. Others might have given up on him, but he had shown such talent and gameness that we all wanted to persevere.

And it was worth it. Carrying top weight and probably needing the race badly, Mick Fitzgerald galvanised *Fleet Street* to the front in Newbury's Greatwood handicap for a memorable victory. I watched the race at home. Racing UK commentator Eddie Freemantle called it "one of the gamest performances I have ever seen." You can actually see *Fleet Street* blowing up two hurdles out before gulping in air and answering Fitzy's urgings.

Fleet Street was never quite the same horse again, although he won his first novice chase at Leicester with ease and at Kempton's Boxing Day meeting in 2008 won a £50,000 three mile handicap chase which encouraged us to run him in the 2009 Grand National. Andrew Tinkler was on board again at Aintree when he was unseated on the second circuit when still in touch with the leaders. He got loose and sadly he was injured again and we retired him.

Biggin Hill's career was modest in the extreme and featured in Henry Cecil's poorest year (2005) with a licence when he sent out only twelve winners from Warren Place. It was perhaps inevitable after Brian Vine, who like me had bought a share in the Alzao colt, wrote a double page spread in the *Daily Mail* of

December 2005. The article boasted that while the Queen and Sheik Mohammed were still waiting for their first Derby triumph, *Biggin Hill* was going to beat both of them to the victory rostrum at Epsom. Unfortunately, Brian had form in his written appreciation of the thoroughbred as he had written glowingly of *Snaafi Dancer*, the world's most expensive yearling (at $10.2 million in 1983) who was too slow ever to be allowed to run.

As a Ponsonby syndicate horse, *Biggin Hill* was always going to exercise his limbs. But he got progressively slower and his final race was at Haydock in the lowest possible grade, a selling race. He again finished unplaced and had the distinction of being Cecil's final runner in that grade. His previous race was at Warwick where Brian, gamely fighting terminal kidney problems, was present and had his customary £20 each way on the colt. Ten days later my good friend and mentor died. *Biggin Hill* was so named after Henry's Derby runner *Gatwick* was sold to Hong Kong for £295,000 after a successful career in England. Henry liked wartime associations, so it was *Biggin Hill* rather than Heathrow.

The third Ponsonby horse I want to chronicle was altogether of a different mettle to *Biggin Hill*. *The Betchworth Kid* was named after my good self when Ponsonby attended my sixty-fifth birthday celebrations at Ealing cricket ground in February 2007. Determined to get me involved again, Henry promised to name the Tobougg colt *The Betchworth Kid* if I would take a share along with Maurice Manasseh who was also at the party.

The colt was sent to our mutual friend Michael Bell to be trained in Newmarket. I had attended Michael's wedding to Georgina Lillingston at the Hyde Park hotel in 1989. Having forgotten to give them a wedding present I agreed to take a quarter share in *Fitzroy Belle* who, in 1990, proved to be as bad an investment as *Biggin Hill* – a very expensive wedding present! Since then

Michael's training career skyrocketed and he trained the 2005 Derby winner *Motivator* and Classic winners in Italy. Just the man to train us a Derby winner.

The Betchworth Kid won his second race as a two-year-old at Brighton of all places, very easily under a quiet ride from Ted Durcan. The latter apologised for the six-length gap back to Clive Brittain's runner-up and favourite, not realising how easily our colt had won. Bell also expressed some surprise at the ease of the victory, achieved on firm ground which wasn't supposed to suit our horse.

This win resulted in *The Betchworth Kid* having a rather elevated and uncompetitive rating of eighty-five in his subsequent nursery races. He ran well but not fast enough to win again that season. His three-year-old career coincided with my retirement. A slow start to the season got better and better as he won a handicap at Nottingham before taking in the valuable Mallard Stakes handicap at Doncaster at the St Leger meeting in September. Hayley Turner, who was employed by Michael Bell, was given the chance to shine in a top handicap and she didn't let us down, bringing the stocky bay through from the back of the field down the expansive straight at Town Moor to win by three lengths. This was a £50,000 race complete with a large solid silver cup which sits proudly on the bookshelf in my drawing room to this day, thanks to the generosity of my fellow shareholders in the horse.

Hayley, who in 2008 became the first female jockey to register a hundred wins in a season, had a light touch in the saddle. She formed a wonderful partnership thereafter with *The Betchworth Kid* who went on to seven victories and numerous placings in top races achieving a rating of a hundred and five after he was third in the 2009 Goodwood Cup. I was looking forward to attending Glorious Goodwood that year but fate intervened when Ronnie Biggs was released from prison on Goodwood Cup day.

Instead of cheering Hayley home on our 33-1 shot I was completing a lengthy obituary of the Great Train Robber who, it was thought at the time, had been released because he had only days to live. In fact Biggs lived for another four and a half years.

At Ascot in September the bay gelding was fifth of six to *Electrolyser* and the plan was for the four year old to go jumping with Alan King. Some of the partners were not too keen, believing that he didn't have the scope to jump hurdles. As Henry was not at Ascot, I did a spot poll among those there and most agreed he wasn't a potential jumper. This infuriated Henry and we did not speak for two months.

The horse duly went to Alan King and won his opening novice hurdle at Plumpton from the useful *King Edmund*. But he wasn't a natural jumper and he never again won in another eleven races over timber. However he was fourth in the competitive Betfair hurdle in February 2011, beaten just under two lengths by *Recession Proof*. This was the race that was delayed by five days because two horses had died in the Newbury paddock the previous Saturday due to electrocution. It was horrible to witness and the remainder of that card was called off. Legal action by the owners of the dead horses and those unable to run continued for more than a year before compensation was finally offered.

The Betchworth Kid ran sixty-four times, winning seven races and being placed twenty-six times plus several fourth places which yielded prize money. Among his wins were the Further Flight Listed Stakes at Nottingham. His total earnings amounted to £185,000. He was returned to Michael Bell aged seven and rewarded him with a handicap win at Salisbury, partnered by Hayley. We kept him going a season too many, retiring him at the end of 2013, but he was a terrific, fun horse to be involved with.

At the Breeders Cup in Santa Anita, with the wonderful backdrop of the San Gabriel mountains, the biggest danger to the action were the forest fires. Gouges of smoke descended regularly threatening to destroy the annual equine Olympics. But on the day, everything was fine and Sir Michael Stoute's wonderful filly *Islington* burnished her reputation with a comfortable victory in the Filly and Mare Turf ridden by Kieren Fallon whose riding had improved even more under the former's tutelage. Shortly afterwards, *High Chaparral* won the Turf for Aidan O'Brien and Mick Kinane.

Buoyed by this European success – two winners at any Breeders Cup, especially on America's West Coast, was considered a good return – I made my way to the Melbourne Cup where it was hoped there might be more European joy following *Media Puzzle's* victory in 2002 for Dermot Weld. Weld, of course, had broken the mould of antipodean domination of the race when *Vintage Crop* won in 1993.

Melbourne was abuzz, not only with the race that stops a nation, but also with the Rugby World Cup which the city was hosting. In the run-up to the big race I was able to get a ticket for the Ireland-Australia game in which the hosts scraped a 17-16 win. I use the word scrape advisedly because the *Daily Telegraph's* Aussie Jim McGrath had secured me entry to the game.

It was Jim who revolutionised racecourse commentary in Britain when he arrived from Australia via Hong Kong in 1986. I remember him describing a chase at Ascot with the words "Professor Plum is scraping the paint as he makes headway into the straight". This meant that his jockey had taken the shortest route against the running rails. That phrase became part of the commentators' vernacular and was ruthlessly copied by locally bred talent.

The Cup was a disappointment for the visitors but it marked a very striking winner in *Makybe Diva*, a filly who went on to win the race for three consecutive years. She was outstanding and holds a place in every Australian racing fan's heart. The nearest European finisher was the useful stayer *Jardine's Lookout*, trained by Alan Jarvis, who ran on to be third.

I watched the race from Robert Sangster's private box. He had spotted me earlier in the day in the crowd and extended an immediate invitation to lunch which was typically generous. Robert was still a huge player in the racing game although financially he was being outpaced by the new Coolmore team and the Dubai billionaire sheiks. I didn't appreciate how little time Robert had left; tragically he died from pancreatic cancer only five months later aged only sixty-seven.

The late *BBC* commentator Julian Wilson commented of this giant of the racing game, "His pleasures were boxing, champagne, golf, racing, and beautiful women, and often more than one at the same time."

Robert inherited his money from his father who created the pools company Vernons. He teamed up with the legendary Irish trainer Vincent O'Brien and it was their foresight that engineered the purchase of *Northern Dancer's* progeny. They then raced them with the idea of creating viable stallions. This is the philosophy that makes the Coolmore stud tick to this day. As Robert's finances dwindled, he sold some of his best progeny to Sheik Mohammed and then sold his share in Coolmore to John Magnier.

I was able to be at his well-attended memorial service at St Paul's Knightsbridge where my namesake, the cricketer Colin Ingleby-Mackenzie, gave the address. Colin, who played his cricket in the manner that Robert enjoyed his racing, was hilarious and fun. It was doubly sad that he should also go to that pavilion in the sky too soon just twenty-two months later. No more would Ladbrokes confuse our identities by sending me his losing bets, which included backing six horses in one race. That was the year he memorably said, having lost on the previous twenty-three races that week, "This is what I'd call a character-forming exercise!"

When Colin was asked how, as Captain in 1961, he managed to transform a journeyman Hampshire cricket team from also-rans to their first County Championship he remarked, "Iron fisted dictatorship. I absolutely insisted that they got to bed before breakfast."

Azertyuiop – supposedly the top line on a computer keyboard – may have been a commentator's nightmare but he was a very talented chaser who landed the Queen Mother Champion chase in 2004 for the rising team of trainer Paul Nicholls and jockey Ruby Walsh. John Hales, the man responsible for inflicting the *Teletubbies* on an unsuspecting younger generation, was the owner.

Paul Nicholls was that rarity, a good jockey who became a better trainer. He was probably too big at six foot and a natural twelve stone to make a huge success of riding. But he had some notable wins to his name on *Playschool* (Welsh National) and *Broadheath* who won the Hennessy Gold Cup. Regular struggles with his weight (he now tops seventeen stone) meant he packed in his riding licence early to become a trainer in 1991, aged only twenty-nine. He was recruited by owner Paul Barber to take over his Ditcheat yard, Somerset, where Jim Old had been training.

Barber's enthusiasm and Nicholls' ambition matched perfectly and they soon became a formidable partnership able to rival champion trainer Martin Pipe. Nicholls was open and very straightforward with the racing press which made him a popular go-to trainer when anything needed to be said or written about.

He realised that getting the fourth estate on side would help boost his business.

Every penny Nicholls made from his early successes was invested in bettering facilities at Manor Farm stables, Ditcheat, a little hamlet seven miles from Shepton Mallet. New gallops, new barns, and most importantly, wealthy owners who could afford the prices of top Irish and French imports became his priority. And it paid off. Soon he was mano a mano with his county rival, an intriguing and at times fiery confrontation that ended only with Martin Pipe's sudden retirement in 2006. Paul maintains a much friendlier rivalry with Pipe's son David who took over the licence at Nicholashayne.

Nicholls now dominates the jump racing scene alongside Lambourn's Nicky Henderson. The two men have a high regard for one another and their rivalry is healthy for the sport. Nicholls' daughter Megan is an accomplished rider on the flat. She has now moved north to ride for northern trainers such as Richard Fahey and owner John Dance.

The 2004 flat season began with the stunning victory of *Attraction* in the 1,000 Guineas. This filly, owned and bred by the Duke of Roxburghe, was trained by Mark Johnston who regarded her as the best filly he had ever handled. She went on to win the Irish 1,000 Guineas and the Coronation Stakes at Royal Ascot. And she would prove to be a wonderful broodmare for his enthusiastic owner who sadly lost his battle with illness in 2019.

This was further evidence, if it was needed, that Mark Johnston could train at the highest level. Soon Godolphin were sending him top class two-year-olds on the understanding that the best of them would be returned to Dubai at the end of their juvenile careers. *Shamardal* was the best colt Johnston has ever trained and he was nominated Europe's best two year old colt in 2004. Johnston had taken a chance when bidding 50,000 guineas for him at the sales in 2003 because he had been diagnosed a wobbler, a horse whose spine was damaged and could possibly be unsuitable to be trained. Johnston always said that he never saw any sign of this deficiency and so it proved. His brilliant career as a stallion ended in April 2020 when health issues caught up with him and he died at only eighteen.

Kieren Fallon was riding at the top of his game in 2004 and landed a rare Oaks/Derby double with *Ouija Board* and *North Light*. The former, bred and owned by Lord Derby, was to prove the best horse the latter had ever owned. Teddy Derby had been kind enough to give me a little exclusive when he announced his engagement to his wife Cazzie Neville on the eve of the 1995 Derby while posing in front of the Epsom grandstand together. It was a great picture story to have on the front page of the *Daily Mail* on Derby day. It was Teddy's ancestor who had won the toss of a coin with his friend Bunbury to determine what the great race should be called. Thereafter Derby was the signature name for the three-year-old championship race in every country that valued thoroughbred racing.

Cazzie, daughter of the Lord Lieutenant of Essex Lord Braybrooke, had been exhibition assistant for the Surveyor of the Queen's Pictures. As such she had an office in Buckingham Palace and had been seen on the arm of Prince Andrew from time to time. Teddy had inherited the title from his uncle the 18th Earl of Derby the previous November. He told me of his fiancee's relationship with Prince Andrew, "I don't think anything of that is true. But I am a lucky man to have found Cazzie."

Ouija Board went on to win the Irish Oaks and then triumph in the Filly and Mare Turf, ridden again by Fallon, at Lone Star, the Dallas, Texas home of thoroughbred racing. She would be runner-up the following year and win the race again in 2006 to complete a wonderful racing career during which she accumulated more prize money than any other European filly: $6.31 million. She was the most travelled racehorse as well, having gained air miles in the USA three times, in Hong Kong and Japan, and all over Europe. As a broodmare she has produced the 2014 Derby winner Australia.

Dallas was an eye opener, even for well-travelled racing hacks. The Breeders Cup parties outdid anything that California or Kentucky could offer. Country star Willie Rogers was the guest singer at the opening party where margaritas were as common as cowboy hats. Not only did *Ouija Board* win her race but *Wilko* proved to be a surprise victor in the Juvenile for Jeremy Noseda and Frankie Dettori.

American racing journalists used to observe Her Majesty's fourth estate with a degree of astonishment. Our expense accounts and relatively modest salaries were the subject of considerable envy. Things have undoubtedly levelled out since the millennium but it is true that we were better looked after and wore our status a little arrogantly perhaps.

After the Breeders Cup, I took a week's holiday in Las Vegas and Linda joined me. It was an eye opener for both of us to visit the Kennedy Conspiracy museums, all three of them. Whatever the various theories of the president's 1963 killing might have been, they were explored at length. For what it's worth I am fairly sure that the so-called third bullet which shattered the President's skull was accidentally shot from one of his outriders' weapons. That explains the extraordinary decision by Congress not to allow details of the killing to be revealed until 125 years from 1963.

Our next port of call was Gladys Knight and the Pips at the *Flamingo* hotel on Las Vegas's famous strip, or so we thought. We had arranged to meet my colleague Geoff Lester and his wife Gerry at the *Flamingo* hotel theatre for which we had booked tickets. And we were going on to eat a steak dinner at 9pm. Imagine the horror when Gladys called off her concert with ten minutes to go. No voice, it appeared.

We had to cool our heels for two hours before there was an available table at *Smith & Wollensky's* as both of us had agreed not to burnish the casinos with our hard earned. To cap an irritating night, by the time we got our refunds for the concert the dollar had waned in value and each couple lost $35 on the refund. It needed a plane trip to the magnificent Grand Canyon a day later later to restore our spirits.

Kieren Fallon was appointed retained rider for the Coolmore team in 2005. It had become apparent that Mick Kinane, the immensely accomplished jockey who had held the job since Jamie Spencer had been deemed too inexperienced four years earlier, was no longer the flavour of the month. For his part Kinane was happy to be joining the affable John Oxx who was still training for the Aga Khan.

Fallon, who did not come from a racing background when he was born in County Clare in 1965, had transitioned from a journeyman jockey in Yorkshire to the best job in racing inside a decade. It was some achievement. But there was always the risk with Kieren that he would at some moment employ the self-destruct button. We would have to wait less than three years for this to happen.

The 2005 season could hardly have started better for the new O'Brien/Fallon partnership when *Virginia Waters* and *Footstepsinthesand* won the 1,000 and 2,000 Guineas respectively. Fallon was riding with rare confidence, safe in the knowledge that he was probably partnering the best horses for a man who always had the jockey's back.

This became even more apparent when *Hurricane Run* won the Irish Derby, following up four months later with a famous win in the Prix de L'Arc de Triomphe which was getting more valuable and prestigious by the year. The first signs of a crack in the relationship between Frankie Dettori and his Godolphin masters appeared when the Sardinian partnered *Scorpion* for O'Brien to win the St Leger.

Meanwhile Kinane was proving that he was no back number with victories in the Irish 1,000 Guineas on *Saoirse*, *Azamour* in the King George VI and Queen Elizabeth Diamond Stakes, *Proclamation* in the Sussex Stakes and *Electrocutionist* in the Juddmonte International. This was a prestigious quartet of Group One successes for someone so recently passed over by Coolmore.

The 2005 Derby was won for the first time in living memory by a syndicate owned colt in the form of *Motivator*, trained by Michael Bell and ridden by Johnny Murtagh. Officially the horse was owned by the Royal Ascot Racing Club which boasted more than four thousand members. Membership entitled shareholders to their own dining room in the grandstand plus lunches and drinks during the season. Whether the three horses they ran were owned or leased became a matter of public debate once they involved the winner of the Derby (probably worth £10 million to go to stud).

Ascot's CEO Douglas Erskine-Crum, who did so much to modernise Ascot with its new grandstand and enhanced paddock facilities, now found himself in unwanted territory as members besieged both him and racing manager Henry Herbert as to precisely how much they would receive. It was their misfortune that the noisy Sir Clement Freud was a fully paid up member of the awkward brigade. He was in no doubt that the prize money and breeding rights should be split among the membership, of which he was one.

Erskine-Crum, formerly the army's youngest ever general, wouldn't retreat from his position that the colt was leased to the members but owned by the Ascot Authority. And somewhere in the small print of the membership form he found proof of his position. In the end, despite huffing and puffing from the lugubrious Freud, it was agreed that members would each receive a free membership for 2006, worth around £8,000, or the cash equivalent if they decided to end their membership.

None of this detracted from Bell's joy at training his first Derby winner. Michael was always a good friend to the racing press and had made both himself and the colt very accessible in the run-up to the big race. For this and many other reasons he was made the Horserace Writers and Photographers Association Flat Trainer of the Year at the big December lunch in the Royal Lancaster hotel.

One of the bonuses of Bell's Derby winner was to demonstrate to the world that there were trainers capable of Group One success outside the inevitable Coolmore and Godolphin teams. And this theme was to be continued in 2006 when the unconsidered *Speciosa*, trained and bred by jump specialist Pam Sly, won the 1,000 Guineas. She was owned by Pam, her son Michael, and Middlesex GP Dr Tom Davies. She was also ridden by the unfashionable Micky Fenton who might have partnered *Motivator* had he remained with Michael Bell a little longer.

Because of the creation of the new grandstand, 2005 was the year that Royal Ascot was transferred from the manicured lawns of Royal Berkshire to the bucolic charms of the Knavesmire in York. Many regard York as the finest racecourse in Great Britain and I always loved going there. But the Knavesmire's most famous and notorious resident was and always will be the highwayman Dick Turpin who was hanged there in 1739 aged thirty-four.

Yorkshire folk embraced the concept of the Royal meeting with all the enthusiasm of a puppy on his first walk. For starters, York racecourse acquired a full round course to accommodate the Queen Alexandra Stakes over two miles and six furlongs. Hitherto the longest race at York was fourteen furlongs. And the full round course has enabled York to stage two mile plus races ever since.

Then there was the fashion. I had discovered that the Beau Brummel of Yorkshire, Spittin' Mick Easterby, had agreed to model for a Harrogate outfitters who were anxious to sell and/or hire out morning suits. Mick, who has more millions in his current account than teeth in his smile, didn't exactly need the modelling fee. So what was the motive?

"The money's going to the Yorkshire Air Ambulance team," he proudly told me. "How do I look?" It was a question I couldn't answer, but Worzel Gummidge on speed came to mind as I giggled some inane response.

Mick, who kept his age a dark secret but was quoted as seventy-five at the time, had one crucial condition in his modelling contract – he would not sacrifice his comfortable broad brown brogues (which cushioned the barnacles on his feet) for any black versions that were de rigueur for his morning suit. "I prefer comfort to chic," he added.

A hilarious morning trying to sell me a horse I couldn't afford was followed by pleadings of poverty. I can honestly say that Lord Vestey's biggest Brazilian farm could not have accommodated the land that had the Easterby logo writ large. I wasn't put off by the shabbiness of various outhouses – where there's muck there's brass is the watchword of the Easterby squires. And what Mick doesn't own in North Yorkshire is probably the property of his elder brother Peter and nephew Tim.

I was much assisted in this feature article by Mick's son David who was preparing point-to-pointers while he waited to inherit the training licence from his father. Fifteen years later the youthful looking and rather handsome David still awaits the call as he acquires the grey hairs that come to all of us in maturity. Like Prince Charles he is a monarch in waiting.

York's hostelries rose to the occasion whilst Royal Ascot regulars relished the racecourse's policy to charge far less for champagne than any racing venue south of Hadrian's Wall. It was an exhilarating and exciting week which the racecourse hosted with great aplomb and style.

Sir Percy, a cheap yearling buy unlike most Blue Riband winners, was victorious in the 2006 Derby. The colt who had won the 2005 Dewhurst Stakes – always a good pointer to Derby success – was trained by the popular Marcus Tregoning and ridden by scouse jockey Martin Dwyer. Tregoning had been Dick Hern's assistant for fourteen years before setting up as his successor after the latter's retirement in 1997. He'd have been a poor student had he not picked up the skills necessary to succeed at the highest level.

Sir Percy was owned by Anthony Packenham who stepped in when Tregoning couldn't find an owner for the *Mark of Esteem* colt despite his modest sales cost of only 20,000 guineas. He won five of his ten starts and might have won more but for injuring his shoulder in the tight finish at Epsom where he short headed Geoff Wragg's *Dragon Dancer*.

Dwyer, a graduate of the Ian Balding group of apprentices has a great sense of humour, persuading his father to imitate him when I called to congratulate him the next day. I was fooled – for about ten seconds. Dwyer, a great Everton fan, was fond of comparing himself with the aristocratic trainer Hugo Palmer, scion of the biscuit company. "We've got a lot in common," he would say in his thick Liverpool accent. "We were both brought up on an estate!"

The Oaks was won by *Alexandrova*, trained by O'Brien and ridden by Fallon. This was significant because she was the final Classic winner sired by the great *Sadler's Wells* who was about to cede his status as Coolmore's prepotent stallion to his young and up and coming son *Galileo*. *Sadler's Wells* was champion sire for fourteen seasons and was responsible for three hundred and twenty-three Stakes winners.

Brian Vine entered the racecourse in the sky in September 2006, the first of three giants of the *Daily Mail* to die within a year. His wife Beverly asked me to do a reading at his funeral at St Lawrence church Hungerford and I used part of Paul Mellon's poem "The 16th pole", with the final stanza:

In my interview, of course
I'll ask St Peter for a horse
He'll lead me down the heavenly sheds
Past miles and miles of thoroughbreds
And say "Since you've escaped Old Nick
They're on the house, just take your pick.

I told the congregation of Brian's habit in later life to fall asleep in front of the television. Poor Beverly could never wake him up by shouting "lunch is ready". That's when she devised a fool proof method of gaining his attention. She would assemble all her decibels and yell, "They're off!" Apparently Brian always responded and padded his way to the dining room thereafter.

Brian taught me a huge amount about reporting from my first day in Fleet Street. Behind his bluster he was a kind and brilliant newspaperman, holding down the position of bureau chief in New York for the *Daily Express* in its pomp. It was only after the paper's proprietor Lord Matthews read an article in the *New Yorker* magazine about this monocled journalist who had a yacht, a weekend house on Shelter Island (off Long Island), and a pair of racehorses, that he was summoned back to London to explain himself and his "fortune". It was Matthew's misfortune not to make him editor of the paper he had served so well. Like many before and after him he succumbed to the blandishments of the *Daily Mail* and completed his career there.

Brian's service at St Bride's in 2007 was one of three memorials for distinguished *Daily Mail* writers that year, the other two being Ian Wooldridge and Nigel Dempster. Woollers' memorial was in the Guards chapel, Wellington Barracks, in sight of Buckingham Palace. He had not been well for several years and was on his way to my birthday party in February 2007 at his old stamping ground Ealing cricket club when his wife Sarah telephoned to say they would have to go home because he had had another turn. He died four months later.

The great and the good turned out for this memorial service including former prime minister Sir John Major, Dame Mary Peters, Sir David Frost, Michael Parkinson, Richie Benaud, Terry Wogan, Bruce Forsyth, and Peter Alliss. *Daily Mail* editor Paul Dacre, Richie Benaud, and Michael Parkinson gave the addresses, praising not only his writing skills but also his humanity.

I could not laud Woollers more accurately than his son Max did in a warm tribute. He wrote, "It wasn't always a wise move to introduce a girlfriend to my dad. Like countless other people who met him they adored Dad's wit and charisma. They loved his mix of old-world charm and understatement. He represented a simpler, gentler, and easier time when Britain owned all the pink bits on the map. The good old uncomplicated days when wholesome folk who resembled Ian Carmichael ran the civil service and Terry-Thomas the country. In an age when gobby shameless self-promotion is all the rage, my father remained endearingly unfashionable until the end. Even if he thought he was the best sportswriter of his generation he had the grace to keep it a secret."

In October of that year we lost Nigel Dempster, who liked to call himself a diarist even when he was King of the Gossip Columnists. Two years earlier when Nigel had already been diagnosed with the dreadful creeping killer progressive supranuclear palsy, Brian Vine and I took him for lunch to the *Foxtrot Oscar* restaurant in Chelsea. Although Nigel could not speak by then he could understand everything. Brian and I reminisced about the old Hickey days for two hours, leaving Nigel falling off his chair with laughter. He was officially separated from his wife Camilla but she generously took him back to her home in Richmond and nursed him devotedly for the final two years of his life.

Paul Dacre and Charlie Brooks gave the two addresses. While Paul concentrated on Nigel's glorious career and contribution to the rising *Daily Mail*, Charlie gave us an insight into Nigel as a racehorse owner. How many owners not only slip the lad £20 whenever the horse runs but also send a thank you letter for looking after the animal so devotedly? Apparently Nigel did. Nigel's prose may have had a barb – his nature was a generous one.

Cockney Rebel, who won the 2007 2,000 Guineas at 25-1 was another shock in that he was trained by the unfashionable Geoff Huffer and ridden by Olivier Peslier. He would have been partnered by Mick Kinane but for the latter deciding to placate Aidan O'Brien by partnering the outsider of his entries even though he had been replaced by Fallon as Coolmore's retained jockey. Big mistake. O'Brien rewarded him seven months later with the Breeders Cup ride on George Washington, winner of the 2006 2,000 Guineas. Sadly the colt, who had failed at stud earlier in the year, broke a leg and had to be put down.

Huffer had been training for only four years under his own name and was subsequently warned off over the running and riding of *Sabre Light* in 2009. But he knew he had a good horse in *Cockney Rebel* who went on to win the 2007 Irish Two Thousand Guineas.

"I've had a bit of a chequered career," Huffer admitted. "But I'm back training twenty-five horses and this one is by far the best I've had."

The horse was owned by Phil Cunningham who was a big fan of the pop group of that name. Lead singer Steve Harley was a big follower of racing and tried to be present whenever the horse ran. Harley had been a messenger boy and trainee accountant on the *Daily Express* in 1968, and that's when I met him before he went on to fame and fortune. He still tours at the age of sixty-nine.

In a year of comebacks, Henry Cecil landed his 8th Oaks victory with *Light Shift* partnered by Ted Durcan. Henry was emerging from the abyss some seven years after *Love Divine* gave him his 7th Oaks win. His reception at Epsom was redemptive and gave him the ambition, despite the return of his stomach cancer, to undertake the final remarkable six years of his career. You could argue that this victory was the springboard for the arrival, three seasons later, of wonder horse *Frankel*.

By the time the charming and somewhat foppish Cecil finally succumbed to his illness in 2013, he had assembled a wonderful record of twenty-five Classic wins and ten championships as a trainer. Latterly his courage and resilience won him thousands of new fans, and racegoers – whether they had backed his horses or not – always accorded him great affection and support.

As a press man I found him delightful to deal with: modest, informative, and self-deprecating. He was a gift to Rory Bremner's comedy apprentice Richard Phillips who mastered the Cecil mannerisms with his head on one side imploring his interrogator to give him his views on life and horses. Richard, who tries very hard to be a successful trainer, always bridles when told he is a comedian – in the nicest possible sense.

Kieren Fallon was seldom out of the headlines during the latter part of my career as a racing correspondent. In early October 2007 he was demonstrating his undoubted skill in the saddle when persuading *Dylan Thomas* to win the Prix de L'Arc de Triomphe for his Coolmore bosses, narrowly denying *Youmzain* who could be considered unlucky as the winner crossed him a hundred yards from the winning post.

Less than twenty-four hours later, the six times champion jockey, winner of sixteen English Classic races, was in court at the Old Bailey charged with conspiracy to stop horses for profit, alongside jockeys Fergal Lynch and Darren Williams, Lynch's brother Shaun, barman Philip Sherkle, and syndicate manager and punter Miles Rodgers.

The British Horseracing Authority (it had changed its name from the British Horseracing Board that summer) had handed a file to the City of London police alleging that all sorts of skulduggery had gone on resulting in certain individuals – notably Rodgers – benefitting from inside information. It was alleged by trainer Alan Jarvis in court that the BHA's head of security, former police officer Paul Scotney, was heard to say he was "out to get Fallon".

Fallon may have seemed an easy target to the BHA having had a poor disciplinary record. He was suspended for six months after pulling Stuart Webster off his horse at Beverley in 1994. He won £70,000 in damages at the High Court after the Top Cees trial found that he had been libelled by the *Sporting Life* for allegedly not trying on the horse in 1995. As previously mentioned, he had been sacked in 1999 by Henry Cecil who wrongly believed that he had seduced his wife Natalie, and his own wife Julie divorced him alleging he was the father of an illegitimate child.

More recently he was suspended for three weeks after his mount *Ballinger Ridge*, who had been six lengths clear with two furlongs to go in a minor race at Lingfield in March 2004, had been caught and beaten a short head by the favourite *Rye*. He had looked behind him when clear and had not ridden the horse out with enough purpose, according to Lingfield stewards.

To most professionals it was an error of judgement rather than anything more sinister – but the incident convinced the City of London police that Fallon was stopping horses. They alleged that Rodgers had called Fergal Lynch several times before the race and that Lynch had sent Fallon a text ten minutes before the race. Rodgers then began to lay the horse to lose over £72,000. After *Rye* caught Fallon's mount, Rodgers won over £26,000.

I had been to the Old Bailey before – once as a witness and a couple of times reporting trials – and it is quite a daunting place. Even for someone like Fallon who had enjoyed a measure of success traversing the legal minefield, this was his career on the line. One of the former champion jockey's problems was that he tended to associate with the Arthur Daleys of the racing world rather than the Aga Khans. Much of the police evidence was circumstantial but the presence of these characters did not assist Fallon's path to innocence.

The case largely revolved around Miles Rodgers whose Betfair account was the subject of much debate. He had turned over £2.1 million in one period, a sum the prosecution's chief police witness Detective Sergeant Mark Manning mistook for profit. This immediately alerted the Judge Mr Justice Forbes to the potential weakness of the prosecution case.

A further weakness emerged when Paul Scotney, the BHA security chief, gave evidence. For a man who must have given evidence many times in his 20 year police career, Scotney was nervous and unsure of himself. He may have handed all the evidence to the City of London police himself but he did not appear to be on top of his brief.

Then there was the prosecution's expert witness Ray Murrihy, the senior stipendiary steward for New South Wales. He had looked at seventeen races in which Fallon was alleged to have ridden improperly. Murrihy was unhappy with six of the rides. Unfortunately for the Aussie stipe, in two of the six rides – on *Barking Mad* and *Beauvrai* – Fallon had won the race concerned. To any experienced British racing man, it was a nonsense to suppose malpractice. But in Australia Murrihy knew that jockeys could be penalised for easing down their horses even when they were winning. The two legislations were furlongs apart in their interpretation of the rules of racing.

No one had thought to tell the hapless Aussie that this rule did not apply in Great Britain. Immediately, his evidence was undermined by his assertions that Fallon had ridden the six horses illegally. The £10 million trial was going west, most observers believed. Then evidence emerged that Scotney was trying to recruit Manning to join the BHA security team once the case was completed. This piece of intelligence impressed neither the Judge nor defence counsel.

Fallon had first been arrested in 2004, following the *Ballinger Ridge* episode. He was charged with conspiracy two years later. Amazingly he had since landed the job of No 1 rider at Coolmore and had continued to be Sir Michael Stoute's retained rider before that. The case against him was weak and as the doomed scenario unravelled it became increasingly clear that we were in for a second episode of Southwark (in which five alleged dopers were cleared after the case collapsed).

After Murrihy had stated on oath "I am not an expert in respect of UK races; it's not incumbent upon me that I verse myself on UK or other jurisdiction rules," Mr Justice Forbes had just about had enough. He said, "This is an extraordinary admission." Within a few hours he told the jury that the six defendants had no case to answer.

Outside, a sombre and unusually reticent Fallon said, "I am of course relieved and delighted but also outraged. There was never any evidence against me."

Coolmore spokesman Richard Henry who had attended most days of the trial said, "A jockey's riding career is a short one and Kieren was cruelly disadvantaged at the peak of his career. Kieren has been nothing less than superb in his riding of our horses and his record is there for all to see. This has been a terrible time for Kieren and we are delighted that it's finally behind him."

Was it though? I had discovered, as the trial proceeded, that Kieren had failed a drug test in France that summer. As it was his second such offence across the Channel, he would be subject to an eighteen month riding ban, as had Dean Gallagher when found guilty of the same offence two years earlier.

Instead of being back in the saddle after the trial was over, Fallon faced a ban so lengthy that his job at Coolmore was at risk. My exclusive back page story on the Saturday morning was met with astonishment, not least by John McCririck who read it out somewhat disbelievingly on *Channel 4's Morning Line*. I later discovered that Fallon had failed his drug test after riding the aptly named *Myboycharlie* (charlie is street slang for cocaine) to win the Prix Morny at Deauville in August.

My prediction that the forty-two year old would lose his job at Coolmore would be confirmed a few weeks later once the full implications of his ban were realised; it would essentially encompass the next two flat seasons. It was a huge blow to the rider who was at the top of powers. And although he came back with plenty of support from Newmarket, he never again reached the sublime heights he had enjoyed with Messrs Cecil, Stoute, and O'Brien. In just a decade he had ridden sixteen Classic winners in Britain and been champion jockey six times. His career winning total amounted to 2,253 winners.

Fergal Lynch continued his riding career in the USA where he worked for his brother. He has since returned to Ireland and the UK where his licence has been restored to him. Miles Rodgers was warned off indefinitely by the BHA who continue to believe that he was corrupting jockeys for financial gain.

Yet again the racing industry learned to its cost that the level of proof needed to win cases of corruption in court is above that needed in its own arbitration hearings. And the police and the Crown Prosecution Service would be loath to take on another case involving racing unless "the horse is past the post" or the conspirators are "bang to rights". It is patently absurd for police, with little or no knowledge of the intricacies of the sport, to take charge of criminal proceedings against its participants, especially when clever QCs familiar with the sport are defending those charged with corruption.

Kauto Star was one of those "once in a lifetime" horses that chanced upon the right trainer to manifest their unique talent. And just as *Arkle* had *Flyingbolt* quartered alongside him at Tom Dreaper's yard in the mid 1960s, so *Kauto Star* had the very imposing presence of *Denman* in his shadow at Ditcheat. The two horses would give rising trainer Paul Nicholls much pride and joy. They would also enable him to finally overtake Martin Pipe as champion trainer, having finished runner-up on seven consecutive occasions.

Kauto Star won the King George VI chase at Kempton on Boxing Day 2007, the second of five occasions in which he won this mid season championship chase. His statue now adorns Kempton at some distance from his famous predecessor *Desert Orchid,* who won four King Georges.

While *Denman* was a power house stayer, *Kauto Star* was a nimbler, more athletic chaser, quick enough to win the Tingle Creek chase over two miles at Sandown Park and yet possessing the stamina to win the Cheltenham Gold Cup over three and a quarter miles twice − the second time beating 'The Tank', as *Denman* was affectionately known in Paul Nicholls' stable.

While *Kauto Star* was bred and sourced in France, he cost owner Clive Smith a cool 400,000 euros as a four year old; *Denman* was a graduate of Ireland's point-to-point academy. Adrian Maguire, surely the best jump jockey never to be champion, had trained him. He was purchased by Nicholls' landlord Paul Barber who passed on a half share to professional punter Harry Findlay. The extrovert Findlay and the quiet cheese-making farmer made an odd but very complementary team.

Kauto Star's fall at the second last fence at Exeter in a minor prep race before the Cheltenham Festival in 2005 resulted in a significant rule change. Ruby Walsh had remounted the bay with the flashy white blaze on his head and failed by only a short head to get up and beat *Mistral de la Cour* who had been left twenty lengths clear. The following morning, *Kauto Star* was found lame behind and the Jockey Club ruled eventually that no horses should ever be remounted in a race once they had fallen.

Happily, *Kauto Star's* injury was not career ending and he was back at Exeter in the 2005 Haldon Gold Cup in which he was runner-up to *Monkerhostin.* Then he won the Tingle Creek but fell in the Queen Mother Champion chase at Cheltenham in March 2006. He won his first King George the following Boxing

Day as 4-9 favourite by 8l from *Exotic Dancer* and was 5-4 favourite when beating the same horse in the Cheltenham Gold Cup.

In the 2007 King George, *Kauto Star* again had a David Pipe runner, *Old Vic,* in his slipstream as he powered home by eleven lengths with the aforementioned *Exotic Dancer* another length and a quarter away third. At the 2008 Gold Cup, *Denman* had his day in the sun when he beat *Kauto Star* by seven lengths before the latter regained his crown in the 2009 Gold Cup where he beat *Denman* by thirteen lengths amid scenes of unbridled joy among spectators who were evenly divided in their loyalty to these two wonderful horses. *Kauto Star*, at 16.2 hands and 520 kilos, the perfect shape for a chaser, won a total of £2.12 million in prize money, winning twenty of his thirty-four races.

Denman, at seventeen hands and 555 kilos, was a full size larger. Racing fans loved his never-say-die front running style especially in the 2009 Hennessy Gold Cup at Newbury where he gave masses of weight away to good horses like *What Friend* and *Niche Market* to win by three and a half lengths and three and three quarters lengths. *Denman* won fifteen races from twenty-one starts garnering £1.011 million in prize money. Both horses, foaled 29 days apart in 2000, were a tremendous credit to their ambitious trainer who remains at the top of his game.

My final assignment for the *Daily Mail* took place at the Aintree Grand National meeting in April 2008. *Comply Or Die*, trained by David Pipe and owned by the late David Johnson, won the race. In doing so he took some pressure off Pipe junior who took over the training licence from his father Martin two years earlier and felt he had much to live up to. It's extremely testing to follow a genius, and that's been David's burden. But he is making a very good fist of it, keeping the stable in the top ten, season in and season out.

I said goodbye to my racing editor Brian Giles and to his able deputy Marcus Townend who was inheriting my role. Marcus has proved to be the right man for the job, winning the Derby award as Racing Journalist of the Year twice. He has even taken on the role as president of the Horserace Writers and Photographers Association. This has become ever more important with the rise in freelancing.

16.

Retirement

The 'R' word finally hit me when Aintree's chairman Lord Daresbury generously presented me with a farewell silver memento to mark the end of my writing career as the *Daily Mail's* racing correspondent. In fact I had acquired a little role as the European correspondent for the American publication *The Blood Horse* which I carried on for another year until Linda and I were free to travel the world.

Later that month we were invited to lunch by the trustees of Ascot, and Johnny Weatherby, Her Majesty's Representative, kindly asked us to present the trophy for the Sagaro Stakes. Then Rod Fabricius, the clerk of the course and director of Goodwood, invited us to the Glorious meeting where I received a silver trophy at the media dinner in Goodwood House where we had enjoyed so many similar events in the past.

In late April 2008, ninety of my colleagues and friends hosted a dinner for Linda and me plus five of our six daughters. This was a wonderful occasion when several colleagues made speeches which had me consulting my lawyers – again. In fact they were slanderously generous to me in word and deed. It was humbling that they had somehow amassed a leaving present of £5,000 which was handed to the Chancellor of the Exchequer (aka Mrs Mackenzie) to fund two round the world air tickets. There was an outrageous suggestion (principally from Linda) that the money might otherwise have been directed towards Mr Ponsonby and another of his syndicates. I suspect that one or two bookies' representatives had persuaded their bosses to return a percentage of my lifetime's losses to their source.

At the annual awards ceremony for the Sports Writers Association I was nominated for Scoop of the Year for the Fallon story. My *Daily Mail* colleagues were hopeful I'd win but I received a Highly Commended (runner-up) prize – the winner being the *News of the World* and its coverage of Freddie Flintoff's antics on a pedalo in the Caribbean.

I received an award at the annual Horserace Writers and Photographers lunch at the *Royal Lancaster* hotel that December when I won the President's Trophy and I felt very honoured to be in the illustrious company of previous winners such as Dick Hern, Jack Berry, and Lord Oaksey.

After a little persuasion I was also appointed the tennis correspondent of the *Ealing Gazette*, my local paper. Through the *Mail* sports desk I had been accredited to Wimbledon for some years but this would end with my retirement. The cherry I dangled before the sports editor of the *Ealing Gazette* was that I would work for free. And I did – until the paper, like so many local publications suffering financial hardship, went totally on line and sacrificed its sports department.

In *The Ealing Gazette* I ran a little campaign which succeeded in acquiring an English Heritage blue plaque for the house where the legendary Fred Perry lived as a schoolboy. He had come down to London from Stockport as a fifteen year old international table tennis player when his father became a Labour MP. Within weeks of joining the Brentham Park tennis club in the Ealing suburb of Pitshanger he had mastered the grass game, and ten years later in 1934 he won the first of his three consecutive Wimbledon singles titles.

On New Year's Day 2009 Linda and I set off on our round the world journey which was to involve a month in New Zealand, a month in Malaysia (where my stepdaughter Alex had moved to teach in Kuala Lumpur) and a month in India and Kashmir. Our twenty year old Jack Russell bitch Bobbie was rehoused with friends and relatives while our Ealing home was borrowed by recent exile to the countryside, Cornelius Lysaght, my sometime chauffeur and *BBC Radio Five Live* colleague. Within two weeks we had pictures from Cornelius of our garden under twelve inches of snow.

We set off for New Zealand via Los Angeles where, because of US regulations, passengers in transit have to go through customs. Our luggage went missing, which we didn't discover until we reached Auckland. Thanks to the efficiency of *Air New Zealand* our cases were delivered to our hosts Chris and Dee Whitby's home within four hours on the next flight out of LA.

I decided to write a blog about our trip and was astonished to learn halfway through that it had received quite a following, and not just from family members. With our photographs, we turned this into a little book for our daughters. When we finally admitted to spending a few days in Kashmir, Alex emailed us – "naughty parents" – because at the time it was considered one of the most dangerous places in the world. And her opinion was justified, as we were to discover.

New Zealand was enchanting and gorgeous but also something of a time warp. Rural Britain, circa 1955, would be a rough guide to the quaint shops with B&Bs run by ex-pat Brits only too glad to exchange the nasal twang of a New Zealand accent for the Home Counties version. Having traversed continental Europe many times and received a welcome made cautious by the British reputation for drunkenness and debauchery abroad, it was doubly pleasant to receive such warm welcomes from people we had never met.

Two weeks in the North Island included visits to the magical peninsular of Coromandel with its Driving Creek railway that snakes twelve hundred feet into the clouds to reveal magnificent views of the South Pacific. We attended an international tennis tournament in Auckland where we cheered on British hope Anne Keothavong, who beat the higher ranked Spaniard Carla Suarez Navarro. Cathedral Cove, and Hot Water Beach where you can enjoy a mud bath in the hot sands, were somewhat overrated in our view.

We drove on to a fabulous lunch at the Tauranga home of David Barons and his wife Anna. David had been a top National Hunt trainer who employed Paul Nicholls as his stable jockey. I reminisced with him about the good old days of Playschool and Broadheath. They emigrated to New Zealand in 2003 making a new life for themselves as house builders and developers.

David's son Chris owns a hotel in Napier where we stayed two nights later. Linda was delighted to be staying in a room that had harboured Cliff Richard a few months earlier. The art deco hotel was one of only two buildings that survived the 1931 earthquake which devastated the east coast port. Chris also has the New Zealand Wine Centre display opposite his hotel which draws crowds from the cruise liners that regularly ply their trade up and down the east coast.

Bungee jumping (not for us) is worth a watch on the Waikato River which winds its way from Lake Taupo to the coast. We inhaled the sulphur fumes of Rotorua before following white water rafters as they negotiated the Okere Falls and river. The countryside surrounding Lake Taupo is a cross between the Lake District and Wensleydale – spectacularly beautiful.

After ten days enjoying the North Island, we flew to Christchurch in the South Island to enjoy the contrast and to see what excited Captain Cook in the eighteenth century when he named the fjords Doubtful Sound and Milford Sound. First we stopped in Queenstown, the gateway to the fjords and glaciers. As a sixty-seventh birthday present Linda bought me a flight in a seaplane which took off from the nearby lake to traverse the southern Alps, giving us a magnificent view of Doubtful Sound.

My late father always boasted of having flown in sixty different types of aircraft, including a Sunderland flying boat in which he flew from Lake Victoria to Cairo, Rome, and onto Southampton in the 1950s. But he was jealous of my having flown in Concorde in 1985 – a flight to introduce the refurbishment of the aircraft's narrow interior – and he would have been even more envious that I, as a latecomer, managed a flight in a Spitfire which he never achieved. In 1949, he flew in a prototype Comet, the first ever commercial jet, piloted by his good friend, the test pilot 'Cats Eyes' Cunningham at Hatfield aerodrome.

A seaplane flight finally put me on a par with my dear dad. The flight was thrilling, as we traversed some of the highest peaks in New Zealand, flying through rain, snow, hail, and sunshine. You could almost touch the mountain tops as pilot Allan Remnant zig-zagged through the peaks onto the magical Doubtful Sound so named because Captain Cook wasn't quite sure if it was a river or a fjord.

Staying in a motel on Lake Matheson we were able to view the awesome Mount Tasman and Mount Cook, both peaks in excess of thirteen thousand feet, although we learned that the latter had lost thirty feet due to a rock fall in 1991. We were also able to walk up to the two extraordinary glaciers – Fox and Franz Joseph – both of which snake down to sea level. I understand there is only one other glacier in the world so accessible to the avid tourist.

From the cool of New Zealand's west coast, we drove in only three hours to Kaikoura on the east coast to indulge in whale watching. The temperature rose to thirty degrees and the town is surrounded by mountains so dry and bare that the resort resembles a picture postcard from southern Spain. Whale watching – being tossed in the swell for forty-five minutes and getting seasick (although Sea Captain's daughter Linda was unaffected) – is something of an acquired taste. But we finally saw one whale, which saved the boat owners an eighty per cent refund which tourists receive for a wasted voyage.

We tasted wines in the Marlborough region and were astonished to realise that the much vaunted Cloudy Bay wines are grown no more than two metres away from the much cheaper Oyster Bay variety. Marketing is an exercise which clearly appeals to the New Zealand palate, not that we objected to testing the delicious Cloudy Bay whites.

After two weeks we returned to the Whitbys' home in Auckland – satiated by the sheer variety and beauty of the New Zealand countryside. But we were ready to board our *Singapore Airlines* flight which would eventually get us to Kuala Lumpur. On our last day in the Land of the Long White Cloud we chanced upon the returning New Zealand America's Cup yacht anchoring in Auckland harbour and witnessed it being winched out of the water to reveal its controversial submarine shaped keel which enabled the crew to be victorious yet again. It was a talking point as we celebrated Burns night with our hosts.

It was exciting to be reunited with Alex and her boyfriend Craig (later to become her husband in 2010) on our arrival in Kuala Lumpur. She was a little stressed because this was the week that Ofsted were inspecting the Alice Smith school where she taught. She had a further surprise for me – would I like to address year four (nine and ten year olds) on the subject of journalism as a career option? Not really, but I'll do it.

On arrival at the school the following morning I was confronted with 110 enquiring and intelligent looking, mostly ex-pat kids. I told them about the places I had visited in the course of my work, including Brazil, America, Hong Kong, Australia, and so on. I also included the names of some of the better known political leaders, such as Nixon, Ceausescu, Clinton, and Mrs Thatcher who I had interviewed. I also included the name of Manchester United manager Sir Alex Ferguson who I had met on the racetrack, and his was the one name that resonated throughout the audience which included several teachers.

All went well until the question and answer session afterwards. One bright boy put his hand up and asked the immortal question, "Did you cover the assassination of Abraham Lincoln?" I had to disappoint this particular nine year old with the answer, "I'm old, but not that old."

It turned out to be a delightful experience but when the Head Teacher arrived to ask if I would like to repeat the exercise with year six the following day, I thought I would quit while I was ahead and I declined. We had some serious sightseeing to do in Penang and Langkawi, where we were looking for wedding venues for Craig and Alex's nuptials in 2010.

Penang is an old colonial delight. Fort Cornwallis is named after a former governor general and a venue where you can sample *dim sum* and Indian curries. The old boy's statue is missing his sword which had apparently been melted down by the invading Japanese to assist with their war effort in 1942. We also visited the home of Dr Sun Yat Sen who established the modern republic of China in 1911 following the Cantonese uprising.

On Langkawi we looked at the Tanjung Rhu beach resort which did not disappoint. Situated at the north end of the island the bridal suites would dwarf the whole of many London flats. The beach and the views were picture postcard perfect. Twelve months later Alex and Craig opted for a similar calibre of hotel on the Thai island of Ko Lanta.

After all the humidity and warmth of Penang and Kuala Lumpur Alex took us five thousand feet up to the Cameron Highlands where we stayed in the old schoolhouse just outside the main town of Tanah Rata and enjoyed the "cool" 23 degrees. The hills, where tea and vegetables are grown, are named after William Cameron who first mapped the area in 1885. The major tea plantation is called *Boh* but has been owned by the Russell family since 1929. It was fascinating to watch the workers harvesting the crop using small mechanised hovercraft which sweep the leaves off the tops of the bushes every three weeks.

One of the great delights of Malaysia is the cuisine which is varied and tasty. We enjoyed cocktails in the Sky Bar at the top of the Traders Hotel which boasted a spectacular view of the impressive Petronas twin towers. Not even a massive thunder and lightning storm which lit up the towers as if they were giant Christmas trees could dampen our enthusiasm for a lovely city.

To India. The calm mood created by the tranquillity of Malacca, Penang, and even Kuala Lumpur, was soon forgotten as we arrived in Delhi to be transported by the world's worst taxi driver to the world's worst hotel which – even at midnight – was not ready to receive us. We put up with filthy sheets and a noisy room for one night in order to assemble our thoughts and find our travel agent Javed to arrange a twenty-one day tour of Rajasthan.

Before that, we met up with my old colleague Richard Edmondson of the *Independent* who had forsaken the hard graft of racing correspondent to become some sort of Indian Maharajah while his energetic award-winning wife Alex Crawford held down her important job as *Sky TV's* Asia correspondent. Edmo, as he was always known, masterminded the education of their four children while trying out great restaurants such as *Punjabi by Nature* where we enjoyed a terrific lunch.

Evidence that *Sky* are better payers than the *Independent* was immediately obvious when we arrived at the Edmo mansion to be greeted by a guard who resembled 'Jaws' from the James Bond movies. Early retirement clearly suited our talented host for whom the description of house husband would be slandering that profession.

Back at the travel agency, Javed was persuading us to take the "journey of a lifetime" to Kashmir where we could enjoy the lakes and mountains for four days for an unbeatable price. It would be, said Javed, a pleasant twenty degrees celsius during the daytime and a little cooler in the cabin of the houseboat where we would be laying our heads at night.

This was misinformation on a grand scale. As it was early March the temperature on arrival in Srinagar was barely ten degrees while at night it dropped to minus ten inside our cabin. Our host had to provide paraffin heaters and seven layers of blankets to keep the Memsahib warm. Furthermore, we hadn't bargained for the army presence (650,000 Indian troops) in the Kashmiri capital which meant that there was a daytime curfew once we had set off on our various tours. In other words, once we had set off, we could not return to our boat on Lake Dal until after 5pm.

This became relevant on our first tour, a riding trek in the foothills of the magnificent Himalayas which dominated the skyline. Linda was suffering from altitude sickness and a bruised knee and I had pulled a muscle or two in the Cameron Highlands which, coupled with our inappropriate warm weather clothing, combined to make riding in freezing temperatures a near impossibility. We conceded defeat after two hours. Unable to return to our base we had to spend several hours in the guide's primitive home where his wife was nursing three children under three years of age. She generously made chapatis and Kashmiri tea for us – and we didn't have so much as one rupee to give her. Receiving their hospitality was both embarrassing and humbling.

We warmed up only when our driver, aged nineteen, finally removed the mobile telephone from his ear to concentrate on getting us back down a sheer mountain path in his four wheel drive jeep with thousand foot gorges either side. Finally we got back to Srinagar and were able to locate the shikara wallah (boatman) to get us back to our cabin.

That's when the hard sell began. Stranded aboard the boat we could not avoid the multifarious carpet, jewellery, and spice sellers that quietly wafted alongside to sell their wares. I am sure Kashmir would be lovely in summer when the lotus flowers and water lilies are at their best. But it is by no means a winter resort – hence the unforgettable "bargain" we had been offered by the Delhi travel agent.

Back at his office we arranged a twenty-one day tour of Rajasthan, including a visit to the Taj Mahal. Rather naively I accepted his claim that my credit card wasn't working and that he could take only a debit card. Another big mistake, because it wasn't until I was back in London four weeks later that I discovered this rogue had charged me twice the price he had quoted for our tour. We were out £3,000! It was little consolation that we posted emails to this effect and that he went bankrupt within months.

The Taj Mahal, the tomb of Mumtaz Mahal, Emperor Shah Jahan's second wife and beloved mother of fourteen, lived up to its billing. We had the late Princess Diana in mind as we posed for photographs in front of this seventeenth century masterpiece which took twenty thousand workmen twenty-two years to complete. It cost the then equivalent of £100 million. The marble inlay work is astonishing in its detail and magnificence.

India is a country of enormous contrasts; close by this majestic monument we witnessed lame, mange-ridden feral dogs, wild pigs, and cattle all foraging for the same street detritus. Nearby there were mothers and babies begging piteously and once you have given to one the remainder will surround you. They were always gentle but very demanding.

The tour of Rajasthan was memorable. Tigers went missing in the Ranthambore National Park so sadly we saw none even though we were granted two goes. The main excitement was that our jeep twice suffered from punctures – armed with my long serving racecourse binoculars, I was in charge of spying any would be predators. Until we were leaving the park, when we saw a couple of leopards, there was nothing. The leopards are regular tenants of the exit caves because they too go scavenging in the nearby town.

We visited the pink dwellings of Jaipur and took an elephant ride the eleven kilometres to the Amber Fort. It was worth the two hour tour by which time we felt we had earned a visit to the *Polo* bar at the *Rambagh Palace* hotel where turbaned staff complete with waxed handlebar moustaches served the Maharajah of Ealing a Kingfisher beer while the Maharanee took a gin and tonic.

We traversed the state, visiting Pushkar, Johdpur, and Bundi. We stayed in a hillside hotel in the latter town having wiped the blue, yellow, and red powder from our bodies, acquired as we drove through villages celebrating Holi day which marks the end of winter and the onset of spring. Teenagers sprayed our car with the powder paint, having placed boulders in the road so that we had no choice but to stop and give them money. After a dozen occasions it became truly tiresome.

Settling down for a siesta we were awakened by a giant monkey charging through our door and belting the window opposite in an attempt to gain egress. So shocked was the memsahib that she was practically at ceiling level by the time the monkey had about-turned and retraced his steps. At breakfast on the hotel's roof the following morning we were not surprised to see the restaurant manager holding a gun to frighten off unwanted guests.

We visited a small lakeside palace called the Sukh Mahal where Rudyard Kipling wrote part of *Kim*. Sadly the building was closed and in bad need of a lick of paint. But it was easy to see how Kipling could be inspired by the peace and beauty of the lake which was surrounded by imposing mountains. Eventually we retraced our steps to Delhi and enjoyed a few days of R and R at the five-star *Park Hotel* in Connaught Place. A little upgrade from *Virgin Airlines* gave us a pleasant flight home to London where there was to be action aplenty on the domestic front.

17.

Family & other animals

When Linda wed Colin, the mix
Of their three doubled daughters made six
It's a bit of a bore
To have six sons-in-law
Unless you've got gadgets to fix.
(Jeremy Hornsby, Daily Express 1959-68, poet, lyricist good
friend)

As the above indicates, being the father of six involves many a
wedding, together with speeches from the father of the bride. I
made four of those – Alex's father was unable to be in Ko Lanta,
Thailand, for her 2010 nuptials so the understudy had to perform.
What I have learned is to be brief – no more than twelve minutes
– be funny (without upsetting your daughter), and above all be
generous.

When Tara wed Roo Lecomber in 1995 his parents kindly lent us
their house and grounds near Backwell in Somerset which saved
us the cost of a venue. A jackpot win at Bath, plus a Ponsonby
tip that *Captain Miller* would win the Queen's Prize flat race at
Kempton's Easter meeting (20-1 thank you very much) ensured
that the right quantities of champagne and food were on hand for
the hundred and fifty guests.

Actress Georgia's 2004 wedding to fellow thespian Richard
Coyle was held in Usk Castle, Monmouthshire, a fifteenth
century edifice with the roof missing and an outdoor chapel.
Again luck played its part when the weather was kind. There
were enough well-known faces from television and film such as
Michael Fassbender, Jack Davenport, Ben Miles, and Anne Reid
to keep the catering staff ready with their autograph books.

The father of the bride faced a testing audience but just survived while the bride's sister Cate made her debut as a public speaker to such comedic effect that stand-up became her hobby. She would later appear twice at the Edinburgh Festival with her husband to-be Paul Wogan.

Kate, Linda's younger twin, married Jamie Codrington in August 2009 at the Royal Mid-Surrey Golf Club, Richmond. I had a lovely relaxed time as the bride's father John Sharman took on the onerous duty of speech making. Jamie, who runs a design company, is a talented sportsman who as a teenager played a lot of soccer with England international Peter Crouch.

I was back in speech making mode when Alex married Craig Kaye on the gorgeous island of Ko Lanta in April 2010. The couple had taken over the *Royal Lanta Resort* hotel which overlooked the Straits of Malacca and the romantic service took place on the beach. It was extremely hot and the "father of the bride" resembled an undercooked lobster. Friends from all over the world, including Craig's family from Barnsley, had made the journey. The Icelandic volcano Eyjafjallajökull, which erupted on the wedding day, caused so much consternation that international flights were cancelled leaving many stranded for an extra week. There are worse places to be.

Older twin Helen married *Sky* television producer Simon Cole in August 2010 in St Peter's Square, Chiswick, the then home of her father John. Again I was on a happy and relaxed furlough as speech maker and, trust me, weddings are more enjoyable in these circumstances. Helen, a relocation executive, is a computer whizz and an indispensable aide to her stepfather in matters technological.

My final act as Father of the Bride was delayed until 2015 when my eldest Cate tied the knot with Paul Wogan whom she had met on the stand-up circuit. Paul has an uncle Terry (no, not that one) but much fun was had at the poor man's expense during the speeches. The wedding reception was in Battersea within sight of our first house. Cate had come full circle, as it were.

I now have nine glorious grandchildren, including William and Natasha whose mother is Tara, Purdy who is Georgia's daughter; Alex has Charlie and Lily, while Helen has Maisie and Thea, and Cate has Seren and Elsie. Lily and Elsie both have Downs Syndrome and their close family are so proud of them and of the wonderful love and devotion they receive from their parents.

I have to credit my lovely wife Linda with the great sensitivity and love she has brought to our complex family. She has been the glue and the inspiration for bringing us all together as such a caring unit. She provided the backbone to my racing career when on many occasions I was filled with self-doubt. And she has even brought about a caring reconciliation with my first wife Tina. Sharing children and grandchildren is made simpler when love abounds and I have won the jackpot in this regard.

One day in 2011, my brother Charles Marriott, who is a film director and cameraman, suggested that I make a documentary about Ronnie Biggs, using the tape recordings I had kept from my 1974 escapade in Brazil. He had partnered up with ex *Sky* producer Stuart Strickson. Through Timothy Spall's production company Bargepole, we made a one-hour documentary which was shown as part of *Channel 5's* "Revealed" series. The great actor was the narrator. It was also sold to the *Sky Crime Channel* who subsequently broadcast it more than a hundred times.

John Humphreys and Michael Brunson, who had covered the event for the *BBC* and *ITN* respectively, kindly agreed to be interviewed about the media circus that enveloped the story. Brian Hitchen, the former *Daily Express* news editor who had masterminded the input into the paper on that February day in 1974, flew over from Spain to provide insights. And Peter Jones, the detective sergeant who had accompanied Jack Slipper to Brazil, evinced the police perspective. Sadly, by this time, Slipper himself was dead. I'm afraid viewers also had to withstand my mug for much of the film, which received some critical acclaim.

There is no money in making documentaries but a certain satisfaction can accrue if they are successful and well received. At seventy I felt in need of another stimulus and I asked Andrew Morton if he would reminisce about authoring his Diana book. In 2012 it would be the twentieth anniversary of the publication of *Diana – Her True Story* which had caused a sensation when serialised in the *Sunday Times*.

After Andrew agreed, it was a matter of getting together *Sunday Times* editor Andrew Neil to explain why he took a chance on the publication of such controversial material which had the potential to dethrone the Royal Family. Sir Max Hastings, former editor of the *Daily* and *Sunday Telegraph* gave a contrary opinion. He said to us, "I just could not credit the idea that Diana could have confided in someone like Andrew Morton. I dug my hole even deeper (with his *Telegraph* executives) when I turned it down. I want British institutions to survive and prosper."

To someone like Andrew Morton, this was a coded implication that his working class, Leeds-born background would not have appealed to a member of the Royal Family. The word "oik" had been used quite unfairly by others to describe Morton. In fact on a royal tour five years earlier, Diana had adjusted Morton's tie for him while giggling. It was clear she appreciated his Clark Kent good looks.

Alongside other Royal correspondents such as Richard Kay, Jennie Bond, ex Royal press secretary Dickie Arbiter, and royal snapper Kenny Lennox, the programme detailed how Morton had acquired the scoop of the century, way outscoring my modest efforts. And it was riveting to learn how Morton had been the pariah of Fleet Street when the book first appeared. Only after Diana's untimely death five years later was he able to reveal her participation in the enterprise. Then his reputation and honour could be redeemed.

Mariella Frostrup narrated the programme entitled *Diana – The Book That Changed Everything* – on her *Sky Arts' The Book Show* programme. It was very well received, especially when Morton revealed that his flat had been invaded – possibly by MI5 – and photos and material removed. Wisely he kept the tapes of Diana answering all his questions with intermediary Dr James Colthurst, a radiologist friend of Diana's, so they were untouched.

I had always admired the campaigns in the *Sunday Times*, and earlier in the *Daily Mail*, to assist the victims of the Thalidomide scandal of the early 1960s to get justice. With this in mind my next project was called *Thalidomide – The 50 year Fight* which would eventually find its natural home on *BBC2*, narrated by the lovely actress Juliet Stephenson. I soon discovered that Sir Harold Evans, the former *Sunday Times* editor, had a similar project in mind, so we were in a bit of a race.

There was total lack of co-operation from the German company responsible for the invention of the drug namely Chemie Grunenthal GmbH. The drug was originally created in the 1950s as a sedative or tranquiliser. But its use was widened later on to include other conditions such as colds, influenza, nausea, and more specifically morning sickness in pregnant mothers.

The drug which is now used effectively for treating leprosy, affected women and their babies most damagingly during the third month of their pregnancy. And it became apparent from 1961 onwards that babies were being born with deformed arms and legs. It was shocking to parents and doctors alike. Although generally the children themselves were naturally bright and intelligent.

The company marketing the drug in the UK was the giant drinks conglomerate Distillers. Once they had admitted liability, following lengthy court deliberations, they and Diageo, which eventually took over the company, have behaved with generosity and compassion. There is a Thalidomide Trust which administers funds to victims and their families.

This only happened after one man, Mayfair art dealer David Mason, stood up to Distillers and refused an initial offer of around £3.5 million for all nine hundred plus sufferers in the UK. He was determined that victims, including his own daughter Louise, should be better compensated for the lifetime of disability they would suffer. Following lengthy legal proceedings and despite facing hostility from other parents who wished to settle for the original amount, he won through for all the victims.

This was the background against which we interviewed thalidomide victims, now in their fifties and sixties, including Louise Mason who sadly was no longer in touch with her father David. We also interviewed Mr Mason, a very articulate and successful businessman who devoted much of his adult life to making things better for the five hundred or so survivors (by 2012). The documentary received rave reviews and was even considered for a BAFTA nomination. And, despite being up against the final of *Master Chef*, it received viewing figures of well over one and a half million.

My next project ended in abject and expensive failure. Through police contacts I acquired the address and whereabouts of Michael Fagan, notorious for breaking into Buckingham Palace on July 9, 1982, and parking himself on the Queen's bed having a cup of tea while she anxiously telephoned for help. Her favourite Page in Waiting Paul Whybrew, who would normally have been outside her chamber, was walking the corgis at the time. The armed police guarding her quarters had come off duty at 7am and were due to be replaced an hour later.

Fagan's timing was fortuitous to say the least. Thanks to the calm of the Queen, Fagan never really represented a threat – but she wasn't to know that. Just after my attempts to persuade Fagan to appear in my documentary failed, the episode was made into a drama entitled *Walking the Dogs* which was shown on *Sky One* starring Emma Thompson as Her Majesty.

When Fagan got together with me, my brother Charles, and producer Stuart in a pub off the Holloway Road in North London he was happy and prepared to do the documentary about his part in royal history. Gradually however his interest waned and he disappeared as fast as the financial inducement I had given him. Fagan, now seventy-two, had been in and out of psychiatric wards and I should have known that he was unreliable. But it was frustrating.

Interestingly, an episode of the Netflix drama *The Crown* (series 4) was devoted to this event, within which Fagan was portrayed correctly as a dysfunctional and bitter working class painter and decorator. However *The Crown's* creator and chief scriptwriter, Peter Morgan, made the classic mistake of imposing his own political ideals on Fagan's dialogue. The man I met and interviewed was inarticulate and very tense. There is no way he could have expressed himself to the Queen in the language used. This alone made me wonder about the veracity of some other episodes in this best selling series.

My good friend James Whitaker – known as the Red Tomato to Royal watchers and to Princess Diana – passed away far too young at seventy-one in 2012. We knew James was suffering from sarcoma of the stomach but it was a shock when he died so soon leaving his wife Iwona and three children. He was courageous to the end and made a unique mark on Fleet Street having worked for all five great tabloids – *the Mail, the Express, the Sun, the Star,* and *the Mirror* in that order. Not for nothing is his one of the few graves at St Brides, the journalists' church.

Linda and I were on a cruise in South America when the news of James's death was confirmed. My daughters Cate and Georgia were able to read my tribute to him in his local Chiswick church. Three months later I upgraded my encomium at his memorial service in St Brides where my *Mail* colleague Robert Hardman and the *Mirror's* Anne Robinson also gave touching tributes.

Funerals and memorials are sad companions as one approaches the final furlongs of one's life. Brian Hitchen was killed in a car crash in 2014 near his home in Spain. I lost my good friend Stephen Freud in 2015 having outlived his younger brothers Lucian and Clement. There was a touching picture of him on the lap of his grandfather Sigmund on the order of service.

The voice of racing, Sir Peter O'Sullevan, was silenced in July 2015 at the grand age of ninety-seven. Hughie McIlvanney gave the address and described him thus, "His admirers are convinced that had he been on the rails at Balaclava he would have kept pace with the Charge of the Light Brigade, listing the fallers in precise order and describing the riders' injuries before they hit the ground." Rory Bremner, who had so often imitated the great man, described his last conversation with Peter, "I remember *Arkle* beating *Mill House* as if it was yesterday. The trouble is I can't remember yesterday."

Bremner's was a punch line I ruthlessly purloined for my own dear mother Hazel's funeral a few months later. She was ninety-five and her memory was just starting to fail. She received some wonderful obituaries in all the serious newspapers for her ground breaking career in film and television. Her time as chair of the

Writers' Guild was recalled with her famous victory over Lord Grade concerning repeat fees for scriptwriters.

She always felt guilty about being something of an absentee mother as she forged her writing career on radio, television, and film. She was famous for her soaps, *Emergency Ward Ten*, *Compact,* and *Crossroads.* She was generous to a fault to her six children (she adopted three girls when I was eighteen to add to my two half brothers). And despite her slight lack of maternal instinct she always wrote to me very lovingly when I was at boarding school and adored her grandchildren and great grandchildren. She had only one rule for them, "never, ever call me Granny as it makes me feel old." She became Daisy to one and all.

We lost one of the finest sports writers of any generation when the boxing ring in the sky finally beckoned Hughie McIlvanney in the spring of 2019. He was able to translate the mundane into literature, the commonplace into a thriller. He brooked no compromises whether in the written form or in friendships. Fleet Street won't see his like again.

I hope it doesn't seem lugubrious to write of the dearly departed as I conclude this opus. They are all people for whom I entertained admiration, friendship, and in some cases love. They were all, in their special ways, superstars. And there is one more – still very much alive – for there is little doubt that the Barbury Castle stables of Alan King contains the most talented horse I have ever had anything to do with.

Trueshan is his name and my ownership percentage would scarcely grant me three hairs of his tail. But I am one of twenty-four shareholders in the Barbury Lions V partnership run by my sometime bridge partner and former Chairman of Warwick racecourse David Hill. David knows a little about partnerships having owned one sixth of Whitbread Gold Cup winner *Docklands Express* and other good chasers in the past.

By the conclusion of the 2020 flat season, *Trueshan* had won seven of his eleven races and over £320,000 in prize money, a truly phenomenal achievement for a relatively cheaply bought horse. In 2019 he ended his season by beating William Haggas's good stayer *Hamish* in a rousing finish of a £32,000 stakes race at Newbury. He had previously won the competitive £120,000 Old Rowley handicap at Newmarket, enabling his owners to dream of the £1 million Ebor handicap at York in the summer of 2020. A jumping career was put on hold – and then what happens?

We hoped normality and rain would return. It did. Racing resumed with *Trueshan* winning his Listed prep race at Haydock. Unfortunately, prize money had been badly hit and the Ebor was worth little more than a quarter of 2019's £1 million which made it the most valuable flat handicap in Europe. He did run in the Ebor and finished no closer than eighth. Eleven days later, our mare *Tronada* won a valuable race at Bath to make it seventy wins for me as an owner. Happily, *Trueshan* then ran in a Listed race at Salisbury and resumed his winning ways. He is now six wins from ten starts – phenomenal for most racehorses.

Trueshan then exceeded all his previous noble efforts when winning the Qipco British Champions Day Long Distance Cup at Ascot, beating the hugely talented triple winner of the Ascot Gold Cup, *Stradivarius*. He was ridden by Hollie Doyle, who will surely become the first female champion jockey one day.

Because of Lockdown, only six of his twenty-four owners could be present. I was lucky to be included, but we could not enter the paddock or winners' enclosure. It hardly diminished the pleasure we felt, however. We can dream that he will be even better next year, shortening the winter months until his reappearance in the Spring of 2021.

The thing about racehorse owners is they are a supremely optimistic bunch. Disappointment is the usual bedfellow. But with seventy-one winners to my name I have been more than lucky in my owning career. For that I thank the trainers, the jockeys and my partners for being so patient and kind to a noisy latecomer to the sport. Without the intervention of Maurice Manasseh in my academic career, I would have been lost to racing, I have little doubt. And I have enjoyed every moment of the ride.

Index

Acknowledgements

I'd like to thank many former colleagues for their help in remembering events of long ago. In particular thanks go to Jeremy Deedes, Geoff Levy, Adam Helliker and Helen Minsky. John and Barbara Jackson read early drafts and made many helpful suggestions, as did Dennis Sheriffs and Tim Richards. I'd like to thank friend and colleague Brough Scott for his encouragement, while John Maxse, formerly press officer of the Jockey Club, has a forensic memory of the recent past. David Gandolfo checked the text for equine facts and figures and recalled the horses I owned forty years ago. Richard Griffiths was generous in allowing me to use material from his book *Racing in the Dock* on the doping trials I was unable to attend myself. My lack of technological expertise reared its head on many occasions when the text was rescued from oblivion by step daughter Helen Cole who found chapters I had thought were consigned to heaven (or hell). My editor Sue Fitzmaurice was kindness itself in suggesting improvements – more especially as she has no knowledge of the esoteric world of horseracing.

A huge thank you to my three lovely daughters, Cate, Tara and Georgia for their unwavering support and skill in setting up a website and other social media. Cate's contribution especially has been a wonderful bonus for me.

Finally, a big thank you to my lovely and long suffering wife Linda whose patience knows no bounds. Lockdown was made more bearable by her love and persuasion that it would canter by all the faster for completing my memoir.

About the author

Colin Mackenzie was a Fleet Street journalist for 44 years, having worked on the *Daily Express*, the *Daily Mail* and the *Racing Post*. His Ronald Biggs scoop was named by the UK Press Gazette as one of the top ten of the 20th century. After his retirement he made three acclaimed documentaries for television. He is married with three daughters, three step daughters, and nine grandchildren. He lives in London and still plays squash, tennis, and bridge.

www.colinmackenziejournalist.com

REBEL
MAGIC
BOOKS

www.rebelmagicbooks.com

Printed in Great Britain
by Amazon